THE CHILDHOOD OF MAN

THE VILLAGE OF SECOTON, NORTH AMERICA

A bird's-eye view, showing a cluster of houses among scattered trees with three crops of maize, inscribed: *Corne newly sprong, Their greene corne,* and *Their rype corne.* In a corner of the last is a man sitting in a raised hut to scare birds away. In the foreground is *The place of solemne prayer* and a place for ceremonial dancing.

From the original water-colour drawing in the British Museum by John White, Governor of Virginia, 1587.

LEO FROBENIUS

translated by A. H. Keane

THE CHILDHOOD OF MAN

MERIDIAN BOOKS, INC.   *New York*

LEO FROBENIUS

The German ethnologist and explorer Leo Frobenius was born in Berlin in 1873. The author of many books, he is known for his theory that civilization undergoes an organic development similar to that of plants, animals, and man. Professor Frobenius was also an authority on prehistoric African art. He died in 1938.

M

Published by Meridian Books, Inc. August 1960
First printing July 1960

English edition originally published 1909
Library of Congress Catalog Card Number: 60-12989
Manufactured in the United States of America

IN an Introduction printed only in the first edition of this popular work, the gifted author took the reader into his confidence, and explained that, as nephew of Dr Bodinus, he passed his early days in the Berlin Zoological Gardens. Here he came into constant contact with Eskimo, Laplanders, Indians, Bedouins, and Blacks, and thus gained the sympathy and even the love of these primitive peoples. The knowledge in this way acquired of their feelings, temperament and views of the world soon satisfied him that the pictures of savage life painted for young and old in such current literature as Cooper's novels and the like are untrue to nature, and, in fact, for the most part "frauds." Convinced by his youthful experience that the "one touch of nature" was the key to the interpretation of all human activities, of all the outward manifestations of the mental qualities of the rudest no less than the most cultured races, he forthwith resolved to approach the study of mankind and his manifold faculties from this new standpoint, and devote all his spare hours to this, for him, all-absorbing subject.

But, after much groping in the dark, and many more or less successful essays, he found that no real progress could be made without first bringing together the necessary documents, that is to say, the "raw materials," the endless products especially of infantile crafts and industries, from the four quarters of the globe. This was a labour of many years, and was effected chiefly by establishing direct relations with officials, seafarers, traders, explorers, missionaries, and others engaged in various pursuits

TRANSLATOR'S PREFACE

amongst rude and barbarous peoples all over the world. Through their friendly and sympathetic co-operation, and partly also by his own personal efforts, Dr Frobenius has contrived to transform his domicile into a sort of private museum of primitive and more advanced artistic and industrial objects, somewhat analogous to that of the late General Pitt-Rivers now in Oxford. These are often accompanied by the donors' descriptive notes, greatly enhancing their value.

In the present work, which is enriched by over four hundred illustrations drawn largely from the author's storehouse, he not only describes the nature and action of the various mechanical and other contrivances, but also endeavours to trace them, as well as the traditions, legends and general folk-lore of the lower races, to their origins in remote prehistoric times. Here ample scope is naturally afforded for much speculation, and some of the theories advanced may not be accepted by every anthropologist. But all alike may be welcomed as honest attempts to sound the unfathomable, and in any case as highly suggestive and supplying much food for thought. Here it will suffice to refer to the sections on the origin of labour, Bushman folk-lore, the discovery of fire and the early history of warfare, with the accompanying commentaries. Evolution, in the Darwinian sense of this term, is at the root of all this speculative matter.

Attention may here be drawn to the reproductions of some excessively rare water colours with which, thanks to the courtesy of the British Museum authorities, the publishers have been able to supplement the illustrations in this English edition. They are over three hundred years old, being taken directly from the volume of admirable drawings in water colours executed by John White,

TRANSLATOR'S PREFACE

one of the pioneer settlers in Virginia, to which he made five voyages, and of which he was, for a short time, made governor by Sir Walter Raleigh in 1587. He probably made earlier journeys to the East of Europe, the Caucasus and Greenland, which explains the drawings of natives of those parts in the British Museum volume. Several of these were engraved in the first volume of Theodor de Bry's *America* (Frankfort-on-the-Main, 1590). During a visit to London de Bry had made the acquaintance of Richard Hakluyt, by whom he was introduced to Governor John White.

Thanks to their great accuracy, fully confirmed by contemporaneous and later research, these drawings are highly instructive as illustrating the habits, pursuits, dwellings and other features of native American life in the sixteenth century. Thus Morgan points out that the oblong, round-roofed houses of the Virginia and North Carolina tribes, seen and described by Capt. John Smith and depicted by Governor John White (see p. 236) were of the communal order, that is, were built to accommodate two or more families. Again, White's weir (p. 280) corresponds exactly to the wattle-work fish trap of the Virginia Indians, shown in Hariot's *America* published in 1585 and reissued in 1874. Here, too, we see in the shallow lagoon the spearing of fishes attracted to the surface by the fire which is tended by two men crouching in the middle of the canoe, while a third holds a landing-net ready to toss them ashore. With this compare J. D. McGuire's statement that "fires or torches were used along the shore or in boats, the gleam of which attracted the fish to the surface, when they were easily taken by hand or with a net" (*American Indians North of Mexico*, p. 462). Again, at p. 286, we have the broiling of fishes

vii

over a fire, and read how "great supplies of fish were cured by drying in the sun or over fires," etc. (ibid. p. 463). Lastly, in our frontispiece, may be noticed the deftly-pictured scene of a ceremonial dance, which is still a characteristic feature of religious life amongst the Iroquois and others, especially in connexion with agricultural pursuits at the sprouting, growing and harvesting of the maize crops seen in the picture. Hence this is no doubt " the green-corn dance" performed in thanksgiving for bountiful harvests (J. N. B. Hewitt, op. cit. p. 382). From this instructive picture we also see how true it is that before the advent of the whites the natives were not exclusively hunters, as is commonly supposed, but combined hunting with tillage, and were largely of sedentary habits, as indicated by the bird's-eye view of the village of Secoton here figured.

A. H. KEANE

CONTENTS

AND

LIST OF ILLUSTRATIONS

ix

CONTENTS

CONTENTS

xi

CONTENTS

CONTENTS

Chapter XV. SECRET SOCIETIES AND MASKS   198

Chapter XVI. THE MIDE   226

Chapter XVII. SACRED ANIMALS   240

CONTENTS

xiv

CONTENTS

Chapter XXII. MANKIND ON THE PATH OF THE SUN   330

Chapter XXIII. THE CUNNING SPIDER   349

Chapter XXIV. ORIGIN OF THE WORLD, FALL OF THE SKY, THE FLOOD   373

Chapter XXV. THE THEFT OF FIRE   386

CONTENTS

CONTENTS

CONTENTS

FROM DRAWINGS IN THE BRITISH MUSEUM
BY
JOHN WHITE,
GOVERNOR OF VIRGINIA IN 1587.

REPRODUCTIONS OF NATIVE DRAWINGS
AND CARVINGS

THE CHILDHOOD OF MAN

The Childhood of Man

CHAPTER I

PERSONAL ADORNMENT

THE European observer finds two distinct classes of aborigines, the primitive wild tribes, and the slightly civilized peoples who have come into contact with Europeans. There is a wide difference in their outward aspect. The original wild man in his savage

Figs. 1-5. African Combs (from the Kassai River). In the author's possession.

splendour, hair crowned with a huge plume, glittering shells strung in rows round neck and arm, topped by a conspicuous comb, cheeks and forehead, arms and breast covered with graceful incisions or coarse scars, such is the natural man, man as independently developed. Here we have a certain unity, in which our perceptions of the beautiful lose their power of discrimination. And I my-

PERSONAL ADORNMENT

self, who live a double life, one in the enjoyment of our own culture, the other buried in the past, absorbed in the original elements of savage life, will frankly confess that the outward appearance of those strange and now vanishing men compels me to a peculiar kind of respect. For just herein lies quite an extraordinary range of independence, since there have been so many, such endlessly diversified types of these strange peoples. Every tribe has been constituted in its own particular way, has acquired such a special form of culture that we must stand amazed at the infinite fulness of independent social phenomena.

Fig. 6. A "King" on the West Coast of Africa.

Just think: the Brazilian in his gorgeous feather array; the African stiff with his iron embellishments; the Siberian in his fur-trimmed garb; who could mistake one for the other? And withal, it is certain that anyone who knows them can surely distinguish the hundreds of African and American tribes, the thousands of Asiatics and Oceanic peoples. And this he can do from the outward forms of their own invention; I mean from their dress and adornments, in contradistinction to their natural

PERSONAL ADORNMENT

racial characteristics, such as the form of the face, the shape of the skull and of the body.

While, therefore, Anthropology begins the study of races by classifying men according to their colour and type of head, I start with a consideration of those outward forms that man has invented for himself. Hence, my first expression is amazement at the diversity of independent phenomena.

When the native enters into relations with the European, he seems in most cases to be seized with the desire to shape his outward appearance as far as possible to that of the stranger, of the much-admired white man. Here the African Negro is a typical case in point. As quickly as may be he procures a "chimney-pot," a dress coat, spectacles and a pair of patent leather

Fig. 7. African Chief, Aruwimi River. After an original sketch by Ward.

boots. As trousers do not seem so necessary, and the old native-woven loincloth is replaced by a gaudy strip of cheap printed calico, the result is a caricature which stands in the most glaring contrast to the old natural harmonious costume. It is as if the native had suddenly lost his critical sense, all feeling for outward form. This is disconcerting; but whoever has once seen the picture, will acquire a better understanding of the old independent type, and readily see that amongst the natives the development of ornament has proceeded on definite lines (see figs. 6 and 7).

The human body presented quite simple possibilities for embellishment. First of all there is the hair, which allows of endless modifications such as pleated coiffures, partly combed out and partly gathered up in top-knots. But this is not enough. By introducing rods and strips of cane, there arise domes, crowns, quite magnificent super-structures. The whole is smeared with clay or mutton fat to give it greater firmness, and is also dyed. Less pleasant is the hair dressing of the Dinka Negroes in the Upper Nile region. Amongst them the reddish tint is the result of constant washing with cow-dung and water. In some cases a like result is obtained by a compact mass of dung and ashes patiently worn for fourteen days, as Schwein-furt tells us.

On the other hand, the Brazilians have a decidedly more noble style. The beautiful feathers of parrots are woven into a resplendent sort of crown in the hair; though, indeed, amongst these natives the hair is often shaved off. I subjoin a passage from Carl von den Steinen, who clearly explains this treatment in his account of the tribes about the Xingu, a southern affluent of the Amazons.

The head-dress of the men forms a calotte or coif with a tonsure, the hair being combed out in all directions from the crown. It falls in front over the brow, reaches on the sides to the aperture of the ear, and behind, not quite to the nape of the neck. While the Suyas usually shave the front bare, and wear the tonsure of the Apostle Paul, all the Kulisehu Indians have the tonsure of the Apostle Peter, a cross-shaped bald patch on the scalp, nearly three inches wide. When the young Lukhu, a member of the Bakairi tribe, strutted about in Vogel's brown woollen poncho, he looked like the convent student in Ekkehart's book about Charlemagne. Hence it would appear that the tonsure was not first introduced by the monks. But, after all, the removal of the hair is a far from rare custom, and amongst these tribes all the rest of the hair, except the eyebrows, was shaven or simply plucked out. In this process the eyelashes are not laid on the fibre of a tukum palm, and then torn out with a single wrench, as amongst the Yurunas of the Lower Xingu, but pulled out one by one in early childhood.

Dr R. Brown has told me what a lively picture of homely family life may at times be observed in the south-western villages of the Mobali district north of the Congo. Round about a warm fire are seated father, mother, sons, daughters and grandchildren, one behind the other, and pluck out each other's hair with little primitive iron tweezers. Brown thinks this does more good than harm, and the whole group looks like a family of monkeys comfortably enjoying themselves. The scene was even unpleasantly like, from the fact that, when one of the group had the luck to discover a pediculus, there was a pleasant grimace and the little beast disappeared like a flash between the teeth of the fortunate "collector." Note that the Mobali are not the only lovers of these titbits. In one of his fine and very learned treatises the late Professor Joest has shown that the gourmets amongst

PERSONAL ADORNMENT

many peoples highly appreciate these vermin, which are so little to our taste. Science, however, has supplied Gottlob with more weighty proofs of the kinship of man and the ape.

Fig. 8. Boar's Tusk Ornament. In the possession of Dr Brandt. From the Ubangi, north of the Congo.

To decorate himself with chains, strings of beads, rings, man had ample opportunity, which he utilized in very large measure. The objects, however, which are available for such purposes, did not, generally speaking, fall from the clouds.

As a rule any natural, pretty, graceful, bright-coloured finds, such as variegated stones, the bits of gold, valued by the old Americans for their brightness, also snails, mussels and the like, could be strung together as ornamental chains. But in special cases these

Fig. 9. Leopard-teeth Ornament of the Balolo within the great Congo bend. In the possession of Dr Brandt.

objects have not rarely another value. The hunter, proud of his captured quarry, hangs round his neck the tusks of wild boars (fig. 8). But it is by no means rare for the autocratic power of an African chief to deprive the skilful trapper of his legitimate honours. So it is a widespread custom in the interior of the dark continent, for the canine teeth of captured leopards and lions to be given up to the head of the tribe and worn by him arranged on a string as a necklace—a proud symbol, not of his own but of his subjects' skill in the chase (fig. 9).

Fig. 10. Ornament of imitation leopard-teeth Sanga District Inner Africa. In the possession of Dr Brandt.

In this connexion it is very curious to see how those in a measure deprived of their booty are able, so to say, to indemnify themselves. Thus a certain giant of the Sanga district, a renowned leopard hunter, whenever he brought down an animal and had to hand over the trophy to his chief, contrived a sort of compensation by carving two wooden teeth, taking them to the smith and getting them plated with brass. He thus kept for himself an outward sign of his hunting prowess (see fig. 10).

PERSONAL ADORNMENT

Ancestor-worship, again, offers another important material for neck pendants. The brave sons of the Abanza wear round their neck a string of the finger-joints from the bodies of their deceased parents. A Walonga native of the Mongala district wore suspended from a thong three heads, carved in wood, in memory of his three murdered bro-thers. This pendant was to keep him constantly in mind that he had still to avenge his brothers' death. Such is the custom in the Walonga village. Each of such wood-en heads demands an expia-tion, the death of a man be-longing to the tribe that killed his relatives. When the vic-tim is slain, a great feast is held in the Walonga village. The murdered man is eaten, and his wooden head burnt.

Fig. 11. Necklace, Mongala District, In-ner Africa. In the Author's possession.

In this way such an appa-rently harmless necklace may be the witness of a long and very sad family record (fig. 11).

Here is another picture. When Stanley reached the present Stanley Pool on his first famous crossing of Africa from the east, he found that brass had already penetrated so far from the west by the intermediate trade from tribe to tribe. But how? This yellow metal was here esteemed as the most valuable of wares, and the wealthy king, Chumviri, had caused rings of it to be forged round the necks of his wives to the weight of from 44 to 90 pounds! The question then arose whether, after the death of his

28

wives, the metal should be consigned to the grave with them.

What?

The answer was a line, full of meaning, drawn with the finger round the neck. Good heavens! Will the wife lie in the grave with or without her head? Ugh!

Here we have ornaments already treated as currency, as so much capital. Here is unfolded a very long chapter in the history of civilization, which I shall have later to deal with in a separate section.

So much for outward adornment. But we must now see how man, dissatisfied with these outward and easily lost symbols, seeks to make them imperishable, by engraving his decorations, his emblems, the very language of his embellishment on the body itself, so that they may persist to the end of his days.

CHAPTER II
TATTOOING

IN the year 1895 a French trader started with a small expedition at his own expense up the Middle Congo, to reach the southern part of Lake Leopold, and there open a trade. I saw the young man when he set out, buoyant, confident of success, full of great hopes, and I saw him on his return. What a difference! His ruddy cheeks blanched, his eyes sunk deep in their sockets, his spirits gone; but, above all, on each temple a small thick boss, over each cheek an oblique stroke. The poor fellow had met with a strange experience.

Without much difficulty he had pushed forward through the Wangala and Balolo districts, and always at the head of the caravan, he had bravely cut his way with his forest knife through the dense thickets, and at last came to a halt among a small Mongo tribe somewhere in the neighbourhood of the river Bussera. Here he was quite comfortable, ivory and rubber seemed to abound, and the friendly natives so well-disposed that it seemed as if a few metal spoons, spectacles and pocket mirrors were all that would be needed in order rapidly to make a big pile. All went swimmingly for a few days, so that our little dealer decided to build a permanent station. But scarcely was the axe applied to the first tree when one hand of the village chief fell on the woodman's shoulder, while the other indicated with unmistakable emphasis that this

TATTOOING

business was to go no further. So a palaver was held, and the gentle Mongos only asked that the trader should become a member of the tribe. He was rejoiced. Nothing more? He nodded assent, and through his Wangala interpreter asked how it was to be done. In amazement he saw how the Congo carriers began to grin sarcastically, and was horrified at the answer:

"You must receive our tribal scars."

He made a long face, but there was no help for it. Right

Fig. 12. Tattooing of the Bahumbi on the Quango.

Fig. 13. Tattooing of the tribe on the Bussera.

Fig. 14. Tattooing of the tribes about the sources of the Equatorial rivers.

and left ivory and rubber, all for a few gashes—the opportunity of rapidly growing rich—go ahead!

Next morning the *ganga*, that is, the priest of the tribe, introduced himself to our friend. On a leather cloth he spread out all kinds of little objects, a couple of horns, black ashes, red dyes, a few little iron implements, and four small wooden figures tied up in a bundle. Meanwhile outside was set up a great yelling, with much jubilation.

To put it briefly, the white brother of the tribe was first of all manipulated on the temples, a black mixture rubbed in, and his head scored with all possible red lines. Meanwhile the outside crowd held high feast, dancing, eating good things, drinking palm wine—all at his expense.

Fig. 15. Tattooing of the Mongo tribe on the Maringa.

Fig. 16. Tattooing of the Mongos on the Maringa.

Fig. 17. Tattooing of the Gombe east, of the equatorial rivers.

Fig. 18. Tattooing of the Sukuru in the Aruwimi district.

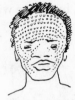

Fig. 19. Tattooing of the Malema in the Aruwimi district.

Fig. 20. Tattooing of the Lokele in the Aruwimi district.

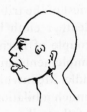

Fig. 21. Temple tattooing of the Niumba, Lake Leopold.

Fig. 22. Tattooing of the Yalelima on the Lukenye.

Fig. 23. Tattooing of the Moliro west of Lake Tanganyika.

Fig. 24. Tattooing of the Wemba west of Lake Tanganyika.

TATTOOING

Even that was not enough. Inflammation set in with the wounds, which festered, and when the patient wanted his carrier to get him some chicken-broth, the ganga put in a veto.

So for four long weeks he had to fast, for four weeks he was down with the fever, was ill and suffering, and

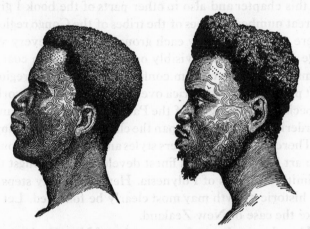

Figs. 25 and 26. Bashilange on the Upper Kassai.
After Drawings by Prof. Dr Max Buechner.

all the time not a thought could be given to business, for the Mongos kept continually away from him and his people. After four weeks the ganga presented himself in the hut. Freedom, thought our merchant. But alas! before the young man was aware of it, the scorings were repeated, he bled profusely, and the crowd again feasted, of course at his expense.

Again he fell ill; more feasting, nothing to do but sleep away an idle life. Then he lost all patience; in a few days he packed up his goods and returned to Europe.

TATTOOING

The affair had a sad ending. The poor fellow never recovered, and died in the hands of a surgeon, trying to get the hateful excrescences removed from his temples.

This story strikes us as a remarkable instance of an interesting process which is constantly going on in the life of an immense number of primitive peoples. The process in question is a deep-rooted indication of tribal kinship. In this chapter and also in other parts of the book I give a great number of types of the tribes of the Congo region. Here we may see how each group, how even every village bears, so to say, visibly on its head its own coat of arms. Nor is the custom confined to the Congo region, but prevails beyond Africa over a great part of the world, especially in the region of the Pacific Ocean and the lands bordering on it. Is not Japan the classic land of tattooing?

There are the most divers styles and methods, although the art has displayed its finest development amongst the primitive peoples of Polynesia. Here also many steps in its historic growth may most clearly be followed. Let us take the case of New Zealand.

Here I reproduce a few examples of New Zealand tattooing, especially that of Tupai Kupa, as drawn by himself over a hundred years ago for his friends in Liverpool. When this Maori was being painted by his friend John Sylvester, he looked on with great interest, but he presently shook his head, and declared that it was not at all the picture of Tupai Kupa. Those present and others coming in were greatly surprised. All were agreed that the features had been hit off with rare ability.

But Tupai Kupa smiled with a superior and self-satisfied air. With his finger he pointed to the forehead and said laconically:

"That not me!"

34

Of Florida.

A TATTOOED WARRIOR OF FLORIDA

The hair is drawn up to the top of his head, with a white plume drooping from the top. Small brass plates tied in bracelets round his elbows and knees, and a larger one hanging on his breast.

From the original water-colour drawing in the British Museum by John White, Governor of Virginia in 1587.

A TATTOOED WARRIOR OF FLORIDA

The hat is drawn up to the top of his head with a white plume issuing from the top. Small bone plates tied in bracelets round his elbows and knees, and a jasper one hanging on his breast.

From the original water-colour drawing in the British Museum by John White, Governor of Virginia in 1585.

TATTOOING

But still greater was the amazement when the Maori, asking for the pencil, with extraordinary skill drew his

portrait as he conceived it, and as I here reproduce it (fig. 28).

This, however, was not his actual portrait, but that of the ornamental lines tattooed on his face. At the time it created great surprise, and for several weeks poor Tupai Kupa had to draw the tattoo marks again

Fig. 27. A Maori, Tupai Kupa. After an old woodcut.

and again for all his friends and acquaintance; but, unfortunately, science had not yet acquired sufficient insight to appreciate the full meaning of this remarkable incident. Tupai Kupa gave the name and the significance of each flourish, related the occasions when they

Fig. 28. A Maori, Tupai Kupa. After his own drawing.

35

TATTOOING

were severally applied, and sketched the patterns of all the noble families. But, unfortunately, all the reporters of the occurrence have only recorded the incidents as such, without the details of Tupai Kupa's explanations.

We know, however, as a fact, that in the central islands

Fig. 29. A Maori, from a modern Photograph.

of Polynesia, it was customary to have his tutelar deity or sacred animal tattooed on each person; we know that on festive occasions the tokens were recorded on the breast of all the participators, and we find the same rite in Africa, as, for instance, with the western Niam-Niams. Here the young man carries marks recording his reception as a warrior amongst the elders of the tribe; the married couple has its tattooed sign instead of a wedding-ring,

TATTOOING

Fig 30. Tattooing of the Marquesas Islanders,
After Von Langsdorff.

TATTOOING

and the mother the number of her children permanently indicated in a way legible by all experts.

And this brings us to another important subject, that is to say, the beginning of a script and of historical writings.

Anyway it is certain that body-painting preceded tattooing. Even still the designs are painted on the body in black or red colours before the puncturing needle is inserted or the knife applied for incisions. For this purpose the Bornean Dayaks even use a regularly-carved stamp, as shown in the accompanying figure.

Fig. 31. Block for painting the body; Dayaks of Borneo. After Ling Roth.

CHAPTER III
TESTS OF MANHOOD

IT is now time to be reminded that we are speaking of the boyhood of our race, and I must here deal with some cases of downright wanton mischief. The collar and the armlet are common enough in our society, while the decoration and painting of the skin are prevalent amongst our sailors and soldiers, and on the stage. But what here follows betrays an overflow of the art such as we meet in this ill-regulated and extravagant form only in the childhood of mankind. We still laugh at times at the dainty little ear-lobes pierced for the insertion of a pretty little ring. But we look with horror at the sight of an ear-hole which is distended down to the shoulders —to the shoulders! I feel amazed at men clinging so tenaciously to such violent embellishments as, for instance, the knocking out of the teeth, from which there is no escape for any one not wishing to be boycotted by his fellows. One may also be surprised at the taste which displays itself in the deformation and distortion of the child's head, while still soft, by means of bandages on a frame. And yet such customs are not rare amongst energetic peoples; this very flattening of the head, this forcing of the forehead by tight bandages, are practised amongst advanced peoples, the ancient Peruvians, or the Mangbattus (Monbuttus), whom a man like Schweinfurt is ready to pronounce the most intelligent of all negroes.

TESTS OF MANHOOD

Here I reproduce some woodcarvings of these Mangbattus, from which we may see how beautiful this flattened forehead was thought (figs. 32 and 33).

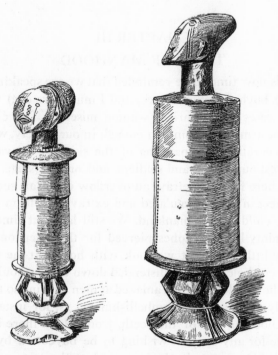

Figs. 32 and 33. Two boxes of the Mangbattus, Welle-Ubanghi Region. Both about one-eighth the natural size. In the Author's possession. Note the foreheads inclined back, which is effected by pressure in childhood.

And these very customs, which on the one hand denote the tribal mark, and on the other serve as a test of youth by strengthening its manhood, must needs prove attractive. So here follow a few instances, first from the debased Australians, and then from the Mexicans.

TESTS OF MANHOOD

Formerly the Bengel tribe of aborigines in New South Wales were regarded as "of age," that is ready to be received amongst the warriors, between their twelfth and fifteenth years. Then they had to undergo an operation, which bore the name of Gua-nung. It consisted in piercing the nasal septum for the insertion of a bit of reed or a bone as a permanent ornament, and at the same time a tooth was knocked out. With the loss of the tooth they entered the ranks of the men, that is, they received their privileges, which consisted not only in the rights connected with war, but also those of the kangaroo hunt, and the like. In the year 1795 Collins witnessed such a ceremony from the summit of Farm Cove. A few days before it began, a place called You-Lang of oval shape, about twenty feet long by sixteen wide, was cleared of the grass, scrub and branches. On his arrival, Collins found the chief actors in the proceedings, who belonged to the Kemmirai tribe, grouped in full array at one end of the scene, and at the other the young men who were to lose their teeth.

The ceremony opened with the armed men advancing singing, or rather, yelling, hurling their spears and throwing sticks at each other's shields, and with their feet raising clouds of dust which covered all the spectators. The moment they approached the youths, a man stepped out from the group of armed dancers, advanced a few steps, seized one of them and turned towards his comrades. These hailed him with shouts, and showed by their gestures their readiness both to receive the young man as a victim and to defend him. In this way each of the fifteen young men present was seized, one after the other, and brought to the group of men on the other side. Here they remained seated with crossed legs, down-

41

TESTS OF MANHOOD

cast head and clasped hands. However uncomfortable this posture might be, Collins was assured that the lads never stirred the whole night, nor raised their eyes, nor would they get a morsel of food until the ceremony was over.

Now the Carrahdis (priests) performed some mysterious rites. One of them threw himself suddenly down, rolled over and over on the ground with wonderful twisting and contortions, shammed frightful convulsions, and then seemed at last to get rid of a bone which was to serve for the next ceremony. And all the time the other savages danced and shouted round about him, and some kept beating him on the back until the magic bone was extracted. Thereupon he seemed relieved from his sufferings.

Scarcely had one risen from the ground, bathed in perspiration and thoroughly exhausted, when a second went through the same farce and also produced the bone. It was explained that the pretended sufferings of the Carrahdis were to convince the young men that the operation they would have to undergo the next day would cause them but little pain, since they would have the less to endure the more the priests suffered. Thus was concluded the ceremony of this first day.

Soon after sunrise on the second day the Carrahdis quickly advanced, one behind the other in Indian file, to the You-Lang, raised a great uproar and ran three times round the clearing. Then the youths with bent knees and clasped hands, were brought forward, and now a series of ceremonies were gone through, as pleasant interludes, one after the other, each representing something particular, but one and all strange and grotesque. Of these I here reproduce eight scenes.

TESTS OF MANHOOD

Fig. 34. The fifteen youths were seated at the upper end of the You-Lang, while those who were to perform the operation ran on all fours several times round the place, in this manner imitating the attitude of walking dogs. In order to make the scene as true to life as possible, their boomerangs were stuck behind in their girdles, so that they stood out like dogs' tails. Every time they crawled by the place where the lads were seated, they threw up sand and dust with their hands, these remaining all the time, with doleful mien, squatted and motionless, still as mice. They acted as if they never caught sight of the comical procession of the men. Presumably this ridiculous canine display was intended to yield the control of the dogs to the youths, and exhibit to them all the useful qualities of these animals.

Fig. 35. The youths still seated as above. A powerful savage advanced, bearing on his shoulder a kangaroo made of grass, while another carried on his shoulder a bundle of twigs. The others sat some distance off, singing and beating time to the step taken by the two Carrahdis, who seemed nearly to break down under their burdens. They would for a moment stand still, and then again go forward, staggering along till they reached the young men, at whose feet they laid their booty, and then withdrew from the You-Lang as if relieved of a heavy tribute. The man carrying the bunch of twigs presented all the more singular appearance, since he had inserted in the nasal septum two little flowering stalks. The kangaroo indicated the permission henceforth to kill this animal.

Fig. 36. The boys remained seated a full hour at the end of the clearing, while the operators withdrew to a neighbouring hollow; and now, instead of the boomerang they stuck a long bunch of herbs in their girdle. Then they set

TESTS OF MANHOOD

off like a herd of kangaroos, now springing on their hind legs, now standing erect, now scratching with their claws. At the same time a man standing on one side kept beating a shield with a club. Two other armed men followed as if they were at a hunt, and wanted to overtake, spear and kill the game. This was, of course, the symbol of a

Fig. 34.

kangaroo hunt, the future important pursuit of the youths looking on, a pursuit reserved for men.

Fig. 37. Having again reached the clearing the troop of men playing the kangaroo show swept by the youths like a small herd. But now they suddenly drew out their grassy tails and threw them away. Then each seized a boy, put him on his shoulders and carried him off to a place where the last great scene of the whole comedy was to be acted.

Fig. 38. After a few steps the lads were taken from the men's shoulders and set up in a group, where they awaited the next move with clasped hands and head bowed down on their breasts. While some of the chief actors removed to a distance of about ten minutes in order to arrange for another scene, Collins was requested to retire, so that he was unable to witness one part of the ceremonies. This particular scene was regarded by the natives as a pro-

Fig. 35.

found mystery, and as a necessary preparation for the following proceedings.

On his return Collins found the whole spectacle exactly as depicted in fig. 38. In the left group stood the boys and their attendants, before them on both sides two men, one of whom was seated on a tree-stump, while the other sat astride on his shoulders with outstretched arms. Behind them the other men lay on the ground at the foot of a stump with down-turned faces and as close together as was at all possible. As the youths and their leaders approached the two men at the first stump, the leaders turned now on one and now on another side, and began to put out their tongues, to make fearful faces, to open their eyes as wide as possible and roll them wildly about, altogether presenting a most frightful appearance. After these grimaces had lasted a few minutes, the boys were led over the bodies lying on the ground. Then these

Fig. 36.

began to stir, turning about and writhing as if they were at the last gasp. At the same time they made a muffled noise like that of thunder rolling away in the distance, all of which was to express pain and terror. After this strange walk over the bodies, the youths were presented to the two men on the second stump, who made the same grimaces as the first. But then the whole procession moved on.

This ceremony was called Buru-Murung, the exact meaning of which was not explained. On being asked about it they replied that it was very good and was done in order to make the young men of the future brave and daring warriors.

Fig. 39. The whole troop came to a halt some distance off. The boys had to take their seats beside each other in a row, while the men, armed with spears and shields, formed a semicircle in front of them. In the middle stood

Fig. 37.

Budirro, conductor-in-chief, his face turned towards the men. Holding a shield in one hand, a club in the other, he beat time with the two, but at the third stroke the others aimed their spears at him and stuck them in the centre of his shield. Thus ended the spectacles preliminary to the operation on the teeth, the last scene being apparently intended to indicate that the young men should henceforth regard the spear as their chief weapon.

Fig. 40. Now arrangements were made for knocking out their teeth. The first lad, ten years old, was lifted on to the shoulders of a man kneeling on the ground. Now

they showed him the bone which the previous evening
the first Carrahdi had pretended with his jugglery to
have extracted from his inside. This bone was sharply
pointed at one end in order to cut through the gum.
Were this not done, the blow might easily break his jaw.
Then a womera, eight or ten inches long, was sharpened

Fig. 38.

to serve as a chisel. When the gum was loosened from
the bone, the chisel was applied to the tooth. Then a
flourish in the air, another, and yet another, when at last
the heavy stone bounded with a great swing against the
wooden wedge—always three flourishes in the air before
the actual blow was delivered. With the first lad the
operation lasted ten minutes, as, unfortunately, the tooth
proved very firm.

At last it yielded, and his friends took the little patient
aside and pressed the gum together. Then they dressed
him in the garb in which he was to be arrayed for a few

48

days. This was a girdle and a boomerang, with a bandage round the head, its white colour producing not at all a bad effect. The patient kept his left hand to his mouth, which had to remain closed, eating and talking being forbidden for the whole day. From that hour each youth added to his own name that of his bearer.

Fig. 39.

All the youths present were treated in the same way, and one only, eight years old, was so overcome with the pain that he ran off. During the whole operation the spectators kept shouting at the top of their voices, either to distract the boys or else to drown their cries of agony. But the young fellows had evidently a rather strong sense of honour, for they suppressed all groaning and moaning to the utmost.

A further peculiarity was that the blood was not wiped away, but allowed to trickle on to the breast of the patient and to the head of the man beneath him, and it so

Fig. 40.

remained for several days on both of them. Later the young man received the title of Kebarra, a name which evidently has reference to the instrument used in the operation, for Kebah means a stone or a rock.

Fig. 41.

TESTS OF MANHOOD

Fig. 41. Now all the youths are brought together; they have undergone the operation, and are seated in a row on the trunk of a tree. One only, named Nanbarry, has suffered too much. So his cousin, a man named Kolbi, comes and applies a broiled fish to his gum, which should relieve the pain.

But at a given signal all spring from their seats and chase everybody, men, women, spectators and operators, into the camp, and those that cannot run ahead fast enough respectfully withdraw.

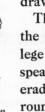

This puberty rite gives the young one the privilege of carrying club and spear and marrying. The eradicated tooth is worn round the neck as a valuable memento.

Fig. 42. Gobu-Bubu of the Ubanghi west of Mokoangay with simple labret.

Fig. 43. Gobu-Bubu with labrets in the upper and lower lips.

So long as such customs are confined to people like the Australians, who are recognized by all as standing at the lowest stage of civilization, the European shrugs his shoulders, remarking that after all these are but savages.

But how if one meets precisely the same brutality, the same violence in disfiguring the human features and their natural form amongst the renowned and much-vaunted Aztecs and Incas?

And, in fact, so it is. Gomara tells of an eminent order of merit, in a measure a knightly order, which was called Tecuitle, and consisted of the bravest and most distin-

TESTS OF MANHOOD

guished men in Mexico, including the monarch himself. If anyone aspired to become a member, he had to undergo a long probation, a year of the severest hardship and physical ill-treatment, with manly pluck and endurance.

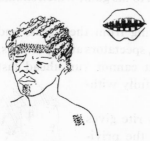

Fig. 44. Tattooing and tooth-filing of the Zakaras on the Ubanghi.

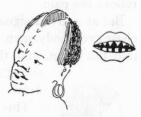

Fig. 45. Enlargement of the ear-lobe and tooth-filing of the natives at the bend of the Ubanghi.

At the beginning of the probation a festive gathering was held, and the whole proceedings were opened by the aspirant kneeling at an altar, when his nose was

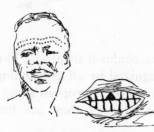

Fig. 46. Tattooing and tooth-filing of the Bakuba between the Zan-kurn and Kassai rivers.

pierced with a sharp bone or an eagle's claw and a piece of obsidian inserted in the hole. Then came the further tortures, derision, every kind of deprivations and blood-letting, all of which he had to endure without turning a hair. When this period was passed through, the hair-shirt was removed from his shoulders, and his hair bound with a red fillet, and he was then decked with many coloured feathers.

Then his pluck was praised, and then he was exhorted at all times to prove himself a loyal Tecuitle, and to fight bravely and unflinchingly for his country and religion; and then he was reminded that the highest honour had been conferred on him by having his nose pierced with a bone and an eagle's claw.

And when the young men of the Inca State had undergone their hard training in work and arms, the Inca himself conferred on them the high distinction of manhood

Fig. 47. The "Pelele," that is, the Labret or ivory disk of Rubi, north of the Congo; natural size. In the possession of Dr Brandt.

by piercing their ears with a gold needle. It is, therefore, clear that we have not here to do with a brutal custom practised by mere savages alone. And, in truth, there is something more implied by it. By examples from Oceania the deeper value of these ethical practices may be easily recognized.

Riedel tells us that on Babar, one of the lesser Sunda islands, the distension of the ear-holes is connected with the notion that access to the land of the dead is allowed to those only who, during life, have effected this embellishment of the ear-lobes to a proper extent. Some Australian tribes think that those are punished hereafter who do not have the nasal septum pierced for the insertion of a bone, a bit of reed, or the like. Amongst the Motu, a tribe in British New Guinea, there are, strictly speaking, no punishments after death. In the popular belief, however, there is one painful experience for the souls of those whose nose is not pierced, that they go to a

Fig. 48. A born Wahoko Woman naturalized Wawira wife (after Stuhlmann).

bad place where food is scarce and there are no betelnuts.

According to the beliefs of the natives of Maevo, an island in the New Hebrides Archipelago, all those whose ears are not pierced must drink no water, while all who are not tattooed will get no good food. For the souls of the natives of Florida Island after death a wandering journey begins, in the course of which they meet a certain tindalo (spirit) on the shores of the island of souls. He examines the nose, and if found pierced they are easily admitted to the kingdom of the blest, but if not, for them begins a period of sorrow and suffering. On Mota, one of the Banks Islands, those fare worse still whose ears are not found pierced when they come before Paget, judge of the dead, and in the Gilbert Islands the tattooed alone reach the abode of bliss. In the Hades of the Fijians all whose ears are not bored are treated with the utmost contempt, and women who are not tattooed are struck down by the souls of their own sex and served up as food for the gods.

Now we should understand that the natives living in the world of the last mentioned customs and beliefs are so utterly selfish that they will on no account receive the members of other tribes into their land of the dead, while, on the other hand, they recognize the goodness of a man in his strict observance of all the tribal customs and old traditions.

It is further important clearly to understand that a bored ear, tattoo marks, a nasal rod, or a lip ornament are permanent symbols, indelible records. Hence the "family effects," which in Germany are sealed by the Civil administration under official and police inspection, find a complete analogy in the treatment by the natives of their labrets and nose-rings, which they regard as part of the "tribal effects," a pass and, as we have seen, a certificate for entrance into bliss.

Such records, however, may in the long run be subject to change. I here give the figure of a woman from the interior of Africa (fig. 48). She was born a member of the Wahoko tribe, and so received seven incisions on the upper lip. Then she fell into the hands of the Wawira, one of whom married her. As an indication of her new tribal connexion she had a disk inserted in her upper lip. And thus were her wanderings and changed relations ineffaceably recorded to the last by documentary evidence. No European police arrangements could have done it better.

CHAPTER IV
ORIGIN OF LABOUR

THUS have all men, even the most debased, at all times sought to adorn themselves. Even were it only with a variegated feather stuck in the hair, or a ring of straw round the neck, or a dash of colour on the forehead, all have tried to decorate themselves, as far as they are known to us. But it is quite natural that some should find pleasure in the smallest trifles, while others cannot overload themselves enough. The great trouble they take to embellish themselves—as may perhaps be asserted of some primitive people—is done to show whether they are rich or poor, or rather to show how rich they are. For we are surely justified in speaking of poor and rich, even among primitive peoples.

In this connexion one thing is pleasant to notice, namely, how man kept decking and decking himself in a thoughtless sort of way, never supposing that there could be such a thing as work. If his genial environment was such that he had only to open his mouth for plenty of food and drink, how could he at all imagine that work, enforced activity, could be needed? But he decked and decked himself, and began all at once—to work. The necessity arose, not indeed from want of food, but just because he had not yet a sufficient supply of ornaments.

There are, of course, many reasons why labour should begin. But this is, doubtless, the most peculiar, and may well engage our attention for a while.

ORIGIN OF LABOUR

One of the materials that are most generally used for adorning the person is a shell. That this should be the case in lands bordering on the sea is not surprising. But it is noteworthy that shells have travelled from the coast far inland, not only across extensive regions but across a whole continent, Africa. This, as we know, is the case with the pretty little cowrie shell, which comes from the Indian Ocean, yet will be found in the hands of almost every tribe in the Dark Continent. It may serve to decorate a little cap or a fillet, or adorn a knife-handle or a loincloth.

Fig. 49. A New Pomeranian with Dewarra collar (from a photograph).

But the wild man was not satisfied with simple shells; they were sliced in pieces, polished to round discs, and strung together. Thus were produced the famous strings of beads with which we are familiar from every part of the world. In the next chapter we shall again meet them in the well-known wampums of the American Indians. In Africa I have seen them in collections from almost every part of Congoland, and they are vastly more varied and more generally used than anything else in the South Sea Islands, especially in the archipelagos to the north-east and east of New Guinea. Famous above all are the shell ornaments which, under the name of dewarra, have reached our museums from New Pomerania (New Britain). This dewarra may have formerly adorned the necks of the natives as simple ornamental shell-chains; but there came a time when the graceful chain developed to an enormous collar (fig. 49). When, however, the Europeans began to settle in the island, this collar was

ORIGIN OF LABOUR

becoming old-fashioned, simply because the dewarra had been changed to currency, and had thus become far too valuable to be squandered on personal adornment. That these kinds of ornaments became money, a means of exchange, may be noticed everywhere. Even the cowrie shell is now a coin, especially in West Africa, while in Oceania there are hundreds of such shell coins. But the most peculiar of all is the dewarra, which we may now study with Parkinson as our guide.

The shells called dewarra, and also *tabu*, are about one-third of an inch long, and, naturally, of a black-brown colour. They are converted to dewarra by boring the upper curved valve, stringing them together on thin reed-stems, and letting them bleach in the sun.

By the natives of the Gazelle Peninsula, North New Pomerania, the dewarra are highly valued. Hence, every effort is made to collect as great a store as possible, since with them they can obtain everything they want. With dewarra they buy their ornaments and their wives; with dewarra they buy themselves free from all troubles and complications; with dewarra they appease their bitterest enemy, even though they may have killed his nearest relative.

In some of the districts about Blanche Bay, sundry items are thus valued in fathom-lengths of dewarra:

> 1 fathom of dewarra, 60 yams weighing 176lb.
> 10 fathom of dewarra, a pig weighing 132lb.
> 20 fathom of dewarra, an elderly woman.
> 50 to 100 fathom of dewarra, a young girl.
> 20 to 50 fathom of dewarra, indemnity to the survivors of a murdered person.

ORIGIN OF LABOUR

In New Pomerania the dewarra represents enormous power. Whoever possesses the largest store enjoys the highest esteem, exercises the greatest influence. The women must pass their whole life toiling from early morning to nightfall in order to pile up dewarra for their husbands, while the men plot and plan how to rob their neighbour of his store.

To meet his little daily expenses, the native usually

Fig. 50. A Kinakinau, a thief Amulet, New Pomerania, front and side view (Ethnographic Museum, Leyden).

Fig. 51. A Kinakinau (Ethnographic Museum, Leyden).

Fig. 52. A Kinakinau (Ethnographic Museum, Dresden).

carries about with him from a yard to four fathoms of this shell money. The rest is deposited in the dewarra-house, a hut specially set apart for keeping the property of all the villagers, the thousands of fathoms belonging to the rich, as well as the smallest savings of the poor. From 50 to 100, or even 250 fathoms are rolled up in a bundle which is wrapped in bright coloured leaves. Lesser amounts are left open in small baskets. The dewarra bank is always guarded by several sentinels, who raise a hue and cry whenever danger threatens. Thereupon men, women and children hurry forward and carry off their loads of dewarra to put them in some place of safety. We are told that a woman pursued by the enemy would sooner let her child drop and get lost than throw away her dewarra money.

Fig. 53. Chain of iron beads. Money in Yimbagere. In the possession of Dr Brandt.

The owner of capital deposited in the dewarra-house will draw it out only on specially important occasions, as, for instance, when he has to pay the stipulated price for a wife. Otherwise the store is not removed till the death of the owner, when it has to be partly or entirely distributed. In the dwelling only so much is kept as may seem required for the usual daily outlay.

But when a native has once saved more than that, he takes pride in being able to deposit a roll of 50 fathoms or more in the bank. Then the drum is beaten summoning the neighbours, who look enviously on while the lucky owner opens the door, well secured with stout sticks, and draws in his treasure. If it is his first deposit, he must be prepared for the spiteful jeers of the envious onlookers.

"Wait till to-morrow," says one; "you may get hungry, and then will have no dewarra to buy food."

ORIGIN OF LABOUR

"Come along, let us see whether any dewarra has been stolen from our huts," cries another.

But even with all this, we have not yet mentioned the full extent of the mercenary displays that have their source in personal adornment. Nay, rather must I confess, to my regret, that, if on the one hand this greed has stimulated the tribal activities, on the other the notion of *meum* and *tuum* and of the rights of property has been obliterated in a very sordid way. For the New Pomeranian is so eager to heap up dewarra that he loses no opportunity of stealing it. This mania for stealing is at present so developed that it is carried on in a matter-of-fact sort of way, and that a regular little group of teachers, and a kind of cult, have been developed, whose sole aim is to protect the thief. Whoever wants to rob a sleeping person has recourse to a very remarkable magic instrument, the so-called *Kinakinau* (figs. 50, 51, 52). This is a lower jaw which is attached to the upper end of a stick and painted with a grotesque face, and is the embodiment of the spirit Taun. Taun possesses the fine faculty of promoting sound sleep. So when any one intent on burglary has to pass by the sleeping owner of the coveted dewarra he waves the Kinakinau to and fro over him to prevent him from waking. This may often succeed, though it happens frequently enough that the sleeper wakes up despite Taun and his Kinakinau. But the belief in the power of Taun is not shaken, for it is then explained that Kaiia, a spirit more powerful than Taun, has protected the sleeper! After all, the belief in spirits always takes a practical turn. If you are deceived in your confidence in the efficacy of one, it is never very difficult to make another still more powerful answerable for it.

If so far the striving after finery has helped to develop,

if not actually to produce, a currency, an instance will now be given of more obvious and more potent inducements to progress being called into existence.

In Yimbagere, a village between the Rubi and the Aruwimi rivers in the north-east Congo basin, there is found a quantity of good and easily extracted iron ore, which is absent from the surrounding districts. Hence the natives of this village are richly adorned with iron, and are specially distinguished above all their neighbours for their beautiful iron weapons. Now, while each villager manufactures and repairs his arms in the open forge, some few have acquired the art of making the beautiful and dainty iron beads which, like the shell money, are threaded on strings and worn round the neck. These artificers do nothing else but turn out iron beads, which have thus acquired a definite value—one chain a goat, twenty chains a woman. Thus, this means that the iron beads have the significance and value of money. None of the weapons are traded with the neighbouring peoples, whereas the iron beads circulate all over the land from the Rubi to the Aruwimi, and always at the same value— a chain a goat, twenty chains a woman. In this way an industry was created, and in this way labour arose out of the demand for ornament.

Nor was this the case in Yimbagere alone. In Polynesia also there were people skilled in the art of making ornaments, people who made a livelihood out of the artistic objects which they supplied to others. Just as there were boat-builders in Hawaii, so there were masters in feather-work (feather mantles and feather collars), and masters also in tattooing, who, although for this they received no wages, were honoured by the particular work on the various parts of the body

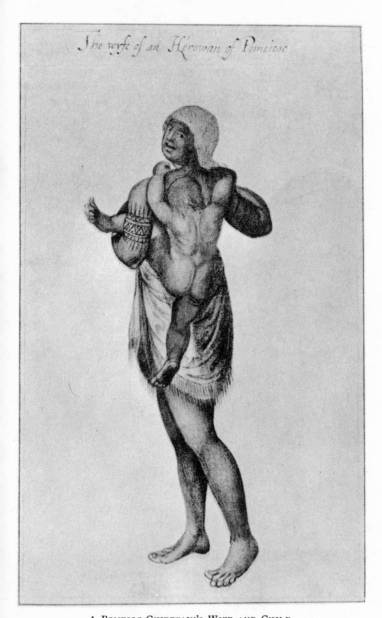

The wyfe of an Herowan of Pomeiooc

A POMEIOC CHIEFTAIN'S WIFE AND CHILD

From the original water-colour drawing in the British Museum
by John White, Governor of Virginia in 1587.

ORIGIN OF LABOUR

being set apart for them in accordance with fixed principles.

I must not omit here to mention a comical incident. In contrast with the practice of all the surrounding people, monogamy prevailed amongst the Benabendi of the Kassai river near the Bashilange (cf. figs. 25 and 26), these last being met with for the first time by the explorers, Wissmann and Pogge, who were both greatly surprised at their rich tattoo marking. Now the Benabendi was very fond of his one wife, and showed his affection by having her tattooed (one sees from this that it is not only in Europe that people show their love for their wives by decorating them!) Now there were three masters of the craft who executed such work, and were paid for it according to long-standing usage. Then, one day, another master of the art turned up. But his fellow-craftsmen enjoyed a high reputation, while he came of a very uninfluential family, being in fact the son of a slave, so that he was unable to make much progress. Now, see how he managed to improve the occasion. One day he openly declared that he would do the work at half-price. Thereupon a great clamour was raised. The "burghers" held a meeting, and in a great palaver it was solemnly decided that such a course could not be allowed. Nothing further was said about the matter, but the young man succeeded all the same. Lawfully he could now work only at the full rate; but in point of fact he at once returned half the amount to his customers as a present! The other masters accommodated themselves to the situation, and in quite a short time the following arrangement was made. To tattoo one arm of a woman costs two double mats. When the work is done, the master receives these and goes home. But next day he returns with one mat, and a little basket of ground-nuts by way of handsel for the proud husband.

From this we may see that in the trade in fancy wares competition has already set in amongst primitive peoples.

CHAPTER V

DRESS-LANGUAGE

"BROTHERS, with this belt I open your ears that you may hear; I take care and sorrow from your hearts; I extract from your feet the thorns which stuck in them when you rode hither; I cleanse the seats of the assembly house that you may sit comfortably; I wash your head and your bodies that you may be refreshed; I bewail with you the loss of the friends that have died since last time we came together; I wash away all the blood that may have been shed between us."

Such a solemn speech was made by the welcoming chief when two Indian tribes met in order to make peace, to deliberate, or conclude any kind of treaty.

"Brothers, with this belt I open your ears that you may hear." Such are the first words, a formal opening that has reference to one of the most remarkable customs of the Indians, to the wampum, one of their most characteristic articles. The wampum has no doubt grown out of the cords on which were strung shell-beads of divers colours for adorning the neck and arms, and which first served as ornaments, but later circulated in the land as real money. The various colours of the shells may at first have led to their being put together as personal badges, so to say, as tokens of ownership of the belts. It is conceivable that amongst the Indians a little exchange may have taken place to cement a friendship or a treaty. In any case it is certain that the wampum-belt acquired an extraordinary measure of importance, that in it was in those days evolved a certain kind of documentary script,

Fig. 54. Conclusion of a Treaty or Production of the Wampum amongst the North American Indians (after Lafitau).

which, however, must have perished before the Europeans thought of studying such a very peculiar aspect of culture.

DRESS-LANGUAGE

Our accompanying picture from Lafitau (fig. 54), depicts a very conventional scene, though doubtless on the whole not a wrong employment of the wampum belt. Two parties to the signing of a treaty are seated each in a row on two sides of a plain. In the background between the two groups is seen the chief who is addressing them, while holding such a belt in one hand. Three other belts lie at his feet, and a fifth on a larger scale may be seen in the foreground, though its ornamental design cannot be recognized.

When two tribes concluded a treaty, they exchanged wampums, as above stated, and these belts served instead of a written document, having a representation of the event woven into it ornamentally. According to Morgan, amongst the Iroquois there was a chief who had the hereditary office of wampum-keeper, and whose duty it was, not only himself to preserve the meaning of each belt, but also to take care that this knowledge should be kept alive among the people. For this purpose, at a fixed time of the year, the belts were brought out of the treasure-house and exhibited to the whole tribe. Then the history and the meaning of each was rehearsed, and this custom is still observed.

Nor was it always belts alone that had these records and significance. At times

Fig. 55. Wampum, Name of a Chief (after Holmes).

67

Fig. 56. Old-time Wampum, formerly belonged to Mr Penn, grandson of the founder of Pennsylvania; hence is probably a document referring to a treaty made with the Indians in the early days (after Holmes).

simple cords or strings of beads were used for the purpose. Thus, when a new chief was installed, he was handed a wampum with ten rows of white beads as a record of the event. Our picture shows three rows, mostly of white beads, which represent the name of a chief. On the other hand, when a chief died, he was mourned for by wearing ten rows of black wampum. But if he was only an ex-chief, ten short rows sufficed.

But the wampum would appear to have had other meanings also. We know that Hiawatha, a tribal hero about whom Longfellow has written a very popular poem, once set out against Leather-bead, the magician of Megissogwon, and fought with him; that Leather-bead was covered from head to foot with wampum; that Hiawatha's darts bounded off from this chain armour, until at last the hero aimed at the exposed roots of the hair. Thus the wampum had also magic virtue everywhere.

It is, however, unnecessary to go back to the wampum in order to bring to light certain written signs forming a kind of ornament or dress-language. Here I will give

DRESS-LANGUAGE

another instance of such signs indicated by ornaments. Among the Hidatsa Indians eagle feathers used as an adornment denote certain distinguished deeds on the

Figs. 57-60. Feather signs of the Hidatsas (after Mallery).

part of the wearer. A plume with a tuft of down or a few horse-hairs attached to the tip (fig. 57), indicates that

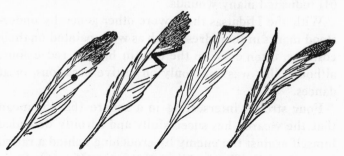

Figs. 61-64. Feather signs of the Dakotas (after Mallery).

the wearer has killed an enemy and that he was, in fact, the first to make the attack on the fallen foe. On the other hand, the man who, as second champion succeeded in striking down the enemy got only one feather, at the wider lower end of which was drawn a horizontal stroke (fig. 58). Then he who, as third com-

DRESS-LANGUAGE

batant at last killed the foe right out, had claim to such a plume with two red cross strokes (fig. 59), and the fourth to such another with three red cross strokes (fig. 60).

More marks of distinction even Indian ambition could scarcely confer on a man.

Analogous marks were used by the Dakota people. A spot on the broader side of the feather (fig. 61) shows that the wearer has killed an enemy, while a notch with

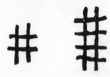

Figs. 65 and 66. Marks of honour on Garments.

a black border (fig. 62) denotes that the enemy had his throat cut and his scalp carried off. But if only his throat was cut, this could be recognized by a feather which was cut off at the top and the edge of the cutting dyed a dark colour (fig. 63). A split feather (fig. 64) indicated many wounds.

With the Hidatsas there were other generally understood marks in their dress, such as were painted on their costume, often even on the toes, in blue or red colour, although this was done only on festive occasions, or at dances.

Four strokes intersecting in a square (fig. 65) mean that the wearer has successfully and adroitly defended himself against the enemy by crouching behind a raised heap of earth. The doubling of this sign (fig. 66) shows that the incident occurred twice. A horseshoe-shaped figure recalls the fact that the man wearing it on his trousers, the blade of his oar, or on any other article belonging to him, has succeeded in stealing a horse from the enemy.

Thus we see that the deeds of which Indian ambition made a parade were not necessarily of a too heroic character.

CHAPTER VI
SIGN AND GESTURE LANGUAGE

LONG before man had learnt to make himself understood afar off by written symbols, he was already using the most diverse means of explaining things without employing articulate speech. We have just spoken of the Indian's dress-language. But it is not only by a

Fig. 67. Finger-post for hunters, Alaska.

Fig. 68. Post indicating the way for people arriving. Abnaki Indians.

feather or some painted ornament that he indicates any great event in his life. Even we distinguish male and female, women's and girls' attire. Our military system has almost created a special social status with its uniforms, so that we also have a kind of dress-language.

On the other hand, we may discover a new method of expression in the sign-language, without, however, pretending that this sign-language is confined to primitive peoples alone. In many schools, and in many of the

SIGN AND GESTURE LANGUAGE

higher and lower classes, quite a distinct sign-language is current, the express object of which is to carry on a

Fig. 69. The long post points to the direction taken by the people departing. As the short post is stuck in the ground at the near end it means: "I have gone off in such and such a direction, but have not gone far." Abnaki Indians.

noiseless conversation behind the back of the teacher amid the deep silence, the solemn stillness of the place. Everybody who knows his Cæsar, and has let some

Fig. 70. Like the foregoing; but as the short stick has been advanced further from the near end it means: "I have gone a long way in such and such a direction." Abnaki Indians.

drops of perspiration fall on the *Bellum Gallicum*, knows how angry Cæsar would get when his dispatches were distanced by the reports of the natives transmitted by bonfires and other signals over the hills. Thus we come to the sign-language that I had in my mind.

SIGN AND GESTURE LANGUAGE

There are in daily use some quite common signs which, one might say, arise from the very nature of things. We signal with our pocket handkerchiefs, the knots in which are themselves signs to aid the memory. We shake our head to say no, we nod to say yes. The pointsmen on our railways signal with red and white (green) flags.

But there are also more distant signals. The Kamerun natives, for instance, thus announce the dawn. They pass the palm of the hand from the forehead over the eyes,

Fig. 71. Like the last ; but as there are five short cross pieces it means : "I have gone in such and such a direction (indicated by the long post) and shall be away five days.—Abnaki Indians.

nose and mouth, and Hutter thinks this is the action which one often makes instinctively on waking in the morning. To incline the head sideways, with ear and cheek on the palm, means sleep, and so on.

In these matters no people seem to have developed their systems in a more interesting way than the North Americans, who are often able to converse in the sign or gesture language, even when they do not understand or speak the language of the stranger. Of this I will give an interesting instance, a sentence which was explained to the American explorer, Dr Hoffmann, by Tce-caq-a-daq-a-qic, "Lean Wolf," a Chief of the Hidatsa Indians in Dakota territory. The whole sentence ran:

"Four years ago the American people contracted friendship with us; but they lied. Finished."

73

SIGN AND GESTURE LANGUAGE

In order to express this the Indian used the following six gestures: Fig. 72. On the left side of his forehead he placed his closed hand with the thumb resting on the middle of the index finger, palm downwards, and then raised the thumb a little way to the right above his head. That meant "White Man."

Fig. 72.

Fig. 73. About 15 inches in front of the right side of the body he placed the naturally outspread hand, fingers and thumb a little apart and pointed to the left, and moved it a short distance from himself. That meant "With us."

Fig. 73.

SIGN AND GESTURE LANGUAGE

Fig. 74. He stretched out the palm of the right hand, as if he wanted to grasp the hand of some other person. That meant "Friends."

Fig. 74.

Fig. 75.

Fig. 75. The right hand, with all the fingers spread out save the thumb, he brought back to the front of the body to within 18 inches of the right shoulder. That meant "Four."

Fig. 76.

Fig. 76. He shut the right hand, leaving the index and middle finger a little apart and outstretched. He placed it, with the back turned outwards, about 8 inches before the right side of the body, and with it rapidly made a slight downward curve. That meant "Lies."

Fig. 77. He brought the clenched fists together before his breast, palms downwards, and then, separating them, brought them with an outward curve to both sides. That meant "Finished."

Fig. 77.

Fig. 78. Question, "Who are you?" Answer, "Pani." After Hoffmann

SIGN AND GESTURE LANGUAGE

It will now suffice if I give a picture (fig. 78) showing how such signs make communications intelligible at great distances.

For the rest it is noteworthy that it is precisely in their intercourse at a distance that primitive peoples have produced the very grandest means of communication. Specially remarkable is the drum-language, to which I will devote a separate chapter.

CHAPTER VII
THE DRUM-LANGUAGE

FIRST of all a scene from the most horrible of all African wars.

Before me lies the manuscript of one of those men who lost their lives in the sanguinary conflict in the east part of Congoland, the upper reaches of the Aruwimi. Our friend was marching at the head of a force of Hausa troops to capture an Arab chief. The road lay continually through the primeval forest—forest, forest everywhere—so that all the forced marching along almost impassable tracks was in vain. The Arab could not be overtaken.

Who does not know the primeval African forest from Stanley's descriptions? Dreary silence, hunger, sickness, and other evils lie in wait for their victims. Our friend was soon worn out, and lay prostrate in a village, a deserted village in the midst of the forest. His people, who had so far been exhausted and tired enough, now began all at once to pull themselves together, and while the leader himself grew weaker and weaker, they started dancing and merry-making the same evening.

"How is it that all of a sudden you feel so much better?"

No answer, only a grin, a puzzling grin. Not a word did they utter till one day the captain himself made a discovery, a ghastly discovery. The men had lain in ambush, and now and then captured, roasted and eaten one of the natives who had escaped from their own

THE DRUM-LANGUAGE

village and taken refuge in the dense woodlands. The leader appeared just as they had gagged a young fellow, and were about to carry him off to their cannibalistic cooking place which lay concealed in a retired corner. Their captain stormed, rescued the lad, brought him to his own hut, and although his provisions were scanty enough, gave him some, and then let him run off. The next night he was wakened by a noise. The lad had crawled to his hut and had brought him some bananas and a fowl, and repeated the gift the following night. Then the officer held him fast, and in return hung a broken opera-glass round his neck. Now his slumbering senses were awakened and there began a lively pantomime between them, ending in a mutual understanding. The white man could clearly see that the young negro wanted to leave his fellow tribesmen in order to start a trade in provisions with the European, though he could not understand how it was to be done. But now the lad suddenly stood up and drew the white man after him by his tattered clothes. They came to a tree which lay across the assembly house in the middle of the village, and was slit open and hollowed out at one end. He took two sticks which lay inside the trough-like hollow and began to beat along the edges of the slit, now with a long, now with a short, rattle, and again with a grinding or hacking sound. Then the officer at once grasped the meaning. "At that instant," so he writes himself, "I felt as if the fetters of this vast wilderness had fallen from my limbs. In this solitude, in which every cry of a bird, every uttered word echoes like some blind sound, there suddenly broke on my ears a vocal concert which I at once realized as the native language, or as one emanating from the spirit of the forest, though I could not yet

THE DRUM-LANGUAGE

Fig. 79. Tree-stem slit open and hollowed out as a Kettle-drum. Malicolo,
New Hebrides (From a photograph).

THE DRUM-LANGUAGE

understand it. For weeks together I had tramped along this route with my northern negroes, and in the north I had understood their nature. Here in the south they

Fig. 80. A Fijian beating the Signal-drum (after Wilkes).

had become strangers to me. Everything was strange, this wild solitude, this dead silence, these shy, ever-fugitive natives. But the moment Rufiro's rat-tat-tat was heard, I at once grasped the spirit of these surroundings, and the stillness which had hitherto seemed everlasting now melted into a half-melancholy clattering language.

And now that the most varied rattling notes responded from all quarters of the heavens—now a sentence from one corner, now a muffled sound from another — the quickening feeling came upon me that I myself now formed part of this environment, that I had learnt to understand it, that, so to say, I was rescued from my own man-eating people."

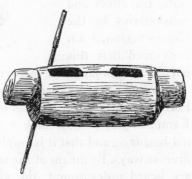

Fig. 81. Signal-drum of the New Pomeranians with drum-stick (Ethnographic Museum, Leiden).

And, in fact, from that moment the situation was changed. Next morning the natives returned to the village, produced bananas and fowls from secluded and

83

THE DRUM-LANGUAGE

hidden places, and even brought in parts of an elephant which had been taken in a snare the day before, and thus all their wants were supplied.

Once in the same war, when Governor Five was re-

Fig. 82. New Pomeranian Signal-drum (after Parkinson).

turning late in the evening to his camp in a secluded village of the Basako district, and sent orders by the drum-tele-

graph to keep his supper ready, on reaching the place a few hours later he found the meal served up. The message had been received long before his arrival, and shortly after the despatch of the "telegram." It ran:

"Bula Matadi come evening; don't eat all up."

From my inter-course with the offi-cials, travellers and missionaries in the Congo region, I am convinced that this

Fig. 83. Signal-drum of the Balubu South-east Congoland (after Cameron).

peculiar drum-language is current throughout Central Africa east of the chain of lakes. But it had already long been known that the Duallas of the German Colony of Kamerun also possess such a highly characteristic sig-nal-language, and that it is employed by them in the most diverse ways. By means of the sounds of the drum, which are heard miles round, the villagers converse on the most familiar subjects. They bully each other, declare war, make inquiries about each other's state of health, hold palavers and courts of justice, and even abuse each other. Yet it is remarkable that all insults conveyed through the drum telegrams are more severely punished than those expressed in words or deeds. The language itself is introduced and specialized by beats on different parts of the drum. There are four distinct notes, which may be imitated with the mouth, and then produce a language which differs absolutely from that in daily use. Example:

To-go-lo-gu-lo-go-lo-gu-lo = madiba (in Dualla) = water, sea, river.

Fig. 84. A Dualla conversing with the Signal-drum. Kamerun (from a photograph).

To-lo-gu-lo-go-lo, or ko-lo-gu-lo-go-lo = bwambo ba mu-tumba (in Dualla) = process, proceedings.

The drum notes cannot only be faintly produced by holding the mouth open and tapping on the cheek, but may also be whistled, which reminds us that the horn-blowing of the Ashanti has likewise a distinct meaning in its signals. Thus the king's own horn proclaims: 'I excel all kings of the world!" The watchword of the head of the town police runs thus: "Bobie sleeps not, he watches for the upholder of the kingdom; in the land of the upholder of the kingdom something watches."

And this language, an independently developed form of speech, indicates a very great treasure in the hands of the not very numerous primitive peoples who possess it. It would appear to be most highly developed in the western parts of equatorial Africa, although scarcely less

Fig. 85. A band of music in Urua, South-east Congo basin. The two in the centre are working the Signal-drum. Right and left of them two are playing the marimba, a wooden piano. To the right in front an ordinary drum (from a photograph).

widespread in Oceania, that is, in the insular lands lying north-west and north-east of New Guinea. In New Pomerania itself the different villages communicate over wide areas by means of the drum-telegraph, which has also a very wide range in the Amazons valley and in Mexico. The North-west Americans, too, possess similar instruments.

The instrument which makes such intercourse possible has a great variety of forms in Africa. The ways in which it is placed differ greatly. In the South Congo lands, as a rule, it is suspended or else carried, whereas in the north it stands on four legs on the ground, or rests on wooden supports. In the south two different forms occur together, one of rounded shape (fig. 83), another like a box, but with the bottom broader than the upper surface with the slit in it (fig. 85). In the north the round, hollowed-out tree-stems lie on the ground under the roof of the village assembly house, and may be 20 inches long. In the Rubi district not much trouble is at first taken to detach the hollowed part from the felled tree. It may happen that the drum is nothing more than the lower part of a fallen tree, 15 to 20 inches long. The Abanza, on the contrary, who dwell in the bend of the Ubanghi, often impart a graceful form to their signal-drum, giving it, for instance, an animal or human shape.

Fig. 86. Bow of the Madi tribe on the Ubanghi, with cane string and little Signal-drum. About one-tenth of the natural size. In the Author's possession.

But the felled tree is not at all needed. Some tribes north-east of the Bakuba are satisfied with a little hollow made in a standing tree. In many parts of the forest such manipulated giants are met with, and such signal-stations are set up wherever there is a pitfall for elephants, a good hunting position where a ferryman on the farther side can be signalled to fetch the prey. In contrast to these gigantic instruments, to this signal system of partly natural growth, are the dainty and charming little instruments

THE DRUM-LANGUAGE

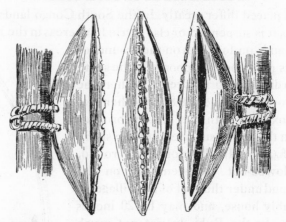

Fig. 87. The little Signal-drum of the Madi bow (fig. 86) about half the natural size—three views.

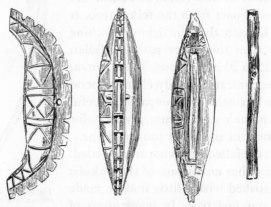

Fig. 88. Little Signal-drum of a bow of the Sango tribe on the Ubanghi; three views; also a little drum-stick (in the Author's possession).

of the north. Being myself the fortunate owner of several of these rare instruments, I may here describe them in some detail.

When the distinguished Professor Schweinfurth for the first time penetrated into the famous Mangbattuland in 1870, he thus described the bow of the natives:

THE DRUM-LANGUAGE

"Their bow is generally about a yard long, with a string of simple split Spanish cane, which in strength exceeds all others. These bows, however, are distinguished from all others known to me by a peculiar fixture to protect the fingers from the recoil of the string. It is a shuttle-like bit of hollowed wood attached to the middle of the bow. In aiming, the arrow is alway shot off between the middle fingers."

In his work on the African bows, Professor Ratzel wrote in 1891:

"But for the authority of Schweinfurth, this attachment as described by him might suggest a musical instrument such as the *gorra*. This gorra, a string instrument common in South Africa, consists of a simple bow on the string of which a calabash is moved to and fro and blown at the points of attachment."

I had long sought in vain for such an instrument, when just at the turn of the last century I managed to get one which was soon after followed by another. The moment I saw the first it was clear to me that Schweinfurth's statement could not be quite correct, since by holding the bow horizontally the poison must inevitably trickle to

Fig. 89. Bamboo drum with wooden stick from Sumbawa, Eastern Archipelago (Imperial Ethnographic Museum). a is the slit of a similar instrument from Celebes, now in the Berlin Museum.

the ground and thus leave the instrument, while, on the other hand, the way of drawing these bows obviates the necessity of any protection against the recoil. I was at once struck by the resemblance of this apparatus to the

THE DRUM-LANGUAGE

wooden drums. Even the dark colour round the slit showed that greasy negro fingers had here played their part. And I was right! From an informant (de Hertogh) I received the following statement: "This little apparatus, which is at times attached to the bows of the Amadi, Abarambo, Mangbattu, Azande, Bangba, serves, for instance, to communicate with each other in the tall grass. The natives have a language which is carried on by slight taps produced by striking the apparatus with an arrow or a little stick. They use the same kind of speech on their large wooden drums." Hence, we have here quite diminutive instruments of the drum-language (figs. 86, 87, 88).

Fig. 90. A Suspended Village Bell, an old Signal-drum. Northern Philippines (after Jagor).

The Oceanic instruments are more varied than the African. We have first of all those of Java and Sumbawa, made of pieces of bamboo. These are separated from the stem on each side of a joint in such a way that a space enclosed between the two partition walls is preserved; and this section of the stem is fashioned to a bamboo drum by a longitudinal slit. These instruments are hung in the trees, and in Java are beaten to call the monkeys to their feeding place. This form I take to be the original (fig. 89).

In the Northern Philippines the Jesuits have intro-

THE DRUM-LANGUAGE

duced an imitation of these in wood to serve as a church
bell (fig. 90).

Fig. 91. Signal-drums and drums-sticks of the
Dayaks of Borneo (after Ling Roth.)

Fig. 92. Signal-drums of Java (Ethnographic
Museum, Leyden).

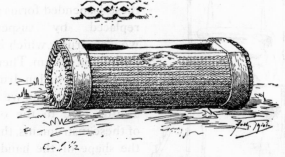

Fig. 93. Signal-drums of the Harvey Islands
(Ethnological Museum, Leipzig).

I take it that this is the normal course of development.
At first these natives made communications by striking

THE DRUM-LANGUAGE

Fig. 94. Signal-drums. Slit tree-stems of the New Hebrides (from a photograph).

against bamboo stems. Then they cut out separate pieces

Fig. 95. New Zealand war-drum (after Angas).

and hung them up. Then these suspended forms were replaced by suspended wooden drums, which is the Philippine system. Then followed the wooden drum in a lying position, and we have a little clue to the origin of these instruments, that is, the shape of the handle at the ends. There is, for instance, the instrument from Borneo (see fig. 91), which still keeps an "ear." This is

THE DRUM-LANGUAGE

a forerunner of the suspended apparatus which we know from the bamboo drum of Sumbawa. The next step in its development (see the wooden drum from Java, fig. 92) is marked by the two ears or handles, both of which persist in the Admiralty Islands and in New Guinea, where we have a superabundance of this kind of carved instruments, ranging as far as New Pomerania. Then the handles disappear eastwards (cf. fig. 93).

There are some other rare forms in the South Sea.

Fig. 96. Teponatzli of the Ancient Mexicans (Ethnographic Museum, Basle).

Such is the pahu, the Maori war-bell which was suspended in the watch-towers of the forts, and with its deadened sound at night proclaimed to the foe that the villagers were on the alert, and to the villagers themselves that their sentinels were eagerly on the look out. The pahu emitted a very sad sound, the strong, heavy strokes breaking the stillness of the night with a solemn monotony, as if it wished to proclaim that it was the death-knell for many who would, next morning, meet the fate of noble warriors (fig. 95).

There are, further, the huge standing wooden drums of the New Hebrides, which consist of entire tree-stems, which are left in the ground, and are much taller than a man. There are whole thickets of such tree-drums, which

93

are often prettily carved above, representing birds, men, and boats in relief (figs. 79 and 94).

Only a very few analogous American instruments have I been able to discover in the European museums. Specially noteworthy is the Teponatzli of the old Mexicans. It is still used on festive occasions in the town of Tepotzlan, Province of Morelos. A few years ago I dug out of a secluded corner in the Basel Ethnographic Museum two old instruments of this kind, one of which is now in Vienna. From the forms hitherto described they so far differ that two tongues project from the sides into the slit (fig. 96).

On the other hand, the affinities of the African and Oceanic forms are quite surprising (see figs. 82 and 83).

CHAPTER VIII

DRUMS AND DRUM-DANCES

SOME say that in the beginning, before the Sun had brought her child into the world, a fight took place between the Sun and the Moon. But when it was over, the Sun called out to the Moon the he (the Moon) was to

Fig. 97. Somali drum which came to hand with the following note: Wooden Mortar as drum (Ethnological Museum, Leipzig).

Fig. 98. Clay drum from the city of Fez, Morocco (Ethnological Museum, Berlin).

take care of her daughter till her return, for she wanted just then to have a wash. Thereupon the moon took the daughter of the Sun in his arms; but he was unable to hold the child of the glowing orb very long, for when he clasped it, it burnt him, and when he felt the heat he let it fall, and it fell on the earth, and that is the reason why it is so hot for the people in the world. Now when the Sun

DRUMS AND DRUM-DANCES

turned round and came back and again saw the Moon, she asked:

"Where is my daughter?"

The Moon answered:

"Your daughter? Well, she burnt me so badly that I let her go, and she fell on the earth.

Fig. 99. Drum made of a pot. Lake Tumba, south of the Congo (Tervœren Museum, Belgium).

Fig. 100. Drum made of an ornamental Goblet. Lukenye River, South of the Congo (Tervœren Museum).

Then the Sun wanted to seize the Moon.

But some say that the path of the Moon was full of thorns and that of the Sun full of sand, and that is also the reason why the Moon cannot travel so fast as the Sun. Now when he is tired of wandering, he is in the habit of getting on to the path of the Sun who then tries to capture him. Now when the Sun has captured the Moon, the people take their mortars, stretch a skin over the opening and beat the drum and pray to the Sun and say:

96

DRUMS AND DRUM-DANCES

"O, Sun, Sun, leave off, or let the Moon fall."

Such is the custom in our land, when the Sun fights with the Moon.

So it is, and it is finished.

This little myth was told to Schön by a Hausa, but what interests us in it just now is the invention of the drum. Evidently the reference is to the action of the Hausas

Fig. 101. Large Drum from Tahiti (Cook's collection in the Historical Museum, Bern).

Fig. 102. Drum of the Dayaks, Borneo (Ethnographic Museum, Leiden).

during a lunar eclipse. They seize their mortars, pass a skin over them and drum upon it. As a supplement to this myth there is in Leipzig a drum with the ticket: "Wooden mortar as a drum; Dulban, Somaliland (see fig. 97). If we have here the mortar as a sound-signal, the same purpose is elsewhere served by a calabash, a clay vessel (fig. 99), or even a beer-barrel. Here I can even produce one of the famous artistic vessels of the Bakuba, which has been made into a little drum by covering it with a skin.

97

DRUMS AND DRUM-DANCES

Now Bücher tells us how the various songs arose in association with the various activities, how the rower composes and sings in keeping with the stroke, how the weaver accompanies the rhythm of the loom in his clattering art, how in like manner the threshing harvester, the hammering carpenter, sings and composes. That in this way from the action of the negro in treading out his millet or pounding his mortar, a musical instrument might have been invented is obvious enough. But I may

Fig. 103. Drummer on the Loango Coast (from a photograph).

here briefly show how the drumskin may have arisen.

The Hottentot skinners take the fresh and smoking hides, and rub them hard with fat until it is worked thoroughly in. Then two of them take hold of the hide, as two housemaids do with a dusty carpet, and beat it might and main with stout sticks.

The Marutse (Barotse) finish off the process of skin-dressing, after removing the scraps of flesh, the sinews, etc., with a metal scraper or any other scratching imple-

DRUMS AND DRUM-DANCES

ment, by rubbing oily or fatty substances hard into both sides of the skin, so that from two to six men in a squatting position may press it with their hands, keeping time and singing, and rubbing it bit by bit together until the whole becomes quite dry and pliant.

According to Fritsch the best leather-dressers in South Africa are the Bechuanas. With them although violent action of the body is unavoidable, the process is carried on with a zeal and energy which are scarcely displayed by the natives in any other pursuit. The tiring work, in which in the case of large hides several persons usually take part, becomes for them a sociable pleasure, which appears to be considerably heightened by the peculiar monotonous humming with which they accompany the measured beat of hands and feet.

The same Bechuanas, who thus enjoy the measured beat of hands and feet in this sociable work, when they celebrate the puberty rites, make an instrument for beating time by several of them holding an ox-hide on the stretch and beating it soundly with sticks to the accompaniment of the same buzzing sound. Thus it becomes a very simple matter. The drum is a hybrid sort of instrument, one part of which, the sounding-case, owes its origin to the pounding of corn; the other, the skin, to the measured beat in leather-dressing. In this connexion room may here be found for the description of a tribe north-west of the Ubanghi bend, for which I am indebted to M. Charles Roland, who on his part took it from his nephew's diary.

It is night, and the full moon has now for the first time risen in its full brightness. Oh, how beautiful, how clear! The sky so splendid! And the wide, wide world! In our camp on the hill we enjoy a delightful prospect over the

DRUMS AND DRUM-DANCES

lovely plain, the bushes skirting the banks of the winding stream—the villages.

It is a glorious night!

Here I am seated at the camp-fire, and scribble with numb fingers in my diary. How can one feel so cold when the world shines so fair? Yet it is cold, very cold!

And all is hushed!

Now, however, something is astir down in the village; it is like a soft murmur, like the moaning of the sea heard from afar off. Are the blacks down below once again consulting and praying to their gods? Or are they, perhaps, uttering a hymn of praise for the beauty of the world?

But now it becomes interesting. In two rows they move out from the village to the open, each fourth or fifth person carrying something. On the right are the men, decked with a wild head-dress, on the left the women their hair cut short. I can see what the women are carrying—their mortars, and now they stop. Then they describe a wide circle round about the men, always standing in twos or threes at a mortar. And now the men spread out within the circle. Now I can perceive what they have, their leather cloaks, which they lay hold of in threes and fours.

But now such an uproar is suddenly raised, as if the devil himself had lighted on the procession. Such stamping, thumping, banging, shouting and singing! And there is an end of the delightful stillness.

Omakiruko has just arrived. With the uproar he can no more sleep than all the others. In this case his friendship is of some value to me. He can tell me the meaning of what is going on below, translate the words of

DRUMS AND DRUM-DANCES

the songs. He stands by my side, and whispers in my ear:

> The pounding of the mortars makes a dull sound.
> "Much millet, much millet; good crops, good crops!
> I will fill the bread-basket of my husband.
> My children will I nourish.
> Much millet, much millet; good crops, good crops!"

So sang the women.
The blows fall with a crash on the leather cloaks.

Fig. 104. Corrobory. Nocturnal festive dance of the Queensland Natives, at which the time is given by the simultaneous beating of boomerang and throwing club (after Lumholtz).

> In the river valley antelopes, so numerous I cannot count them.
> Antelopes, antelopes, antelopes.
> Elephants with heavy white tusks for the white people [Europeans].
> Antelopes, antelopes, antelopes.

How they keep it up!

Dancing and buzzing for two mortal hours! I grow wearied, but I don't know whether with all this row I shall be able to sleep. Omakiruko thinks it will be kept up till next morning. At break of day the women will stretch their husband's cloaks over the mortars and go on cheerfully drumming, while the lords of creation give

DRUMS AND DRUM-DANCES

themselves up to a wild drinking bout. But to witness such a scene as this one does not need to keep awake all night in Africa. So I decide, like the others, to lie down again.

But stay! Omakiruko draws my attention to something that I must at once tell you of.

Apart from the great circle stand three women at a mortar. They are dressed differently from the other women, for strings of white beads hang from their necks low down on the breast. They pound their mortar like the others to a given measure; they also mutter as they do.

But listen! Their muttering has no meaning. They cannot and must not pray for anything, for they are widows, who for one year are excluded from the circle of the merry folk, and pass a sad widowed existence, a period of hard privations in food and drink.

And when they slumber, they slumber each on the grave of her husband who is buried in the middle of the hut.

That was no pleasant conclusion to the revels that Omakiruko sprang upon me. The night had been so beautiful, and now dark thoughts go wandering over the plain.

CHAPTER IX
PICTURE-WRITING AND DECORATION

WITH this chapter we touch the sphere of more advanced peoples, for pictorial writing indicates a preliminary step to a real phonetic script universally intelligible. The difference between a phonetic script and picture writing consists in the latter being always liable to the possibility of a narrower or wider interpretation, whereas the former works with symbols once for all definitely determined. The latter again takes no account of the sound, and represents events, facts or objects alone, while the former is able to reproduce the sound, each sound, or at least the greater part of the sounds. We know that other peoples also, such as the Chinese and Egyptians, had a pictorial script before they reached a phonetic system.

Let us now look more closely into this pictorial script, and this can best be done by keeping to the Indian texts. Here is first of all the life-history of Running Antelope, a chieftain of the Uncpapa Dakotas, who in 1873 depicted it on paper for Dr W. J. Hoffmann in the following eleven scenes. These eleven scenes, which were painted in water-colours in Dr Hoffmann's book, represent the principal events in the life of the chief.

Fig. 105. Two Arikara Indians were killed on one day. The spear in his hand pointing at the foremost enemy means that he slew this one with that weapon. The other to the left was, as we see, killed with the musket, which is going off, and struck down with the spear.

Fig. 105.

Fig. 106. An Arikara shot and scalped. He appears to have tried to make Running Antelope think that he was

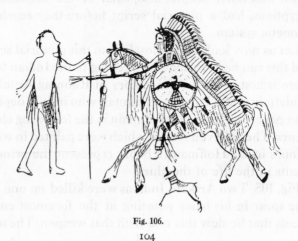

Fig. 106.

PICTURE-WRITING & DECORATION

unarmed, for his right hand points with outstretched fingers outward to indicate the gesture of negation.

Fig. 107.

Fig. 107. An Arikara shot and killed.
Fig. 108. Two Arikaras killed on one day.

Fig. 108.

Fig. 109. Ten men and three women killed.

Fig. 110. Ten Arikara leaders killed. Their rank is

Fig. 109.

indicated by attachments to the sleeves, consisting of weasel skins. The arrow on the left side of the narrator

Fig.110.

PICTURE-WRITING & DECORATION

shows that he was wounded. The scars were still plainly recognizable on the chief's body.

Fig. 111.

Fig. 111. An Arikara killed, being struck down with the bow, which is regarded as the greatest disgrace that

Fig. 112.

can happen to a warrior, a deed which, on the other hand, the hero of the event shows himself very proud of.

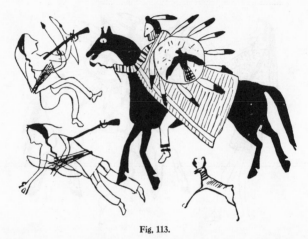

Fig, 113.

Fig. 112. An Arikara killed, and a horse captured.
Fig. 113. Two Arikara hunters killed, shot with the

Fig. 114.

PICTURE-WRITING & DECORATION

musket, as is clearly shown, both of them being represented with the gun. The strokes on the enemy indicate the explosion of the guns and the parts hit by the bullets. The upper figure was in the act of shooting an arrow when he was killed.

Fig. 114. Five Arikaras killed on one day. The dotted

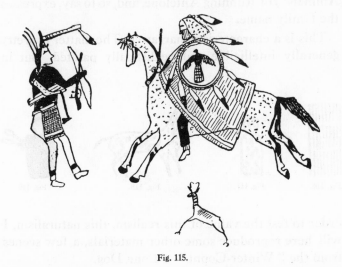

Fig. 115.

line indicates the track followed by Running Antelope. When the Indians found that they were being pursued, they took refuge behind an isolated bush, and were thus killed at leisure. The five guns in a row represent the five armed persons.

Fig. 115. An Arikara killed.

In the foregoing drawings, all of which have reference to incidents in a war between two tribes, and cover the period from 1853 to 1865, Running Antelope is figured with his characteristic insignia. On the one hand, the

PICTURE-WRITING & DECORATION

warrior's name is always indicated by the springing antelope below the horse. This antelope is always drawn in just the same way, as if it were done with a block or stamp, which shows how expert the narrator had become in drawing this signature. The bird on the shield refers to the tribe, or the totem (see the chapter on "Sacred Animals") of Running Antelope, and, so to say, expresses the family name.

This is a characteristic narrative. The matter is pretty generally intelligible and realistically painted. But in

Fig. 116.   Fig. 117.   Fig. 118.   Fig. 119.

order to test the value of this realism, this naturalism, I will here reproduce some other materials, a few scenes from the "Winter-Count" of Lone Dog.

On Plate I have figured the whole "Winter-Count," which represents a record comprising seventy-one years and beginning with the "winter" 1800-1801. Here we see the hide, the buffalo hide, on which, arranged in a spiral line, the more important events of these seventy-one years are represented or indicated. The whole series begins with the figure in the centre containing the thirty strokes.

Fig. 116. 1800-1801. Thirty Dakotas were killed by Crow Indians. The drawing consists of thirty parallel black strokes disposed in three divisions, the outer strokes being continuous. In this art such black lines always mean

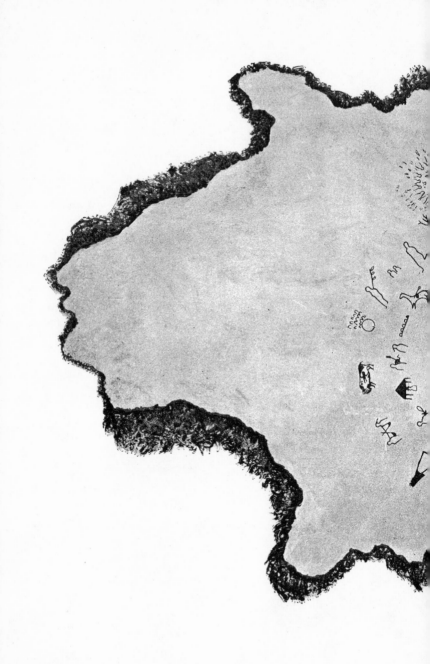

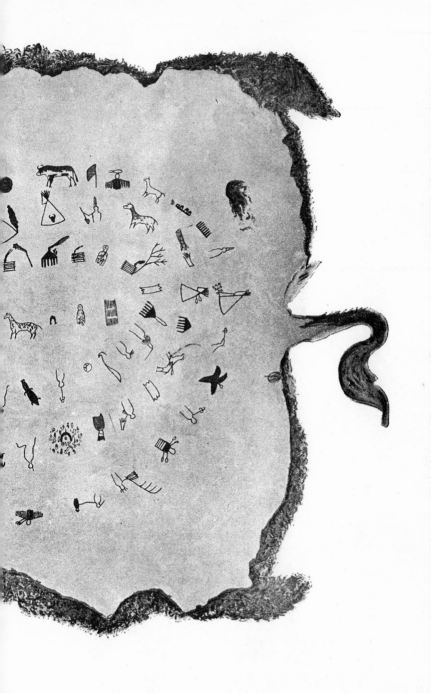

PICTURE-WRITING & DECORATION

death, here the Dakotas struck down by the enemy. The Crow or Absaroka Indians, although akin to the Dakotas and also members of the Siouan family, have been

Fig. 120.   Fig. 121.   Fig. 122.

at war with the Dakotas ever since Europeans have known anything of them.

Fig. 117. 1801-1802. Many died of small-pox. The figure is a head and body covered with spots.

Fig. 118. 1803-1804. A few horses were stolen from the Crow Indians.

Fig. 119. 1807-1808. Red Coat, a chief, was killed. The

Fig. 123.   Fig. 124.   Fig. 125.

figure shows Red Coat pierced by two darts and blood trickling from his mouth.

Fig. 120. 1821-1822. The chief event of this year was the fall of a very fine meteor.

Fig. 121. 1823-1824. United States soldiers attack the Arikaras with the help of the Dakotas. The figure shows a fortified village being fired by a soldier.

PICTURE-WRITING & DECORATION

Fig. 122. 1825-1826. Great floods on the Missouri, by which some Indians were drowned and swept away. In the picture, heads floating in the water seem to be indicated.

Fig. 123. 1831-1832. Le Beau, a white man, killed another named Kermel. This Le Beau was still living in the year 1877, at Little Bend, thirty miles from Fort Sully.

Fig. 124. 1832-1833. Lone Horn had "killed" his leg,

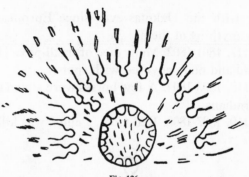

Fig. 126.

as indicated by the picture. The "lone" horn is clearly seen on the figure, as is also one leg, broken or dislocated.

Fig. 125. 1851-1852. Treaty of peace with the Crows or Absarokas. The two tribes are represented by two Indians in different hair-dress, who are exchanging the calumet of peace.

Fig. 126. 1870-1871. The last figure in the record. The Uncpapas had a fight with the Crow Indians, in which they lost fourteen men, and were said to have killed twenty-nine of the foe. In the centre there appears to be a barricaded fort, and bullets, not arrows or spears, are whizzing through the air.

PICTURE-WRITING & DECORATION

When we look at the scenes here reproduced, we are struck by the fact that in general they deal only with incidents; hence that, strictly speaking, there can here be no question of a script, properly so called. They are simply pictures.

Still, quite a number of signs point to a distinct de-

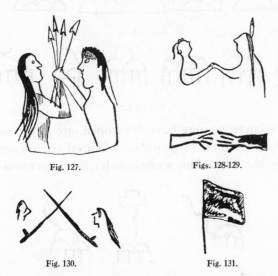

Fig. 127.

Figs. 128-129.

Fig. 130.

Fig. 131.

velopment of writing. In these pictorial scenes there are differences. When a horse is figured, as in fig. 118, that may mean all kinds of things, that a horse has been stolen, that an epidemic has broken out amongst the horses, that some were killed, died, and so on, and it is left to the memory of the chronicler or to tradition properly to interpret the sign. On the other hand, it is otherwise with fig. 116, with its thirty strokes, since such vertical strokes always indicate death. The figure of any man accompanied by such a stroke tells us this man is dead. Hence, such a mark has already a better right to be called a

PICTURE-WRITING & DECORATION

written character. In other words, this latter sign has advanced from the memorandum of a personal reminiscence to a generally intelligible written character.

Our picture (fig. 125), shows the way by which this

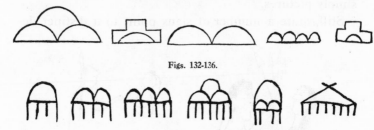

Figs. 132-136.

Figs. 137-142.

picture language may have developed into a true script. The two calumets of peace here figured are universally intelligible. The whole scene is no longer a representation

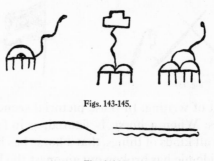

Figs. 143-145.

Figs. 146-147.

of a number of separate incidents, but the production of a symbol. By means of a few more examples it will be shown how such a symbol possesses a higher value as a written sign than a complete representation.

Figs. 127 to 129 represent treaties of peace. In the first are shown two persons with weapons; then two slightly

PICTURE-WRITING & DECORATION

indicated figures joining hands; then two hands alone. Into the first we may still read a great number of things; the second is already more expressive, while at last the third is pat to the point, simple and full of meaning. Further, in fig. 125, a considerable number of signs were figured by the two men round about the calumet of peace. In the following (fig. 130) these two pipes already stand out independently. And when in fig. 131 is represented nothing but a flag as a symbol of peace, although this is

Fig. 148.   Fig. 149.   Fig. 150.

a borrowed sign, we have reached the very acme of brevity and expressiveness, the shortest possible representation of the idea of "peace."

What we here see is certainly one way of development, a way which we may follow in two directions. The first detailed descriptive pictures are altogether the best, considered from the standpoint of the art critic.

The last, on the contrary, must be described as mere scrawls. Thus, as they increase in value as written signs they deteriorate as natural representations. If we look at the accompanying pictures from this point of view, we see it all in a new light. The most informing and the clearest signs from the standpoint of a script (figs. 148 to 150) are the most jejune considered from the standpoint of art.

Now we come to one of the most interesting facts in ethnology. Those races that are the least civilized, that is to say, the African pygmies and the Australians, are by far the most skilful artists in sign drawing of all primi-

PICTURE-WRITING & DECORATION

tive peoples. How is this to be explained? And does it stand in any relation to the subject just discussed?

In order to do the matter full justice, the reader must be good enough to inspect the Bushman drawings reproduced in the next chapter. I will draw his attention especially to one of the very first, the dog (fig. 155); then the hunting scene; then the cattle-raiding, etc. All these are quite superb performances, are little works of art such as are never produced by the infinitely more cultured Central Africans. The drawings of the often despised Australians must also be described as excellent. These also have reached a degree of development which stands indescribably higher than that of the world-renowned Polynesians.

Now if we turn to America itself, we shall find the problem of this phenomenon clearly unfolded and solved before our eyes. In the North we have the Eskimo, a people who, not only in their general state of culture, but above all in their artistic accomplishments, stand on a level with the Australians and the pygmies of Africa. Here we find the same charming designs; but here also we have the same lack of ornamentation, of decorative scrollwork. Southwards the Eskimo are conterminous with those Indian tribes whose pictorial script we have just reproduced, and amongst whom natural and realistic representation seems to pass into a written script, while art in the proper sense tends to vanish.

Lastly, we reach the third stage farther South. Here we have the Mexicans who, as we know, were provided with a somewhat fully developed pictorial script, which displayed an extraordinary richness of ornamentation, but was totally lacking in the power of realistic representation, "picture-work," like that of the Bushmen and

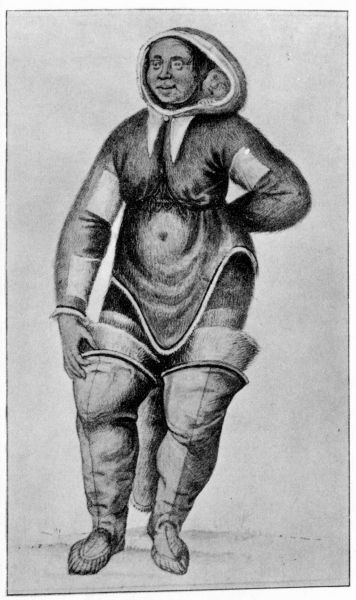

AN ESKIMO WOMAN WITH A BABY PEEPING OUT OF HER HOOD
From the original water-colour drawing in the British Museum
by John White, Governor of Virginia in 1587.

PICTURE-WRITING & DECORATION

Eskimo. Yet another little step, and we reach the culminating point in the Southern Mayas of Yucatan. Characteristic of these is the ideal and fully developed pictorial writing, overdone with ornamentation but quite lacking in the element of realistic representation.

Thus at four different stages one feature dwindles and disappears completely, while a new element emerges from the loss. Thus stand the facts of the case. But how shall we form a judgement of them, how arrive at an understanding of them?

To find a correct solution of the problem that here presses for explanation, we need but mention two facts.

1. Anybody can understand an Eskimo drawing. To explain it we have no need of a native.

2. To decipher the Maya writings the most eminent scholars have worried themselves for several decades past. For the Maya culture died out, and we know very little about it.

That tells us enough. From all these facts we get the broad statement that culture lives in the soul of man, that man has become introspective or self-conscious, that it is an entirely new world in which he lives, namely, the culture created by himself. So far as he distorts the natural images into written characters, so far as he boldly turns from the simple outward forms of nature, so far does he assert his independence in all things, so far is he a man.

But we must now study more closely the mental peculiarities of the various periods, in order to see how man has enlarged his interests, his intelligence and power of insight. I begin with the artists of the early times, with the pygmies, who produce those dainty drawings.

CHAPTER X
ANIMAL STORIES OF THE BUSHMEN

I

CAGN was the first in the world; he gave orders and caused all things to come forth; he made the sun, the moon, stars, wind, mountains. His wife's name was Coti. He had two sons; the elder was a leader and his name was Cogaz; the name of the other was Gewi. There were three great leaders: Cagn, Cogaz and Quanciquchaa, who were very strong, but Cagn gave his orders through the other two.

II

CAGN'S wife, Coti, took her husband's knife and used it to sharpen a digging stick, and she dug roots to eat.

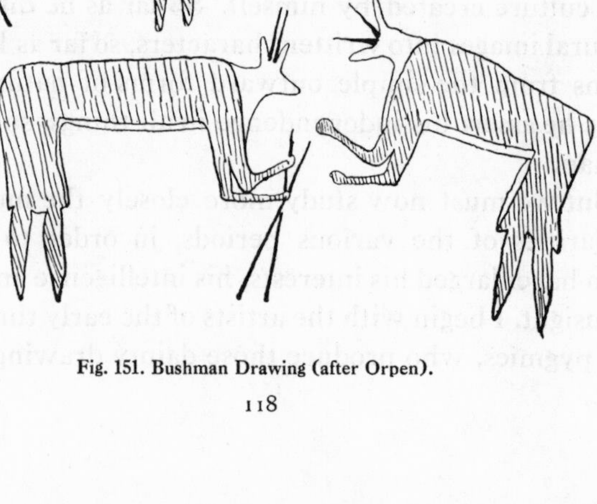

Fig. 151. Bushman Drawing (after Orpen).

ANIMAL STORIES OF THE BUSHMEN

When Cagn found her, she had lost his knife; he scolded her and said misfortune would come upon her. Then she conceived and brought forth a little eland calf in the fields and told her husband. She said she did not know what kind of child it was, and he ran to see it, and when he came back he ordered Coti to rub some kanna that he might learn what it was. She did so, and he went and he sprinkled the magic charm over the animal, and asked it:

"Are you this animal? Are you that animal?"

But it remained silent till he asked:

"Are you an eland?"

Then it said:

"Yes."

Fig. 152. Bush-
man Drawing
(after Barrow).

Then he clasped it in his arms, went off and bought a calabash, in which he put it, and carried it to a secluded cleft in the rock which was surrounded by hills and chasms. Here he let it grow up.

At the same time he made all animals and things, and made them useful for man, and he made snares and weapons. He created the partridge and the striped mouse, and made the wind, that the game might follow the wind, for it always runs behind it. Cagn took three sticks and sharpened them, and threw one at the eland, and it ran off, and he called it back, and missed with all of them, and each time he called it back again. Then he went to his nephew to get poison for the arrows, and he was three days away.

While he was away, his sons, Cogaz and Gewi, went out with young people to hunt, and came upon the eland which their father had hidden; but they knew nothing about it. For them it was a new animal. Its horns had just grown, and they tried to surround and stealthily shoot it. But it always broke through the circle, and when it came back it lay down in the same place. At last, while it was asleep, Gewi, who could shoot well, pierced it through, and they cut it up and took the flesh and blood home.

But after cutting it up they saw Cagn's traps and snares, and they knew he had made them and were afraid.

But on the third day Cagn came back, and he saw the blood on the ground where it was killed, and he was very angry, and when he came home he told Gewi he would punish him for his audacity and disobedience, tore his nose off and flung it into the fire.

But he said:

"No, I won't do this," and put his nose on again; and said:

"Now try to make good again the harm you have done, for you have spoilt the elands when I was making them fit for use."

So he ordered him to take some of the eland's blood, put it in a pot and stir it with a small Bushman stick, which he turned round in the blood, twirling the upright stick between his hands; and he scattered the blood about and it was changed into snakes, and they went far away. But Cagn told him he must not make such dreadful things; so he stirred again, scattered the blood, and changed it to hartebeests, which ran off. Then his father said:

"I am not satisfied, this is not yet what I want. You can do nothing at all. Throw the blood away. Coti, my wife, clean this pot and bring more blood from this disembowelled little beast from which they took it, and stir it."

She did so, and added the fat from the heart; she stirred it and scattered it about, and then the drops became male elands, which surrounded her and butted her with their horns, and he said:

"You see how you have spoilt the elands."

And he drove these elands out. Then they stirred again, and produced a great many elands, and the earth was covered with them. Then he said to Gewi:

"Go and hunt them and try to kill one; this is now your work, for it was you who spoilt them."

And Gewi ran and did his best, but he came back with tired feet and worn out. And next day he hunted again and was unable to kill one. For they were able to run very fast because Cagn was in them.

Then Cagn sent Cogaz to drive the elands towards him, and Cagn shouted, and the elands came running close behind him, and he hurled throwing-spears and killed three bulls. Then he sent Cogaz hunting, and gave him a blessing, and he killed two; then he sent Gewi, and he killed one.

On that day, wild animals were given to men to eat, and the reason of it was that they were spoilt and had become wild. Cagn said he must punish the men and make it hard for them, because they tried to kill the things he had made, which they did not know.

ANIMAL STORIES OF THE BUSHMEN

III

THE big people depicted as deformed are the Oobé. They wielded battle-axes, and are so distinguished.

They were cannibals; they cut off men's heads, killed the women and sucked the blood from their noses. Cagn sent Cogaz to their place of abode to rescue a woman from them and lent him his tooth. His toothache had caused him to send Cogaz. Cogaz went, and when he came back Cagn saw the dust and sent the little bird

Fig. 153. Bushman Drawing (after Orpen).

which flies up and says tee-tee, and in the Sesuto language is called moti, and quoka in the Bushman language, but it said nothing. Then he sent another bird, the tink-tinki, or tintinyane, the qinqininya of the Bushmen, and it brought back no news. Then he sent a third, the qeip, a black and white bird which sings in the early morning, called tswannafike in Sesuto, and he rubbed kanna on its bill and it flew into the dust, and came back with the news that the giants were coming.

The giants seized Cogaz several times, but he had only to apply Cagn's tooth, when he grew so tall that they were unable to reach up to him.

ANIMAL STORIES OF THE BUSHMEN

He generally cooked his food up there and then he used to blow on a reed-flute and this put them to sleep, and whenever he went out they watched and followed him. Then he would again apply the tooth.

At last when they continued to attack him, he killed some of them with poisoned arrows, and Cagn said he would not have those people, and he drove them far away and killed them, as they were cannibals, and he took off his caross (cloak) and sandals and changed them

Fig. 154. Bushman Drawing (after Orpen).

into hounds and wild dogs, and set them at the Oobé giants and destroyed them.

IV

THE head chief Owanciquchaa used to live alone. He had no wife because the women would not have him. A man sent out a number of little boys to cut sticks for the women, and look for ants' eggs. One of these women murmured because she found out that her stick was crooked and those of the others straight.

That same night she dreamed that an ape (baboon) came to take a young girl for his wife, one that had refused Owanciquchaa.

ANIMAL STORIES OF THE BUSHMEN

Next day, when she was digging alone, the ape came to her in a rage; he had been present and had overheard the remark about the crooked stick, and he thought she was jeering at his crooked tail, and he said:

"Why do you insult me?"

On this he threw a stone at her, and she ran home and told the girl about her dream and that it would so happen, and advised her to escape to Owanciquchaa. Then the girl sank into the ground and came up again in another

Fig. 155. Bushmen Drawing (after Orpen).

place, and sank again. She sank three times, and just as often came up again, and thus reached Owanciquchaa's dwelling-place.

Owanciquchaa had killed a red roebuck, and was just skinning it, when he saw the elands running about and wondered what could have suddenly startled them. He let the flesh be, took the skin and went home, where he found the young girl and asked why she came. She said she had been frightened by the ape. He ordered her to fetch water to wash the blood from his hands. She went, and came running back in a great fright and spilled some on Owanciquchaa. He said:

"What's the matter?"

She answered:

"I have been frightened at the ape."

He said:

"Why were you frightened? Is he your husband, and have you come from your home?"

She answered:

"No, I ran off to you through fear of him."

Then he lifted her on to his head and hid her in his hair.

The ape came at the same time to the people she had left and asked for her, and they said they did not know where she was. But he smelled where she had sunk in the ground, and he took great pains to track her out everywhere, and when he came to Owanciquchaa, the elands were startled and ran about and stared at him. He then came to Owanciquchaa with his kirri (throwing club) and asked:

"Where is my wife?"

Owanciquchaa said:

"I have not got thy wife."

He turned on Owanciquchaa and fought him, but Owanciquchaa overcame him and struck him down with his own kirri. Then Owanciquchaa drove him off to the hills, saying:

"Go! eat scorpions and roots, as becomes a baboon."

And he went screaming away, and the screaming was heard by the women in the place he came from, and all the apes were driven away.

Owanciquchaa killed an eland and cleaned himself, because the ape had soiled him, and ordered the girl to go home in order to tell the people that he was still alive. The young men wanted to marry the girl, but she said:

"No, I love nobody but Owanciquchaa, who has rescued me from the ape."

So they began to hate Owanciquchaa; and when he

killed a red eland and put flesh on the fire to roast, those young men took fat from a snake they had killed and let it trickle on the flesh. Now when he cut off a piece and put it in his mouth it fell out, and when he cut off another it fell out again, and the same the third time. Then the

Fig. 156. Bushman Drawing (after R. Andree). The Bushmen have stolen some cattle from the Kafirs and are driving them off, the Kafirs in pursuit.

blood streamed from his nose. Then he took all his things, his weapons and clothes, and hurled them into the sky, and he himself plunged into the river. There were villages down there, and young women who tried to catch Owanciquchaa, but he changed himself into a snake, and said:

"No, by women I was killed."

And he evaded them and threatened them so that they all ran away. The only girl that remained was the one he had rescued, and she made a hut, went and sought about everywhere, made kanna, and laid pieces in a row from the river bank to the hut. And the snake came out and ate the magic charms and returned to the water.

Next day it did the same, and the following night he came and went to the hut, took a mat, climbed up to the sky and fetched his caross. Then he came down and slept on the mat.

When the girl saw that he had been there, she spread out the magic charm again, and set herself to watch. Then the snake came out of the water, raised its head high

Fig. 157. Bushman Drawing (after Orpen).

up, looked round cautiously and suspiciously, and then glided out of the snake skin and went about sleepily; then, picking up the magic charm, he went to the hut.

When he was fast asleep, she came in and forcibly made him take more magic charm in his mouth, and he struggled hard and tried to get away from her. But she held him fast, and when he was tired out, he asked, trembling:

"Why do you hold me, you who are the cause of my death?"

She said:

"Although I was the cause, still it was not my fault, for I loved you and none other besides you."

And she smothered him in the caross, ran to the skin, sprinkled it with kanna and burnt it. And they remained three days there. And Owanciquchaa killed an eland, cleaned himself and his wife and ordered her to grind some kanna. She did so, and he sprinkled it on the ground, and all the elands that were dead came to life again. Some came with the darts in their body which had been thrown at them by people who wanted to kill them. He pulled the darts out; there was a large bundle of them, and they remained in his place. It was a place enclosed by hills and precipices, with a pass which was always filled with cold, numbing fog, so that nobody could get through, and those people all remained outside; at last they ate twigs and died of hunger.

But his (or her) brother, who had wounded an eland in the hunt, followed at its heels through the fog, and Owanciquchaa saw the eland running about, frightened at the wounded eland and the dart sticking in its side. He came out, saw his brother, and said:

"O my brother, I have been annoyed. You see now where I am."

Next morning he killed an eland for his brother, and told him he might go back to call his mother and friends, and he did so. When they came, they informed him how the other people outside had died of hunger, and they abode with him, and the place smelt of flesh.

V

CAGN sent Cogaz to cut sticks to make bows. When Cogaz came to the bush the baboons caught him. They called all the other baboons together to hear him, and they asked him who sent him. He said his father sent him to cut sticks and make bows with them. Then they said:

"Your father thinks himself cleverer than we are. He wants these bows to kill us, therefore we will kill you."

ANIMAL STORIES OF THE BUSHMEN

They killed Cogaz, fastened him to the top of a tree, and danced, singing an untranslatable ape-song round about the tree with a chorus which said:

"Cagn thinks he is clever."

Cagn was asleep when Cogaz was killed; but when he awoke, he bade Coti give him his magic charms, and he took some by his nose and said, "The apes have hung up Cogaz." So he went where the baboons were, and when these saw him coming close, they changed their tune, leaving out the part about Cagn. But a little ape-girl said:

"Sing not this way; sing as you sung before."

Cagn said:

"Sing as the little girl wishes."

Then they sang and danced as before, and Cagn said:

"That is the song that I heard, this is what I wanted; keep up the dancing till I come back."

He went and fetched a bag full of wooden nails, and came behind each of them as they were dancing and causing much dust, and drove a peg into each of their backs; then there was a great uproar, and he sent them off, so that for punishment they should live in the mountains on roots, beetles and scorpions.

Formerly the apes were men, but since then they have tails and their tails are crooked. Then Cagn brought Cogaz down, gave him kanna and made him alive again.

ANIMAL STORIES OF THE BUSHMEN

VI

THE thorns were a people; they were called Cagncagn; they were dwarfs, and Cagn found them fighting together. Now when he went to separate them, they all turned against him and killed him. The biting ants helped them, and they ate up Cagn.

But after a while they and the dwarfs collected his bones, laid them together and bound his head to them, and these (that is, his bones) went stumbling home.

Cogaz cured him, made him well again, and asked what had happened to him. He told him, and Cogaz gave him advice and power, saying how he was to conquer them, and advised him to try the following ruse. He was to pretend to strike at their legs, and then hit their heads. And so he went off, killed many and drove the rest to the mountains.

THE Bushmen have been called dwarfs, and the African pygmy races present a very old problem. Many fables were told about them, but they were scarcely believed in. So long as the Bushmen of South Africa were regarded as a distinct race apart from the Zulu peoples, nobody spoke exactly of pygmy natives. But when towards the middle of the nineteenth century reports began to spread about people of small stature living amongst tall negroes, and representing a distinct negrito race, the scientific world pricked up its ears. At first people laughed incredulously. But then the great pioneer, Schweinfurth, penetrated southwards to the Nile-Congo waterparting, and there he found them, and their exis-

ANIMAL STORIES OF THE BUSHMEN

tence was now scientifically established. Since the year 1871 we have an African pygmy race, that is, a race which in its pure genuine conditions is from about six to eight inches shorter than the negro proper.

Of course, we are not to fancy that these African negritos are at all like the little people of our folk-lore. They have neither a disproportionately large head, nor a long beard; they neither wear pointed caps, nor have they any understanding either of beneficent or malevolent magical arts, although they are in truth mischievous enough. To the ordinary observer one of the Akka tribe, or of the Batwa, or Bushmen, looks just like an ordinary negro, the more fundamental physical differences being perceptible only to very thorough specialists.

At the southern extremity of the continent dwell the so-called Bushmen, distributed somewhat uniformly but becoming more sporadic northwards. Here they are still met only in small groups, so to say, as timid fugitives in the woodlands. Their range is in fact

Fig. 158. Bushman drawing which according to a Bushman's statement represents a leather travelling-bag. From an original copy in the possession of Missionary Bleek.

that of a race that has been pushed aside. They dwell as hunters in the wilderness, in the primeval forests, that is to say in regions that have little attraction for other races. They represent the typical hunters of the whole world, the lovers of freedom and independence. And where they are met as associates or followers of the settled populations, and frequenting their camping-ground, they may be called the "free-lances" of the hunt. Where they are associated with the agricul-

ANIMAL STORIES OF THE BUSHMEN

turists, they are neither slaves nor serfs. They serve the great potentates of the Mangbattu, of the Bakuba, of the Bateke and of the other great agricultural peoples, as free hunters, as independent stalkers of large game.

Thus these little folk represent the hunt, the most original, the most early developed and most vigorous form of the hunt. Free of all hampering property, never settled, never *adscriptus glebæ* by any crafts, industries or duties to the State, the African negrito ranges unfettered over his hunting-grounds. He has no fixed abode, he is not tied to any particular spot, for instance, to the vicinity of an iron mine where he might forge the material for his hunting weapons, or of any pottery works, since his cuisine dispenses with all earthenware utensils. Everywhere he finds the brushwood, which he can entwine as a bower over his and his wife's sleeping place. His arrow is tipped with wood or bone or a suitably worked stone. Where he dwells in the neighbourhood of negro workers in iron, he obtains from them the points for his arrows by barter. He does absolutely no cooking beyond throwing the flesh on the fire. In the forest he would also appear to roast it between hot stones, or simply to eat it raw if no fire is available.

These are the men from whom are derived the above quoted myths or fables or stories, or whatever they are to be called, and also the pictures reproduced in this chapter. These will be easily understood from their life, their usages, their stage of development and its conditions. What we here learn is perhaps the weightiest and rarest of ethnological documents that we possess, since it is the last lisping utterance that reaches us from the childhood of mankind. How wonderfully we are

ANIMAL STORIES OF THE BUSHMEN

affected by this infantile stuttering! how peculiar the sound of this childlike language!

"He, a Bushman, could make no distinction between men and animals, and knew no otherwise than that a buffalo could shoot just as well as a man with a bow and arrow if he had any."

This is a traveller's experience which gives the clue to the sense of the above stories. As they are here told, as they were related to Mr Orpen by a Bushman in explanation of the pictures on the Maluti, they have exactly the same meaning that is expressed in full by the remark

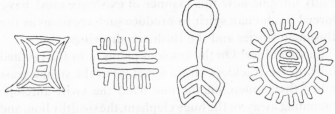

Figs. 159-162.
Bushmen's Drawings (from originals in the possession of Missionary Bleek.)

of another English traveller which I have just quoted. These pygmies have not yet realized the difference between men and animals. We must take them, we must understand them, as they live in their own way, in their solitude.

Primitive men, whom we here meet, after all know nothing but nature and themselves. They are comparatively uninteresting to themselves. They will have naught of each other. They do not understand the notion of individuality. It is not so long ago since the Zulus lived in this same state of development. Hence, they have never been able to reach the level of other races of higher cul-

ANIMAL STORIES OF THE BUSHMEN

tures. Under such conditions, what is there to study in mankind? What have we to learn from other men?

What is ever shifting, what never remains the same, what constantly and always makes demand on the reasoning faculty of man, that is what stimulates us, what we study, what we contemplate. And in this wide nature, which lies so wild and so solitary before us, in which these men, year out year in, daily and hourly, struggle for their sustenance, the animal world attracts man more than does man himself. I regret that space is lacking to describe the struggle between men and animals among these natives. But I suppose that every one will easily imagine how this manner of existence must have forced the human spirit to produce such creations as the Bushman stories and the Bushman drawings.

Just consider! On the spacious plains or in the ravined hills, in the trackless virgin forest or in the steppe-grass taller than a man, on the one hand the swift antelope bounding away, or the huge elephant, the stealthy lion, and on the other the puny little human child, the diminutive Bushman, with his wretched, his miserable weapons. Even to-day the Bushman has not everywhere the bow, nothing but a throwing-club, or an almost ridiculous throwing-spear. And with these miserable weapons this poor weakling must strive to capture these incredibly swift, cunning and powerful animals!

He *must*, I said.

The few roots growing in his district do not suffice to nourish him, for South Africa is singularly poor in such good things, and the Bushman is remarkably inexpert in the use of vegetable foods. Hence, he must almost daily go a-hunting. That in this struggle he has acquired quite an unheard-of experience and knowledge of the mental quali-

ANIMAL STORIES OF THE BUSHMEN

ties of his "foes," the animals, is obvious enough; that he learns to value and respect these qualities is intelligible; and everybody will perceive how all his personal interests, the whole life of his soul, is again and again concentrated in the constant and uninterrupted observation, study and most respectful consideration of these animals. Thus stand the earliest of mankind before us. Assuredly, they are no longer animals; we cannot even say that they have more of the animal in them than the higher and most civilized

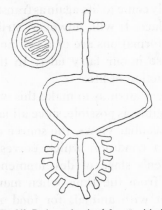

Fig. 163. Bushman drawing (after an original copy in Missionary Bleek's possession).

peoples, since after all they already possess endowments of the very highest significance. They can make fire. They have rules for the family. They have traditions, as we have seen. And they are far more skilled in drawing than any other primitive people.

But we wish here to keep to those peculiarities which they display in contrast with later developments. First and foremost is the fact that they have not yet grasped the difference between man and beast. They have not

ANIMAL STORIES OF THE BUSHMEN

yet thought about themselves. Hence it is that men and animals are always intermingled; hence it is that one can change into the other.

"Change!" That is the most peculiar trait of all. In reading the above narratives one must have been struck with the strange notion harboured by them about death. People die, and lo! they are all at once again somewhere else.

When we look closer, we discover that this dying is nothing more than a transformation, that the dead people quite comfortably come to life again as transformed beings in some other place. It will, however, strike everybody that these transformations are of a far more unpleasant nature than those in our fairy tales. In this idea there lies a deep conviction of life.

I have been very anxious to make this way of viewing nature as intelligible as possible, since all later humanity still entertains peculiar views, the source of which may be detected in a condition which corresponds to the African Bushmen's stage of development. From this primitive state, from the time when man was still in constant conflict with animals for food and even life, flow all the incidents in mythology and all views of the world so far as animals are concerned. When the Indian claims to be descended from a bear, a raven, or a wolf; when the ancient Egyptian thought that his soul would return as a pig, a dog or a crocodile; when the Polynesian lets his sun-god mount as a bird into the sky, radiant and beneficent, or else swoop down destroying and bringing death; when the North German peasant reads an evil omen in the flight of the raven, then all these notions are views and forms of belief which reach us as echoes from the childhood of mankind, from that period when man

ANIMAL STORIES OF THE BUSHMEN

held himself no better than the beast, when man and beast wrestled for the mastery.

This period in the progressive observation of the environment bears the name of *animism*.* It is the view of the world in which the mental qualities of the animal enjoy greater rights than those of man. It is the period in which animals are held in high regard. I pass at once to the next period, to the age in which anim-ism is followed by *man-ism*, to that stage of intuition in which death has been discovered, and in which all views culminate in the measure of influence exercised by the souls of the dead.

* "Animism" means the attribution of soul to all creation, to animals as well as man, and even to inanimate things. This was the prevalent idea of the so-called "animalistic epoch."—*Tr.*

CHAPTER XI

A FUNERAL IN INNER AFRICA

UNDER this heading Professor Dr Max Büchner described at the time a solemn funeral of the Bangala people in the Southern Congo region, at which he himself assisted on Christmas Day in the year 1880. The description ranks with the very best that have ever been made of such incidents among wild people. Büchner writes:

The most notable event during my residence in Kassanye, in the Bangala territory on the Kwango river, was a funeral. Belenge, eldest son of the Bansa (chief), had suddenly fallen seriously ill and was dead in two days. I also was consulted as a physician, but only after the native doctors had exercised their skill on the poor fellow with hot and cold baths, with conjurings, charms and sympathy. I had, however, taken care not to express my opinion openly, and say what was already on the tip of my tongue: "Stop these endless ablutions; your patient is all but dead already." For, had I really made this foolish remark, I should have been punished as a murderer for the death that followed a few minutes later. That is to say, the occasion would have been seized for further extortion.

For amongst the Bangala even the actual fact of the death of a free man must never be announced directly, but only in reply to some question regarding it; and even

138

so the informer must not be the first to utter the ominous word "oaffu" (death), but must wait till this is done by the inquirer. Hence the sad communication should properly be made in this way: A comes and asks B:

Fig. 164. Corpse on the platform. Method of burial in South-East New Guinea (from a photograph).

A FUNERAL IN INNER AFRICA

"How goes it with the Muhongo?"

A shrugs his shoulders with troubled, downcast look.

B: "Dead?"

A: "Dead."

In the present instance the death was soon announced, with the explanation that the Bansa's son had lost his life through the wicked forest fiend Kosh, but probably a wicked wizard in human form had also made his baneful influence felt in the matter.

As with all peoples of the lowest culture, so with the negroes, too, burials give occasion for the greatest festivities, which last the longer the higher is the rank of the deceased. From near and far come the relatives, and often the whole neighbourhood assembles in order to give themselves up for weeks together to a strange mental condition which, in a devilish way, oscillates between grievous wailings, suppressed sufferings and uproarious hilarity. All the drums and other loud-sounding instruments that can be procured are collected. Swine, goats and cattle are killed, day and night are spent in feasting, singing and dancing, broken now and then by loud sobbing; sorghum beer and spirits flow freely, and whoever owns a gun brings it with him in order, from time to time, to blaze away over the heads of the roaring crowds. Probably about half of all the powder imported from Europe into Africa is used up in such senseless displays. The whole night long till the grey dawn these wild scenes are kept up, increasing in intensity and blind frenzy in the flickering and lurid glare of great bonfires. Only during the forenoon there is a little respite, but towards evening it all breaks out again, all are once more on their legs, and the revelry grows fast and furious.

On this occasion, after the drumming, yelling, singing,

A FUNERAL IN INNER AFRICA

dancing and shooting had lasted two nights, the burial was to take place on the third day. Each evening at sunset the deceased had been brought out before the door of his hut, bound fast in a sitting posture to a chair-like frame of rough stakes, the idea being that he also should

Fig. 165. Exposure of the dead in Australia
(after Wood).

take part in the festivities. Then shortly before sunrise he was again hidden away in the hut.

Now to-day also, December 25, the old Bansa came just in the usual way to pay us his morning visit, and while we were taking our coffee he received two famous medicine-men to give them his orders about the burial. The interview seemed to be somewhat ticklish. The men would have nothing to do with the body, and it seemed as if they feared the wicked Kosh might destroy them, too. But it was in vain that they poured out their eloquence in high-pitched voices, though still without failing in respect. They had to yield and obey the chief's orders, going off in a disturbed state of mind and protesting under their breath.

Many other matters still remained to be settled, and as, thanks to its larger size, the white man's house served as a daily "Exchange" for the old chief, much to our own discomfort, all the arrangements were here made. Then came messengers to report that another troop of mourning guests had arrived, and how much each had brought as his contribution to the festivities. Then young men turned up from the village itself to ask whether the twenty fowls and six goats and two oxen, which were to be killed, would suffice. Then again came complaints from the relatives about the outlay for the deceased, but these were found too trifling and rejected. Thus Bansa Nguvu, for instance, had contributed only one flask of powder and four ells of cloth, though the deceased Belenge had been his future son-in-law, and for the daughter, his bride, he had already given at least two pieces of cloth and seven goats as presents for her parents, and they could again put her up for sale, as she was once more free, and thus make further profits by her. For such contemptible niggardliness Bansa Nguvu should expect at most one fowl to eat.

About ten o'clock the medicine-men again appeared to fetch the Bansa, as everything was ready for the interment, and we went with them.

In the open space of the village, facing the hut of the deceased, the chief's relatives sat in groups. The scene presented some picturesque effects of parti-coloured clothes, a few pretty head-dresses, everywhere loud, cheerful gossiping, but not a trace of seriousness. Only in and before the hut, now thrown wide open and already half demolished, were the mourning women sobbing and whimpering, amongst them the dead man's mother and two wives, cowering together close to the body, or stretched flat on the ground and wallowing in the mire. Here they had watched day and night without daring to wash—a most repulsive duty since the body had already

Fig. 166. Drying or mummifying of bodies in Australia (after Wood).

begun to decay, emitting such an odour that even the guests outside held their noses and stopped them with green leaves. It cost me an effort to view the body. The features of the handsome young man could no longer be recognized, the whole face nothing but a repulsive swollen mass swarming with flies. The body was covered with a robe of a flowery red pocket-handkerchief pattern.

We took our seats on mats near the Bansa, on the opposite side of the open space, but soon shifted our places, driven away by the wind, which was just then blowing straight from the body. A few large drums, three marimbas and various rattling instruments played a few muffled notes. But some time passed before the regular ceremony began.

Our two medicine-men of the morning, without any special adornment and clothed only in the loincloth, had meanwhile made a mysterious brew of roots and herbs in two ordinary pots, and now drew near to dip bunches of foliage in the pots and then sprinkle, first the dead and then all round about, within and without, with the mystic concoction. When this disinfection against the influence of the wicked Kosh had been thoroughly attended to, four young men were directed to bring out the corpse. An old woman stood before the door and barred their ingress. So likewise did one of the marimba players by placing his instrument athwart the entrance. Not till the brother of the deceased had bought them off, each with an ell of cheap calico, did they withdraw and allow them to enter.

Now the body appeared, and for a few minutes uncertainty again prevailed as to what was next to be done. After a little wrangling and squabbling—for nothing is conducted quietly and seriously by the negro—the bearers were directed to convey their burden to the back of the hut and lean it against the straw wall. Here some tooth-drawing had first of all to take place; for Belenge had been a great hunter, and in order to prevent his skill from being lost with him, one of his incisors had to be secured and used as hunting medicine. Here, however, it was not a question merely of a rough manual operation, but of a supernatural magical process. All that was needed, so we were generally assured, was to apply a certain root to the tooth, when it would fall out of itself.

The two doctors again approached with the proper

solemn air of the profession. A crowd of inquisitive youths and women, who began at once to press forward, were driven back. Only a few men were allowed to remain as witnesses of the wonderful act now to follow, and I was amongst them, having obtained leave from the Bansa. The two magicians, however, seemed to disagree on the

Fig. 167. Body exposed in a boat as a coffin, North-West America (after Harrow).

point, and now screened off the scene of their art by directing two assistants to lift up their loose upper garments as curtains; whereupon, thus half concealed, they began to operate, muttering the while. As I did not wish to betray any excessive interest, as that would seem undignified, I did not see everything that took place within the enclosure. Still, sufficient peeps were afforded by the space between the two garments and the frequent downward dragging of the screen by other observers. A gentle hammering was distinctly heard, and I really saw through the fissure how one of the doctors firmly held the lower jaw of the dead man, while the other, with a wooden wedge and a stone attached to it, kept tapping round about and was worrying himself, evidently, because he could not effect his purpose. The hammering became louder and louder and less guarded. But the spectators gathered outside only took so far notice of it as to say that was not at all necessary, those stupid doctors did not understand, for if they had a good medicine the tooth must fall out of itself. Presently the tooth was reported out at last, then again no; Belenge was become a Mulosh, a wizard, and even in death possessed the power of baffling the medical science!

All at once the curtain falls. The doctors hurry away, carrying in bleeding hands a small packet of herbs and leaves. The lips of the body were scarified. Kishinta, elder brother of deceased, fires off a strong charge of twenty grains of powder in the air, which means that the tooth has been successfully extracted.

I thought that what I had seen might be explained in this way. The doctors were really bunglers. Being conscious of this themselves, and being at the same time anxious about their usurped calling, they had tried so hard in the morning to decline the Bansa's commission. As they failed in this, they sought by a mechanical process to dispense with the tooth-extracting medicine, which they as firmly believed in as all the others, but which they did not possess. But even in this they acted so clumsily that in the end they had recourse to the simplest and most barefaced trickery, by afterwards slipping another tooth into the packet of leaves which they carried off in such a hurry. Not one of the onlookers, all of whom could have noticed it quite as well as I did, expressed any suspicion.

The body was now laid on the ground, some cloth

Fig. 168. Burial in a hollow tree, East Africa (after Becker).

spread under it, and the whole then awkwardly and tediously lashed round a newly-felled tree-stem in the form of a hammock, and the robe of pocket-handkerchief pattern thrown over the whole. Two young men lifted

A FUNERAL IN INNER AFRICA

the bier on their shoulders, and, while the women re-
newed their sobbing and mourning, brought it into the
open space. Our old chief made them stand on one side
to prevent the keen east wind from blowing the horrible
stench our way. So another group had now to hold their
noses instead of us.

There now followed, if possible, a still more clownish
farce. The deceased had now himself to declare what was
the cause of his death. The two bearers with their load
began to sway to and fro, as if they were being pushed
backwards and forwards by some invisible power. One
of the chief's sons rose, stepped before the body, and
asked in a loud voice, while all was hushed, whether the
dead man was willing to be questioned. A violent forward
plunge of the bearers meant "Yes."

"Whom will you answer? Bansa Kitamba or Banza
Nguvu? or Banza Muhungu? Perhaps your brother
Ginsash? or your younger brother Ngunsa?"

The dead man did not stir from the spot, which meant
"No."

"Would you like, perhaps, to be questioned by Bansa
Moania?"

The bearers fell a-tottering, and were thrust forward,
however hard they seemed to struggle against it.

"So let it be Bansa Moania."

Thus summoned, Moania was visibly disconcerted.
He wanted to have nothing to do with the dangerous
office of "cross-examiner," which could only end in
accusing some objectionable person of witchcraft and murder, and consigning him to the poison ordeal. And when,
after a little struggle, he yielded to the general pressure,
he put his questions in such a low voice and such a faint-
hearted way, that the elder son Kitamba again took the

A FUNERAL IN INNER AFRICA

Fig. 169, Cremation scene of the Rucuyenne Caribs, French Guiana (after Cervaux).

matter in hand, while Moania stood by mincing like a puppet.

I could not quite understand the ensuing proceedings, so was obliged to have them interpreted. Once more the body with its bearers began to tumble about, pressing forwards or remaining quite still. All at once the bearers fell to the ground, bathed in perspiration and thoroughly exhausted. Everybody said it was the women's fault, because they had howled too loud, which was evidently disagreeable and irritating to the dead; only on that account he had thrown down the bearers, and Bansa Kitamba and all the other men cried out that the women should moderate their grief.

Several times the same questions were repeated:

"Tell us, then, what has killed you. Is some vile witch-craft the cause of your death? or was it only the evil spirits? Kosh, perhaps, or the Huiangongo, or some Santo?" (The Santos are originally the Catholic saints, transmogrified in the superstitious belief of the negroes into a kind of hobgoblins.) But no clear answer could be got from him.

At last the deceased declared that he could or would not say anything, because his third brother had gone off to the Tupende land in order to fetch rubber. Then, again, he believed there were both evil spirits and also fetishists concerned in the business, but he seemed unable to be quite sure.

The bearers, who were to deliver the oracle by their movements, were either too tired or too clumsy, or even too biased to do so. Hence, two other young fellows came forward to relieve them. To these some old people had eagerly and excitedly made some secret communications, but did so openly and under the eyes of everybody. Even when they already had the bier on their shoulders, and had advanced to the centre of the open space, a man sprang forward rapidly to whisper something more in their ears.

But even now the deceased did not want to answer all at once. They contended as to who should question him, since, perhaps, personal dislike was to blame for this obstinacy. Several other men essayed in turn to put questions, but, as was obvious, without sure results. The assembly became irritable, and they began to abuse the obstinate dead man. " Speak, then, and keep us no longer in suspense. Do you want us to remain another day waiting here ? A storm is already gathering, rain is falling, and we shall all get wet. You yourself already smell so fearfully (literal) that we can scarcely endure it any longer. So make no further objections, but speak." Such was the language confusedly uttered on all sides.

The bearers again began to stagger, and again to stand still.

Then an ugly old man sprang impatiently forward, seized the front end of the bier with his hand, and pushed and thrust it to and fro or else held it fast according as the questions were to be answered, and the two bearers did willingly what they understood was in this way expected of them.

At last all agreed that the departed Belenge had from first to last declared he had been killed neither by witch-craft alone, nor yet by Kosh alone, but both had worked together; a fetishist had given Kosh power over him, and so he was then struck down. Therewith the questioning was concluded, after it had lasted about three hours.

Now followed a new performance. The malodorous corpse had still to execute the parting dance. The three

A FUNERAL IN INNER AFRICA

marimbas and the great drum struck up, and the two bearers gasping with fatigue began to hop and to caper just before the instruments, so that the body swathed on the bier beat time right and left, swinging like a great bell. Then they made quite suddenly for the old Bansa Kitamba to invite him to the contre-dance. Thereupon he rose, tucked up his clothes, and with a vigour and nimbleness with which nobody would ever have credited him, kicked up his heels for several minutes before the body, which likewise again jumped vigorously up and down. Kitamba's leopard-skin and scarlet robe flew about, and he was hailed with general applause. The children especially shouted loudly and lustily, hastily broke leafy branchlets from the trees, and skipped about behind their old head-chief, switching up the dust with the branches.

In the same way some twenty of the spectators were called upon to dance farewell to the dead, and last of all his mother, too, a hideous-looking dirty old woman, and the blind village cripple. The handsome Kishinta came forward with bow and arrow, and executed a war dance, as if he wanted to fight the whole assembly, and he, too, was joined by the children with much shouting and warlike flourishing of the branches. At the end Kishinta knelt before Kitamba, and presented him with his bow, the string of which he twanged.

Meanwhile, it had grown late. The evening shadows fell, and the distant thunder seemed to get nearer and nearer, and at last to cause awe. Without further ceremony, the body, attended by scarcely a dozen young men, was borne off to that grove marked by three tall palms, which served as the village burial-place. The gathering dispersed, and we went home.

A FUNERAL IN INNER AFRICA

Before us lies unfolded the great problem, the great fact of the second period in the history of man's views of the world. *Men know nothing about the obvious nature of death; they do not yet know that death is inevitable.*

And every time that one departs from amongst them, when the young man lies cold, dumb and mouldering, then they again cudgel their brains, then they again follow up every clue of friendship and enmity, then they again investigate every branch of known and unknown nature, merely to find the answer to the question: "Of what exactly did he die?"

They do not know that man must die, else the question would be: "Why do men die?"

CHAPTER XII

THE GHOST

THE notion of dying, the knowledge of death, the idea of the complete annihilation of the living, the thought that any human being, who to-day dwells, full of joy and vigour, in our midst, could possibly be absolutely extinct to-morrow, all such notions are utterly and entirely foreign to the animistic period, that, for instance, of the Bushmen, as we have studied them in the folk-lore tales. These are the notions which man has struggled with during the second period in the history of primitive philosophies, notions which begin dimly to dawn upon him in this later phase of development, the phase of manism.

In the first period man settled matters easily enough with his dead. He threw them aside without so much as digging them a grave, or at most cast a few stones on the body. That, doubtless, was the expression of a latent sense of fear.

A Bushman of the Kalahari desert told one of the officers of the local German forces that whenever he came across such cairns when hunting, he threw another stone on them. For if the dead are not covered with stones, it might very easily happen that they might rise up again, and "that is not good." But if the body is covered with stones, then it cannot come back again in its old form, but must somehow come back as game, and "that is good."

THE GHOST

But the peoples of the "manistic" period of ancestor worship take quite a different view of the matter. With them, while the pygmy is in the act of simply casting the mortal remains aside, a question begins once in a way to present itself, which has reference to the "how" and the "whereby." In what a crude way these first obscure notions of death are expressed may be better understood from the events related in the foregoing chapter than from any explanation I can personally give. Before all, the first question always is: "In what way has the soul left the body?"

In most cases the answer is, by witchcraft, or, to give it its right name, by the "theft of the soul." The fundamental view of the phenomenon is that body and soul are two distinct things, which no doubt are usually met with together, but which need not at all be always found united in one being.

Not by any means!

A soul may at any time quit its own body. We dream, for instance, that we are wandering in some far-off land. Is it not, then, quite clear to the negro that during the night the soul has indulged in an outing on its own account, without being encumbered with the heavy body, and has escaped to the open? It is certainly not desirable that this should happen too often, but when it does happen, well and good, a little "furlough" must be allowed to the soul!

It is much worse when anything unpleasant takes place, as, for instance, the meeting of two souls in one body. That is something very painful, and, in the scientific language of our advanced way of looking at things, we should call such a poor devil "crazy," and regard him with the deepest compassion. But quite different is the negro's view. For him it is absolutely certain either that

THE GHOST

two souls have encountered each other in this particular body, or else that an alien soul has taken possession of it. And such persons are treated accordingly.

It may happen that the so-called "possessed" are regarded with reverence and held in high esteem, that the convulsive insanity is looked on as a mark of greater spiritual superiority and left to do as it likes. Thus, a few years ago such a possessed person, as he was called, burnt a whole village in the Gaboon district without anyone preventing him. The villagers simply stood by and looked on, not venturing even to save their own effects. When the Government forces arrived there was a great row, and the arrest of the poor idiot almost led to a war.

A similar incident would have caused still greater mischief, if the French officer on the spot had not shot down the maniac just in time. In this case he wanted to shoot his own child, and the Fans were greatly astonished that the European did not let him. They remarked that during the last few years he had been subject to several such fits and killed a number of children. But that had no further significance, except that on these occasions the man had been quite rational and capable. They had altogether fared right well, whence they concluded that their late chief, Cholokke, had taken up his abode in the possessed person in order to procure a boon companion in his sports.

In accordance with these notions it is quite natural that, on the death of a person, his soul should be supposed to have left his body either because it was tired of the worries of this life (this is often given as a cause of death), or because somebody else has stolen the soul. The latter is the more frequent, and hence, especially in West Africa, this is almost exclusively the question put to the dead.

THE GHOST

In this way alone is it possible to understand scenes such as those described in the last chapter. Unfortunately, such questioning of the dead too often ends in tragedy, and at times the whole tribe has to drink the poison-cup. Whoever vomits the draught is free from the suspicion of

Fig. 170. Feeding the departed (offerings to the dead), American Indians (after Harrow).

having stolen the soul. But woe to the wretched victim who retains the poison in his body. On his head rests the charge of having compassed the death or rather stolen the soul. He is despatched to the other world to join the departed, "in order in this way again to release the captured soul."

"Every death is thus followed by at least one murder," I was told by a traveller on the Ivory Coast.

The second question put by the *manistic* view of the world is much more complicated.

What becomes of the soul of the departed?

THE GHOST

There is no exaggeration in saying that the negroes give a thousand different answers to this question. Hence it would be useless, and indeed impossible, to give all the answers separately. We can do no more than arrange them in large groups, in order to ascertain the relation between the general theories. In their answers, in their notions regarding their future state and abode of the soul, men are likewise influenced by their personal feelings, as is seen by the way the body is treated and disposed of at interment.

On the one hand, the negro has a boundless fear of the appalling superhuman powers, the ghostly capabilities of departed souls. Hence, away with them; hence a perpetual effort to keep them in good humour, to appease their wrath.

But, on the other hand, he is amazed that the disembodied spirits are able still to exist, a point about which there can be no doubt at all. The men of this period have the greatest desire to make these infinitely powerful bodiless spirits serviceable, or else themselves to acquire their qualities.

These are the two motives which everywhere emerge from the chaos of the *manistic* views. In order to keep the dead at a distance, they are most generously treated. They receive food and drink, little huts are set apart for them, and farewell feasts are held, more or less jovially, in their honour.

These farewell entertainments call for further explanation.

So long as the body still lies in the house of mourning, or anywhere above ground, so long of course will the soul hover about it. But as long as the soul is still in the vicinity, the people have to struggle with the most in-

FIG. 171. FEAST OF THE DEAD, RUCUYENNE CARIBS, FRENCH GUIANA. After Crevaux

THE GHOST

tense fear of the ghost. Hence all the mourning and groaning, and as this becomes too wearisome for the survivors, especially if they are of good families, mourning women are engaged, who, for good food and refreshing drink, as well as hard cash, keep up the wailing, keening and howling as long as the body is still aboveground. This may often last for weeks together till the burial. When the day arrives for the interment, many of the people of this second period of early development are artful enough either to bury the departed in his own hut, which is then abandoned for ever in order to avoid coming again into collision with him, or else, as on the Shari river, to make a breach in the walls of the hut, through which the blindfolded body, face downwards and head foremost, is carried out, the breach being then again closed up. The people of the Shari explain that they turn the body face down and bandage the eyes to prevent the spirit from knowing which way the body was taken. Then he is carried out head foremost, so that, when he goes on his travels, he may take the opposite direction from his dwelling.

In this connection a comical incident is said to have once taken place. A man who had always been severely "henpecked," and was in ecstasies at the loss of his better half, resolved even after her death to have his revenge, and here is how he set about it.

He simply left the bandage on the body as it was laid in the grave. But man is a creature of habits, as our Bua was now to discover. After a little while the hut began to look very empty, and perhaps on other grounds he felt very down-hearted. It appears further that he also began to suffer from qualms of conscience, that he was tormented by frightful dreams, and that his wife visited him in the form of a horrible apparition. So he sneaked

off to a priest in order to arrange with him for re-
opening the grave and removing the bandage from his
wife's eyes. For he took it as a matter of course that,
since the body was still blindfolded, the soul could unquestionably find no food and would therefore starve,
and, worst of all, would torment him in his sleep.

They went and reopened the grave, but what was their
amazement at finding that the head had vanished! It turned
out that in the interim a European explorer had bought
the skull from a fourth party for an English museum!

But to return to the subject of parting feasts.

When a man is buried, his soul also goes hence, sometimes into the grave, or it may be to a better hereafter.
Anyhow it goes away, and that is a reason for rejoicing;
hence its departure is made easy in every possible way.
In Yoruba (Slave Coast) the priest even sings it a farewell song, in which it is told how lucky it is that it now
at last goes to the delightful after-life, how extremely
beautiful that abode is, how horrible after all was the
life on earth, how wonderfully the survivors have provided for its happy future existence by all kinds of offerings and deposits in the grave, how therefore, all things
considered, it cannot do better than to repair as soon as
possible to that far more beautiful world. But should it
happen to return—so the priest concludes his song—and
injure the people by bad harvests, sickness and other
evils, then these people have also the means of annihi-
lating it, as in that case the body would be dug up and
burnt. Let it, therefore, be pleased to act accordingly.

Moreover, to make things doubly sure, in some places
they hold not only a private but a general, an all-compre-
hensive, parting feast, one that shall, so to say, thoroughly
purify the village. So it is in Old Calabar, in the Niger

THE GHOST

delta, where every two years the town is cleansed from all wicked spooks, who, in the opinion of the authorities, might have taken possession of the place or might be lurking somewhere about. This feast is called Yudok.

At a stated time a number of figures, the so-called *nabikems*, are prepared and distributed here and there in the town. These figures, which are made of sticks and bamboo wickerwork, represent birds, quadrupeds, and also human beings, who are then decked with a fine old straw hat on their head, a pipe in their mouth and a walking-stick, being thus equipped as if for a journey. In the opinion of the negroes these effigies have something exceedingly attractive for the spirits, which makes our informant think that these spirits themselves must be strangely lacking in good taste.

When the night arrives for the general expulsion, one might fancy that the whole place had gone mad. After a good feast of food and drink, the people stream out in groups, laying about them in every empty corner, as if hunting out animated beings lurking there, all the time yelling and shouting at the top of their voice and discharging their guns. The *nabikems* are then furiously set upon, torn to pieces, burned and thrown into the river. The orgy lasts till dawn, and the town is then free from spirits for the next two years.

Delightfully naive are also the notions and the observances of the Kawanda people in the Southern Congo region. They first treat the departed with every mark of kindness, but then shortly before the burial turn the body over on its face and belabour it soundly on the soft parts, "so that he may understand by anticipation what is in store for him, should the fancy take him of annoying the survivors in any way."

CHAPTER XIII

SKULL-WORSHIP AND HEAD-HUNTING

WHEN primitive man brings out his dead and lays them in the grave, he covers them with earth, because he wants to have nothing more to do with them. This, too, is a result of the fear of ghosts. In other words, the process of burial originates in the overmastering fear of the dead.

But should love and devotion, and the effort to keep up relations with the departed, triumph over fear, then the reverse process arises, then the dead are preserved as far as may be. As, however, the children of nature are always wavering between fear and respect of the dead, so also all burial rites oscillate between the destruction and the preservation of the body. Thus it happens that extremely opposite sentiments give rise to most complicated practices and conceptions which are most frequently in flagrant contradiction with one another.

As in the last chapter I took account chiefly of the dread of ghosts, and described the expulsion of spirits, in this chapter I will deal with the preservation, the maintenance of bodies, the "up-keep" of souls.

If the fear of ghosts culminates in the destruction of the dead, veneration for the dead and for ancestors reaches its highest point in the cult of skulls and relics. If one feeling casts the body away, or puts it underground, the other strives, as far as possible, to preserve it. Hence

the practice of mummifying, which is universally prevalent and effected in divers ways. In some places the
corpse is laid on a frame, and a fire kindled at a suitable
distance beneath it. Elsewhere it is smeared with certain
fluids which make the skin tough and leathery. Mummies
of adults from the Torres Straits are
said to be light as feathers.

Although common enough, the mummifying process is not nearly so general
as the cult of human remains amongst
primitive peoples. This is quite natural.
The body itself duly decays and moul-
ders, and is thus not only difficult to
preserve but also has the repulsive
properties of soft corrupting flesh,
whereas it is always easy to keep a
few bones and especially the skull.
Now, in the living subject each separate part of the body has the same
properties as the whole person; that is
to say, what is done to a single particle
may, in the opinion of the natives,
be easily transferred to the whole.
Hence, when the West African negroes
clip the hair or pare the nails, it may

Fig. 172. Mummy of
Darnley Island in Tor-
res Straits (from a pho-
tograph reproduced in
"Globus").

easily happen that some evil-minded person, on finding
these clippings and parings, might bewitch both them
and their former owner. Therefore, all such particles of
the body are carefully destroyed. On the other hand, the
custom of blood-brotherhood, which is effected by mutual
blood-sucking, rests on the assumption that in future each
of the "brothers" will acquire like sentiments, as well
as controlling power over each other's will and thoughts.

SKULL-WORSHIP & HEAD-HUNTING

Hence it is that, of the dead, only a few parts are kept, perhaps some of the arm bones, fingers, nails or (most frequently) the skull. Highly characteristic as a development of this line of thought are the burial customs of the islands in Torres Straits.

The corpse is first of all laid on a wattle frame, resting

Figs. 173 and 174. Sepulchral hut containing the skull of a chief from the Solomon Islands; front and side view (British Museum).

horizontally on four posts. The moisture is pressed out, then, after a long time, the head and perhaps the shoulder-blades or shin-bones are detached and the rest buried or thrown into the sea, after which some funeral feasts are given. Everywhere ceremonial dances are performed by figures which are wrapped like mummies in bundles of reeds, and represent the departed. But an important part of the ceremony consists in the solemn delivery of the skull to the survivors. Sometimes the head is placed at night on the old couch of the departed, so that he seems to sleep with his family as in his lifetime, till at last the paterfamilias or the family chief puts the skull, as a pillow, under his own head.

But something much more significant may occur. On Mabiae Island, near Cape York, a few months after the burial, the bones of the departed are again dug up, and then the chief takes the skull and walks with it into the circle of the men. Now he is allowed to do what he likes, even to commit murder, because he is acting in the name of the departed. In this is clearly indicated the thought animating the skull, namely, that the dead man's soul is active in the hand of the person who possesses it. Still more instructive is the custom of the above-mentioned New Pomeranians with their kinakinau (chapter IV). When they look on the lower jaw of a corpse as a protecting spirit for raiders, it is because at one time their countrymen had believed that the soul of the former owner of the bone assisted them in their undertakings.

Fig. 175. A Mundruku of South America (Middle Amazons) with a mummified head (after Barboya-Rodriguez).

If we understand these views, the whole practice of relic-worship becomes singularly transparent and intelligible. We are no longer surprised to hear that people

SKULL-WORSHIP & HEAD-HUNTING

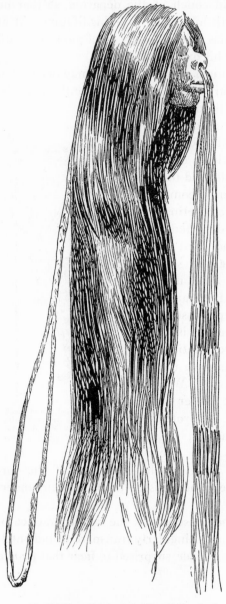

have kept with the greatest care especially the heads of distinguished persons. Cases are on record in which some famous dead man, with his detached head, has been laid on a bed of chalk to undergo the drying process. Then, when the chalk was saturated with the moisture from these remains, it was used by people to rub into their foreheads, under the impression that in this way the souls of the departed would pass into their own brain-caps. Wilson himself was an eyewitness of such an incident on the south coast of Guinea.

Fig. 176. Mummified head of a Jivaro Indian, South America. Head dried and shrivelled (from a private collection in Stuttgart).

SKULL-WORSHIP & HEAD-HUNTING

When such notions once get firmly established, the transition is not very far to the most incredible beliefs.

Fig. 177.   Fig. 178.

177. Scull deity of the Ibo people on the Lower Niger (Private Museum in Lyons).
178. Chinese head captured and decorated with a sweet potato in its mouth, Formosa. The Formosans are ardent headhunters, who pursue their pig-tailed foes most eagerly (after Fischer).

Such, above all others, is the next thing which presents itself and lies directly in a line with this development.

Skull masks! Only think of masks made of skulls!

When in the riotous season of carnival we indulge in

SKULL-WORSHIP & HEAD-HUNTING

the wildest tomfoolery, and see in masks and dominoes nothing more than the outer disguise and cloak of the most frivolous merrymaking, anyone who gives a thought to the origin of such disguises will perceive how the notion of a mask arose from the most weird and horrible mysteries of the human race, that is to say, from the cult

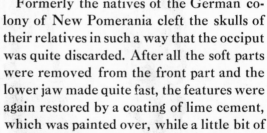

of the dead, from a religious observance the root idea of which was that the dead man's soul passed into the body of the living.

It is a wild, fantastic idea, a notion so gruesome that one might suppose it could not possibly be realized in actual life. Yet so it is.

Formerly the natives of the German colony of New Pomerania cleft the skulls of their relatives in such a way that the occiput was quite discarded. After all the soft parts were removed from the front part and the lower jaw made quite fast, the features were again restored by a coating of lime cement, which was painted over, while a little bit of

Fig. 179. Trum-
-pet made of a
skull; a trophy
of the Brazilian
natives (after a
Spanish wood-
cut).

stick was introduced obliquely in the upper end of the lower jaw, and by this the mask was grasped with the teeth. Now when the Papuan started dancing in the mask made from his relation's skull he doubtless felt that, in the wild excitement which seized him in the heat of the performance, the soul of his perhaps long buried kinsman was descending upon him.

These masks, however, of which I will here reproduce at least one, were already beginning to disappear when the Europeans first settled in New Pomerania.

From the cult of the skulls, bones, teeth, etc., of their

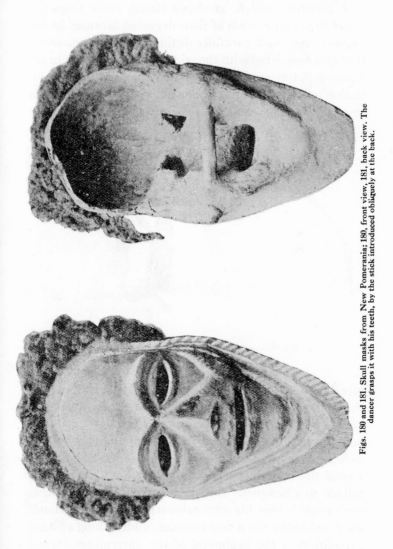

Figs. 180 and 181. Skull masks from New Pomerania; 180, front view, 181, back view. The dancer grasps it with his teeth, by the stick introduced obliquely at the back.

171

SKULL-WORSHIP & HEAD-HUNTING

own relatives, which, as above stated, arose from the effort to keep the souls of their departed kinsmen in the vicinity, we must carefully distinguish the elementary thoughts associated with the widespread custom of head-hunting. A few years ago a French officer of the Bateke station north-west of the Congo undertook an expedition towards the east, and on this occasion obtained inte-resting explanations which enable us to understand this

Fig. 182. Execution of slaves or prisoners of war on the
Middle Congo (after Coquilhat).

utterly cruel custom. Even in his lifetime a rich man of the Babangi tribe endeavours to send forward some of his effects as provision for the after-life. It is mainly a question of "live stock," for a Babangi trader's pride is to have as many slaves as possible. So when he has done a good stroke of business, he one day invites the whole village to a banquet. This does not cost him much, as each guest brings his own palm-wine, while the viands are provided by the whole company undertaking a fishing expedition at the beginning of the entertainment; and those rivers so teem with fish that enough are thus taken to last for several days. Hence, eating and drinking are not precisely the real motive or the main object of the festivity.

What all now await with strained nerves takes place

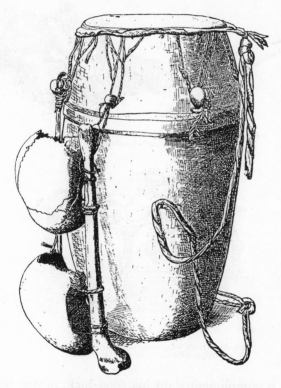

Fig. 183. Drum with skulls, from Togoland
(after Von Luschan).

on the second or third day—the sacrifice of a slave. The actual victim is not announced beforehand, the essential reason being that he has to be taken from the midst of the revellers and there and then consigned to death. Should he escape at the last moment, he is hence-

SKULL-WORSHIP & HEAD-HUNTING

forth free for all time from this fate. But should he fall under the executioner's knife, a great shout of jubilation is raised by the whole assembly, and the owner of the

Fig. 184. Trumpet with human lower jaws from Togoland Slave Coast (after Von Luschan).

Fig. 185. Trestle with human skulls. Trophy in Bunkeya Region of the Congo Sources (after Stairs).

slave is complimented on his good luck, in that he has succeeded in securing an attendant for the upkeep of his future spiritual home and court.

Before the homes of the well-to-do Babangi are generally seen tall posts from which the more or less bleached skulls of slaves killed in this way look down grinning at one. The trader has recourse to this means of making provision for the spirit world because he knows his heirs thoroughly well. He fully understands that, when he is once dead, his legal successors will take very good care

Fig. 186. Skull Dancing-place of the Tagalas in the Northern Philippines
(after a photograph).

not to send human beings after him as was formerly the custom. Their point of view rather is:

"Why should I still send slaves to the man in the other world, when we ourselves can quite well use them for our own comfort hereafter?"

SKULL-WORSHIP & HEAD-HUNTING

Hence the Babangi, too, prefers to provide for himself, and he knows that the slaves whom he has himself dispatched will follow him thither and there work for him, because after his death their skulls will be stuck on his grave.

The neighbouring Wafang people arrange the business in a more matter-of-fact and more seemly way. Similarly

Fig. 187. Iroquois with scalps (f and e) besides a prisoner (b) returning from a warlike expedition. The prisoner is bound with cords (d) (Native drawing from Mallery).

the inhabitants of the East Indian Archipelago are most thoughtful for the spiritual welfare of their relatives and for providing them with a suitable retinue of souls. Who has not heard of the famous "Koppensnellen"?

Below in the village some one dies. Thereupon the relatives steal quietly through the thicket by the wayside to the watering-places and the bee-hives of the neighbouring villages. There they lurk with murderous intent for hours, days, and even weeks together in the bush, waiting for a man, a woman or even only a child to pass that way. And when any unhappy mortal approaches, then the death-bearing steel flashes through the air, then a flow of blood pollutes the fresh grass,

SKULL-WORSHIP & HEAD-HUNTING

then the murderer slinks back home to be welcomed with praise and jubilation. For has he not done something great? Has he not secured a soul for the departed?

And, possibly, it was only the soul of a little child!

Hence, in this head-hunting, in this sacrifice of human lives, a deeper thought may have originally slumbered— a feeling of desire, estimable in its way, to provide for departed relatives. But as it was then later developed, it became the source of unspeakable woes and of incredible loss of life. For the thirst of blood became disciplined and almost sanctioned by the head-hunting custom.

"I have cut off four heads."

"I, seven."

Thus a missionary in Borneo overheard two natives conversing. And a few weeks later the second poor fellow lay still in death. His village friends hooked his body out of the river. But it was now headless. Then they knew, and the missionary too knew, that now the other owned five heads.

And thus grows the rage for collections.

Hence we must very carefully distinguish between the veneration of skulls and head-hunting in its various root-forms. Both, however, are gruesome enough.

CHAPTER XIV
ANCESTOR-WORSHIP AND FETISHISM

NOW the soul soars freely about in the after-world. But where is the after-world?

When people were buried in the shade of a tree, in the tangle of baobab roots, or perhaps in a tall stem, then it was natural to seek the voice of the dead in the soughing of the branches. Then the children of nature suspended in the boughs all kinds of little offerings, calabashes with food and drink, little wood carvings representing the utensils in daily use. Then the wayfarer, on drawing near to the tree, casts a timid glance at the earthly abode of the departed ; or perhaps a survivor, a son or a daughter, repairs to the forest giant in order to relieve natural feelings, to mutter a quiet prayer, or even to shed a tear. Then a European traveller comes along, sees the mound beneath the tree, the calabash in its branches, and enters in his diary, "Fetish tree."

Possibly also, when the tribe in its wanderings reached this district, it had to cross a river. Then it may happen that, as in the Bago territory, the dead are interred on its banks, or else are thrown directly into the stream so as to be on the highway to the land where the tribe was formerly settled. The souls ever yearn after the region where their forefathers were seated, and the river which received the bodies thus became holy. Sacrificial animals

ANCESTOR-WORSHIP AND FETISHISM

were thrown in, and the crocodiles who swarm in its waters were also regarded as holy, because they live in holy waters.

The Bagos call the river "the Way of the Fathers." The crocodiles they hail as "Friends of the Fathers."

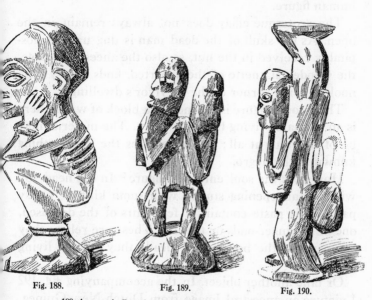

Fig. 188.   Fig. 189.   Fig. 190.

188. Ancestral effigy of the Baluba (in the author's possession).

189. Ancestral effigy of the Bakundu (in the author's possession; a double figure).

190. Ancestral effigy of the Bakundu (in the author's possession). As in the previous illustration it represents two persons joined together at the back. But in a very comical way the positions are reversed so that in the ancestral figure a pair of feet appear above and below. If one stands on its feet the other stands on its head. Unfortunately, the figure is a little damaged.

Now a European comes along, rapidly crosses the Bago territory, sees the people driving pigs into the river, where they are eaten by the crocodiles, and writes about the place: "Great fetish river; crocodiles are fetishes."

On the grave a post is often erected, and scored with a few gashes which rather suggest than represent a

ANCESTOR-WORSHIP AND FETISHISM

human face; it then becomes an abode of the dead. The post is not always placed just on the grave, nor is it always so rudely carved. On the side and the lower part are long notches which mark off the limbs from the body. Male and female are distinguished; man creates the human figure.

The grotesque effigy does not always remain in the open. As the skull of the dead man is dug up and hospitably received in the hut, so also the ancestral image, the wooden statuette of the departed, finds a cosy little nook in some corner of the survivor's dwelling.

The wooden figure is not merely a block of wood, there is an animated living being within it. The material may be of no value at all; but it contains the holiest thing known to the negro.

How does the soul enter the figure? In the head you will find an opening stuffed with some kind of messy paste. This paste contains a few hairs of the deceased, one of his finger-nails or the like. These are relics; they are parts of the body of the dead; they are the living substance.

Or take another object. In the accompanying fig. 192 I picture an ancestral image from Dutch New Guinea. The disproportionately large head is hollowed out and a skull put in. It is the skull of the dead man, which has been dug up again, and is to animate this wood statuette representing him. This notion of an indwelling spirit could not be expressed in a more characteristic or life-like manner.

The little ancestral figures are not seldom brought sociably together, that is to say, they are arranged and represented in groups. In this way the worship becomes simpler, and the root idea more comprehensive. At the same time we are clearly to understand that, *so far as it has been possible to investigate their origin and significance, these wooden effigies have proved to be distinctly ancestral*

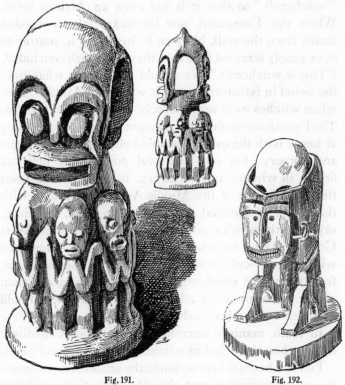

Fig. 191.   Fig. 192.

191. Carved work of the Bakundu (after Von Luschan). Seen from two sides. Numerous little figurini are disposed round the base of a Janus-like image.
192. Ancestral effigy from New Guinea (after de Clerq and Schmeltz). The head is scooped out and a skull inserted.

images. All the artificially built up systems of idolatry and fetishism are not, forsooth, religions in the eyes of the natives, but have been made so by Europeans. Let us ask, for instance, what is the origin and essence of fetishism.

ANCESTOR-WORSHIP AND FETISHISM

Fetishism

THE word *fetish* comes from the Portuguese *feititto*, "witchcraft," so that it is not even an African term. When the Europeans saw the negro take a wooden image from the wall, blow on it, bespatter it, mutter to it, or supply scraps of food to it, they forthwith concluded, "This is witchcraft." We should consider at what time the belief in fetishism arose. It was in the Middle Ages, when witches were most fiercely persecuted in Europe. The Portuguese seafarers were wont to look on everything at home with the eyes of people believing in witchcraft and sorcery. For our medieval populations believed firmly in witches and sorcerers. It must be confessed that this feature of the Middle Ages brands them with the stamp of spiritual decadence. We must, therefore, say that those who established fetishism on the West Coast of Africa by describing the ceremonies connected with ancestor-cult from their own inner consciousness, from their own standpoint, did really nothing else than saddle the negroes for all time with what they should themselves have been ashamed of.

In truth, manism, ancestor-worship, stands infinitely higher than the belief in witches of our medieval times.

I do not hesitate to pronounce the unadulterated ancestor-cult of primitive man, this all-permeating conviction of the immortality of the soul, these gladsome offerings of daily occurrence whenever the dead needed anything, this quiet, deep and heartfelt affection for the dead, all this is one of the finest flowers that the human spirit has ever brought forth. I have myself often reflected how much more loving is this care for the dead amongst the natives than amongst ourselves. Often have I felt that

ANCESTOR-WORSHIP AND FETISHISM

there glows in these men an unfathomable yearning, a profoundly sacred emotion, such as assuredly can never be experienced by us matter-of-fact beings.

We are struck with horror at the son offering human

Fig. 193. Roof prop with human figures, Loango Coast (from a photograph). According to the latest information, the natives hold that distinguished persons are buried under the roof.

beings to his father for the afterlife, at the wife throwing herself into the grave after her dead husband, at the daughter digging up her mother's grave at dead of night to procure her skull, to kiss it, to deck it with dainty network, and keep it ever by her. Certainly there is something wild in all this; but the wildness does not lack grandeur.

ANCESTOR-WORSHIP AND FETISHISM

I want people to start with these facts when they permit themselves to form a judgment on the religion or the "fetishism" of the natives. In a word, I want them in their judgments to shake off the hampering fetters which we have forged for ourselves in medieval times to our own disgrace and that of primitive man. Until in our mental vision we have formed a picture of the real undistorted root ideas, we have no right to consider them more closely in their degraded forms.

Fig. 194. Wooden image from Kuillu (in the possession of Dr Brandt). Formerly an ancestral effigy, now a village deity.

How the early notions inevitably degenerated into frivolous superstitions and lamentable distortions is seen in the very germs of the outward expressions of the manistic period. So long, for instance, as the owners of the ancestral images remember the names and the personalities of the dead represented by them, so long will the object retain the type identical in character, essentially the same. But when the memory dies out while the image remains, it will soon happen that the wooden figures will acquire the general significance of a sacred object without any personal value. I will give a case in point connected with a wooden figure from Kuillu in the possession of Dr Brandt (fig. 194).

Here we see a wooden image which is studded all over with innumerable nails. The traveller who secured it was merely informed that it was Moloko, a kind of war god belonging to the village. His function was to see that the warlike expeditions proved successful. He had also to

ANCESTOR-WORSHIP AND FETISHISM

take care that no wrangling, or palavers took place about frontier questions. If Moloko is remiss, he is cautioned to be more careful by having a nail driven into his flesh by the head chief, who is also the greatest trader and the head man of the village. The village must have had many misadventures, as Moloko's figure is covered over and over again with nails.

When we hear of such tales, we might suppose that the negro had here a regular war god. But such is not at all the case, and the origin of Moloko is to be sought on manistic ground, as our traveller himself ascertained. When he was inquiring into the history of the tribe, an old woman informed him that long ago the people reached their present territory under the leadership of a great chief called Moloko, about whom she had wonderful things to tell. Certain it is that so long as he lived his people ruled the district.

Thus we have here before us a case of the kind mentioned. The chief, as such, is now only faintly remembered, and all memory of him will quite die out. But in the popular tradition the wooden image still bears his name. To it are still referred the characteristics which the warlike chief possessed, and thus the wooden block with its nails becomes a milestone on the road to idol-worship, that is, to the cult of images, of whose actual nature and significance his votaries are unable to give a clear account.

On the other hand, we need not weave all religious notions and expressions on the same manistic loom, as may very easily happen. There are, after all, many things that call for special consideration. When, for instance, the negro sees any unusual object, he is at once taken with a certain feeling of anxiety, a certain perplexity,

ANCESTOR-WORSHIP AND FETISHISM

and he is ready to believe in a display of power in this object, which exceeds the usual, the commonplace, to the extent that the thing itself looks strange or weird. To put it clearly, the negro attributes a supernatural power to every fresh appearance, to any new object which in any way departs from the ordinary, the known, the intelligible. For him it is uncanny.

Example: A man sees a root of singular growth below a tree; he cuts it off, takes it home, completes the resemblance to a human form already suggested by nature, and presents offerings to the puny object, which from that moment is sacred in his eyes. (See accompanying fig. 195.)

Such objects may often occur, but do not give sufficient reason to speak of a lifeless fetishism. In this sense all people have at all times practised fetishism. In this sense even the European does so to this day, when, for instance, from the more or less remarkable or unusual lines of the hand he allows himself to be persuaded regarding particular events in his future life. In this connexion it will be scarcely believed how widespread such little fancies as palmistry, interpretation of dreams and the like still are amongst ourselves. Really, when we think of it, we lose all right to gird at the fetishism of the negro.

Fig. 195. "Fetish" from the Gold Coast (Missions Museum in Basel). Fashioned from a root of remarkable growth.

ANCESTOR-WORSHIP AND FETISHISM

One thing is certain, that the inhabitants of West Africa, for whose views of the world science has discovered and monopolized especially the word "fetishism," are at the present day anything but sober and "orthodox" manists, that, in fact, they live in the same decadent state as the

Fig. 196

Fig. 197

196. A supposed fetish pick-axe. Really the insignia of a Baluba prince (in the author's possession).
197. Supposed "fetish-comb," Kwango district (in the author's possession). Front and side view).

Christians of medieval times. But for this they should not be made alone responsible. For this the European missionaries of the Middle Ages are in large measure answerable. These people were altogether unworthy of their high and noble calling. They came to West Africa with the foregone belief that the black art was possible. Hence they believed themselves in the sorcery of the negroes, and they crowned their missionary zeal by undertaking warlike expeditions, with fire and sword, against this witchcraft, in other words, fetishism. Then,

ANCESTOR-WORSHIP AND FETISHISM

if in their opinion they had triumphed over the devil with holy water, tapers and crucifixes, they set up pictures of the saints, presented the image of the Virgin Mary and other holy effigies to the negroes, converted by means of the lash and imprisonment, and without more ado exacted of them reverence, intelligence and adoration. The negroes obeyed. The holy images were set up and more or less senselessly invoked.

But what became of the saints?

The missionary who to-day goes thither with good and serious intentions is often not a little astonished at the confused notions of the natives. From the jumble of saints' pictures and ancestral images has arisen the very worst kind of idolatry that it is possible to imagine, the real and only idolatry that can be described as such.

Fig. 198. Supposed "fetish-pipe," Bollokoro (in the author's possession).

Fig. 199. "Gratte pour Fetiche," from the Kassai region (in the author's possession.) This descriptive note has caused me very great amusement.

Hence, there is no question that the Middle Ages terribly sinned against these peoples; that the missionaries of to-day would have far more easy work, if those natives had not been thereby corrupted, as they are still being corrupted, in that every preacher of the Gospel approaches them with odious prejudices, with a hateful bias, and regards as despicable notions what he himself has not at all understood. But if we treat as contemptible what to

ANCESTOR-WORSHIP AND FETISHISM

another is sacred, we ruin him and cannot expect that he will hearken with more deference to the good tidings that we bring him, and the sublime and lofty nature of which he cannot at first in the least comprehend. If we sow the wind, we reap the storm.

Even still in the present day the European is inclined to detect fetishes everywhere amongst the negroes.

Apart from the ancestral images proper, there is still a large number of carvings that have nothing to do with the real manistic period. Once the negro had learned to make human figures, he decorated all kinds of objects with human forms or heads, and the European, who is once accustomed to see a fetish in every plastic representation of man, hastens to apply the inevitable name "fetish object" to everything thus ornamented. For my collection I have received all imaginable things of the kind—fetish clubs, fetish pickaxes, fetish pipes, fetish goblets, fetish guns, sceptres, bells, masks and, above all, snuff-boxes. If the collector be asked for the reason of this descriptive title, he will usually answer: "Voilà! C'est la figure humaine!"

A human figure, a human face is there, so it must be a fetish object. It is quite a simple matter, the ticket is right, and when an object bears the title of fetish, then it can be sold for a higher price to the museum.

It is high time to bury this fetish, and I beg all readers of this book to follow me to the interment.

Here I will add another short section on a practice, widespread over the world, which is grounded on other human sentiments. I refer to the *judicium Dei*, the ordeal, the oracle, etc. (cf. fig. 200).

Man often yearns to gain a higher knowledge about past or future things. Then he grasps at any means of

ANCESTOR-WORSHIP AND FETISHISM

acquiring such information. The Greeks had their Delphi, and the Middle Ages had arranged their sanctuaries as well-equipped inquiry offices. The negro has only his ordeal. Here I present the description of such a ceremony from Eugen Zindgraff, one of our very best writers:

Throughout the whole of the Lower Congo, as well as amongst many other negro peoples, there is a kind of God's Judgment, an ordeal, which consists in taking the kaske or cassa. Kaske is the bark of a tree which, when pounded and rolled up in little pills, is eaten by the accused. Poisonous properties are attributed to it. If the accused vomits the kaske he is innocent, and then the accuser has to pay a heavy indemnity. But should the accused retain the kaske for a given time, say, till sunset, he is found guilty and condemned to die by water or fire. The latter is for women.

It is stated that the vomiting of the kaske depends on whether, before taking it, a dose of oil has or has not been given to the accused. This is done by the feticeiro (the chief, or the priest) who conducts the proceedings, so that the whole affair is nothing but a fraud. The issue simply depends on whether the feticeiro is or is not venal. Hence, many accused persons may swallow the pills presented to them with tolerable composure, and then quietly chuckle over the indemnity which will now have to be paid to them.

The charges on which these proceedings are based are much the same as those of bewitchment. Someone is in league with the evil spirits, and is thus himself in a position to practise supernatural arts. The object of the charges, which naturally, for the most part, lack all

FIG. 200. "FETISH DRINK." CASSA ORDEAL IN THE ANGOLA BACKWOODS.   After Capello and Ivens

ANCESTOR-WORSHIP AND FETISHISM

tangible foundation, is to get rid of some objectionable person under the cloak of legal forms, whether it be some old man—white-haired negroes are somewhat rarely seen, as they are carried off by the poison-cup, which is mostly presented to them as useless members of the community—or else some obnoxious woman, or any other troublesome person against whom no certain charge can be brought. It is a singular experience to assist at such a process, as I had occasion to do amongst the Musserongos on the south side of the Congo.

It was at Sumba, and I was just stepping into the canoe in order to reach St Antonio at the mouth of the Congo on the same day, when I accidentally overheard two Musserongos talking about a kaske trial which was to take place in a neighbouring village. As a white person is not as a rule allowed to be present, I repaired at once to the "Court of Justice." The beating of the war-drums was already heard in the distance, and I presently found myself in the forest glade where a circular space had been cleared of grass, etc. The feticeiro and his assistants alone had arrived, as it was still early morning.

In the middle of the circular space four palm branches about five feet long were stuck in the ground to mark off a rectangle, the short sides of which were connected by strips of palm, and from these were suspended at short intervals three times three narrow palm-strips about five feet long. At one corner, where stood a few baskets containing the feticeiro's paraphernalia, an old cavalry sword was stuck in the ground. Groups of natives, men, women and children, gradually gathered round the place, and at last the accused woman appeared and took her seat a little on one side of the "tribunal."

She was perhaps twenty-eight or thirty years old, and

ANCESTOR-WORSHIP AND FETISHISM

was accompanied by her young daughter, both with their faces smeared with red ochre. Now the feticeiro began to dance round the enclosure to the muffled beat of the drums, brandishing the sword and muttering mysterious words. Then he placed on the ground at the east entrance of the court the little basket containing the kaske, knelt before it, daubed his face with earth, and kissed the ground three times. This he repeated at the other entrance, and then danced again round and diagonally across the enclosure, muttering to himself all the while. Then at a sign from him the music ceased, the accused with the woman withdrew more to the background, and the feticeiro with his assistants began to prepare the kaske.

A handful of bark was taken from the ample supply still contained in the basket, carefully cleansed and washed, chopped to pieces, and with a round stone ground to a powder on a flat stone which had already been hollowed out by much use. This brown powder was then moistened and the mess rolled into three balls the size of a small hen's egg. The balls remained on the flat stone covered with a white cloth.

During these preparations a great commotion was heard in the background. The chief fetish was brought forward, and while the accuser was swearing that he would speak the pure truth, and that he did not expect to die an unnatural death, the feticeiro drove a nail into the fetish for the better remembrance of the hour. Thereupon the accuser—the accused herself was not present, but only one of her brothers—asserted that the woman was a sorceress, and had eaten the soul of her recently deceased brother. "Moio" means both heart and the throbbing life, the soul which resides within the body. Possibly the accuser meant by this to say that the woman was guilty of the

ANCESTOR-WORSHIP AND FETISHISM

illness and death of her brother, whom she, of course, had not really killed, and still less eaten his heart.

After the nail was driven into the wooden image, all gathered round the seat of justice; amid the beating of drums, the feticeiro led forward the woman who could scarcely stand on her feet, holding her by the little finger, conducting her to each corner of the rectangle, and describing circles round her and the palm-branches, as if to conjure her into the place of trial, and when it was once more crossed obliquely, he bade her be seated in the middle of the rectangle. Then ensued a deep silence which was painful to me. Was the process now to begin?

My uncomfortable feeling grew more intense when suddenly the branches separated and two Musserongos stepped into the circle. Seldom have I seen such human forms; their gigantic figures were increased by the robe of dark-red stuff hanging low down and worn toga-fashion round the shoulders. If one figure with his European features, Roman nose, and mustachios recalled some Pretorian guardsman, it was impossible to imagine a more repulsive form than the other, whose sinister, bulldog-like countenance seemed the expression of the lowest depravity. These two men, who were evidently under the influence of drink, although they seemed to walk steadily enough, might be taken as distinguished representatives of their tribe. With sullen glance and bloodshot eyes they strode by the white man and stretched themselves in the grass on the opposite side. They were headmen from a neighbouring village who wanted to attend the session.

Now the feticeiro repeated the charges, which the woman denied with tears, while the accuser, an undersized elderly man with really villainous features, sat outside the place of trial, only from time to time muttering something to himself.

Further, the feticeiro unfolded before the woman all her past iniquities, that after the burial of the deceased she had not washed, that once she had eaten with gory hands, that on another occasion she had given a stranger drink without first tasting it herself, and so on. He wound up by handing her the first pill, and calling on her to swallow it to test the truth of the charge. Now the unhappy creature began to tremble and gulp down the pill, while the drum beat slowly and the feticeiro capered about.

One might suppose that the spectators put on long faces at the sight. Nothing of the kind, for these trials are too frequent, and several persons together often swallow the kaske. All kept chatting and laughing with each other as at a festival. One especially of the two fellows described above, the less savage-looking, turned out to be the clown of the piece, while his comrade still kept scowling at everybody. When the woman hesitated a little in taking the kaske, and was encouraged by the feticeiro, the clown also would send her a few perhaps well-meant words, accompanying them with a great guffaw and a complacent rubbing of his huge paws, causing much hilarity amongst the audience.

Twenty minutes passed before the last remnant of the three pills had disappeared. Then the feticeiro bade the woman stand up. Now she had to walk up and down within the rectangle, and at the same time touch the three middle ones of the nine palm-strips hanging down at the narrow side. This had to go on for a long time, until the result was brought about. Thereupon the feticeiro took his fee, a very heavy one, a few bottles of rum passed round, and the main business was concluded. But as I walked away,

ANCESTOR-WORSHIP AND FETISHISM

the muffled sound of the drum echoed in my ears. Whether the woman got off with her life I was unable to ascertain, as I had no time to wait for the issue, which sometimes takes a very long while.

The feticeiro was still a very young man. He wore no special badge of his profession, but had an uncommonly crafty face, which was always on the smile. When I noticed this, I was involuntarily reminded of the old Roman augurs smiling at each other. We two knew very well what a piece of legerdemain was being played before the gaping public, but a few other worthy persons in the assembly seemed also to see through the fraud.

That is a picture of decadent times. Show me a people who have not passed through the same experience, and I will cry *peccavi*, and quietly assent whenever I again hear the negroes addressed in scorn with the words: "You fetish-worshippers, you!"

CHAPTER XV
SECRET SOCIETIES AND MASKS

TWO different attitudes towards the dead must be clearly recognized. Either the deceased is quickly put aside, cast away, or burnt, or else the native tries to conjure the soul of the departed into his own sphere of influence and make it serviceable to himself.

When people became absorbed in the problem of death, in their minds the departed acquired a tremendous power, which became friendly or hostile to them according as the corpse was treated. But, whether friends or foes, the whole world of spirits was constantly wondered at and envied for their extraordinary powers. The amazement grew to such a pitch that the negro and the Papuan at last strove to make themselves "like unto the dead." By this I do not mean to say that in the development of these mortuary rites a conscious purpose hovered dimly before the eyes of primitive man. On the other hand, all notions and practices have grown of themselves. But this amazement and astonishment were the force that brought into existence the spirit-power among these men.

The native arrived at the notion of this power by a spiritualizing process. I have already related above how the Australian takes hold of the skull of the departed, and then all power, all right, belongs to him, either because he acts in the name of the departed or else because the departed acts through him.

SECRET SOCIETIES AND MASKS

This is not yet the spiritualizing process proper, although the example shows us the way by which the power of the spirits is established. The spiritualistic customs have rather their starting-point in another sphere, the rules of abstention, and the interdictions put upon food.

The original rules regarding abstention must, doubtless, be sought in the law that every object that belonged to the dead, or in which he might seek a residence, must be avoided by mortals so long as the soul of the departed still dwells in this world. South Sea Islanders, for instance, leave untouched all coconut-trees belonging to the deceased, because they do not wish to meddle with the property of the departed spirit and thus provoke its anger. Amongst the Africans, on the other hand, the custom prevails of themselves abstaining during the period of mourning from all enjoyments which the deceased must also be deprived of; that is to say, they must not wash nor partake of certain viands, nor speak, but keep aloof from other men. And all this is done in order to live in the closest possible relations with the deceased, and thus become as like the spirits as possible.

Fig. 201. Member of the Tamate Club, Banks Islands (after Codrington).

From these observances we get, on the one hand, the series of rules of abstention which bind each and all closer to their personal ghostly guardians, while, on the

199

SECRET SOCIETIES AND MASKS

other hand, notions and customs become generalized during the progress of the tribe's development.

Of this process some particulars have already been given. I may refer to the chapter about the test of manhood. The education of youths in common I take to be a custom which first began in the period of manism, of funeral rites, of ancestor-worship. For at the base of this school‑like training of the young lies, for the most part, a mythological motive rather than an intentional discipline. I will endeavour to make this clear by an example from the Lower Congo.

Fig. 202. A masked person, Aurora Island, Melanesia (after Codrington).

I. *The Ndembo*

THE *Ndembo* or *Kita* is very widespread on the Lower Congo, and especially in the districts lying to the South. When anyone wants to become a member of the Ndembo, the ganga (chief) instructs him at a given sign suddenly to lie down dead. Accordingly the novice quite unexpectedly throws himself down in any open place; sepulchral shrouds are spread over him, and he is carried off to an enclosure outside the town, which is called *vela*, and he is then said to have died a Ndembo. The young people of both sexes follow in their turn, and when all goes well this pretended sudden death often becomes a sort of hysteria. In this way the ganga receives a sufficient number of candidates for a complete enrolment—twenty, thirty, or even fifty.

It is now assumed that those dying after this fashion in the vela decay and moulder away until only a single bone remains, and this the ganga takes charge of. After a certain time, which in the different places varies from three months to three years, the ganga is believed to take these bones, and by means of his magic power bring every one of the dead back to life. The resurrection is supposed to take place on a certain day, when the Ndembo company returns to the town in a body, forming a grand procession in fine clothes and amid universal jubilation.

Fig. 203. A masked person, New Caledonia (after Codrington).

On their return the Ndembo folk act as if they came from another world. They take new names, which are peculiar to the Ndembo. They demean themselves as if they were utter strangers in this phenomenal world, ignore their parents and relatives, don't know how to eat and require some one to masticate for them. They want to have everything they set eyes on, and woe betide whoever refuses them. The Ndembo people may beat and kill, if so inclined, without having to fear the

SECRET SOCIETIES AND MASKS

consequences. "They know no better," say the towns-people. They behave all alike as lunatics, until the excitement and the interest in the fraud has somewhat abated. When anyone puts inquisitive questions about the land

Fig. 204. Masked Losango people at the burial feast of the Nkosi in Kamerun (from a photograph).

whence they came, they stick a blade of grass behind their ear and act as if they had no idea that anybody was addressing them.

Those who have gone through this rite are called *Nganga*, the "Knowing Ones," while the unenrolled are named *Vanga*. During their stay in the vela the Nganga learn a secret language which gives fantastic names to the most ordinary things.

About these Ndembos in the kingdom of Congo there

SECRET SOCIETIES AND MASKS

is also extant a report which is altogether the best account of the matter from an African point of view. No one has yet succeeded in giving such a genuine picture of their way of looking at things as is here presented by Bastian in the very words of the negro himself.

Bastian writes:

"The Great Nkissi (who here replaces the fetish) lives in the interior of the woodlands where nobody can see him. When he dies the Nganga carefully collect his bones in order to bring them back to life, and nourish them that they may again put on flesh and blood. But it is not well to speak about it. In the Ambamba country everybody must have died once, and when the Nganga (replacing the fetish-priest) shakes his calabash against a village, those men and youths whose hour is come fall into a state of lifeless torpor, from which they generally rise up in three days. But the man whom the Nkissi loves he carries off to the bush and often buries him for a series of years. When he again awakens to life, he begins to eat and drink as before, but his mind is gone, and the Nganga must himself educate him and instruct him in every movement, like the smallest child. At first that can only be done with the rod, but the senses gradually return, so that you can speak with him, and when his education is finished the Nganga takes him back to his parents. These would seldom recognize him but for the positive assurance of the Nganga, who at the same time reminds them of earlier occurrences. Whoever has not yet undergone the experience in Ambamba is universally despised, and is not allowed to join in the dances."

From this description one can see how far the parallelism of the spiritualistic notions has been carried. I will now reproduce the next of these wonderfully clear

SECRET SOCIETIES AND MASKS

descriptions. It is concerned with the Belli secret society in Liberia, and is due to the pen of Dapper, an early author, who writes:

"They have also another custom, which they call

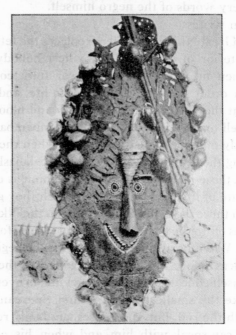

Fig. 205. Large Tortoise-shell mask, from Darnley Island, Torres Straits (Ethnographic Museum, Copenhagen).

Belli Paaro, of which they say it is a death, a new birth and an incorporation in the community of spirits or souls, with whom the common folk associate in the bush, and help to eat the offerings prepared for the spirits."

Here the spiritualistic idea is revealed with remarkable clearness. After these quotations I need not take pains to point out that the members of the association call themselves spirits, that, for instance, the Duk-duk in New Pomerania are called spirits. I need not dwell further on the deeper meaning of the ceremony. It is obvious enough that those who have undergone these experiences wish to be regarded as spiritualized, hence, as having died and having been brought to life again, in fact, as souls of the dead. And the secret society is nothing more than a confraternity of all those who have passed through this training in common.

Things are not always carried so far; the novices are not always required to die. For the most part the society is satisfied if, by rigorous rules of abstinence, the novices are transformed to the spiritual condition.

The activities of the associations differ greatly. Although it may be assumed that as a whole it is nothing more than a system of education for the young, so to say, a course of instruction, many societies have acquired a secondary significance. They aim at certain definite objects, such as are required by the actual state of the country. I will give two cases in point, the first from the land of intestine disorder, where the secret Purrah association has brought about peace and security; the second from the Calabar districts at the Niger delta, where the unstable commercial relations necessitated the safeguarding of the traders' interests.

II. *The Purrah*

BETWEEN the Sierra Leone river Sulima and Cape Mount dwell five little communities of Tulka-Susus, which together form a republican confederacy. Each group has its own officials and its own government. But all

SECRET SOCIETIES AND MASKS

are under a controlling power which is called the *Purrah*.
This is an association acting in union with fighting men.

Fig. 206. Mask of the Purrah (Berlin Ethnological
Museum).

SECRET SOCIETIES AND MASKS

Each of the five communities has also its own purrah, which, again, has its head officials and its court of justice, which, strictly speaking, constitutes the purrah. But from the five district purrahs is formed the great, the general purrah, which holds supreme sway over the five communes. To be received into a district purrah a man must be thirty years old, and fifty to be a member of the great purrah. The oldest members of each district purrah are members of the head purrah.

A candidate will be admitted to the examination for the district purrahs only on the responsibility of all his already associated relations. These swear to kill him if he does not stand the test, or if after reception he reveals the mysteries and the secrets of the society. In each district belonging to a purrah there is a sacred grove to which the candidate is conducted, and where he must stay in a place assigned to him, living for several months quite alone in a hut, whither masked persons bring him his food. He must neither speak nor leave his appointed place of residence.

Should he venture into the surrounding forest, he is as good as dead.

After several months the candidate is admitted to stand his trial, which is said to be terrible. Recourse is had to all the elements in order to gain satisfaction as to his firmness and courage. We are even assured that at these mysteries use is made of fettered lions and leopards, that during the time of the tests and enrolment the sacred groves echo with fearful shrieks, that here great fires are seen at night, that formerly the fire flared up in these mysterious woods in all directions, that every outsider who through curiosity was tempted to stray into the woods was mercilessly sacrificed, that foolish people who would have penetrated into them disappeared and were never heard of again.

If the candidate stands all the tests, he is admitted to the initiation. But he must first swear to keep all the secrets and without hesitation carry out the decisions of the purrah of his community and all the decrees of the great head purrah. If a member of the society betrays it or revolts against it, he is condemned to death, and the sentence is often carried out in the bosom of his family. When the criminal least expects it, a disguised, masked and armed warrior appears and says to him:

"The great purrah sends thee death!"

At these words everybody stands back, no one dares to offer the least resistance, and the victim is murdered.

The Court of each district purrah consists of twenty-five members, and from each of these separate courts five persons are chosen, who constitute the great purrah, or the High Court of the general association. Hence this also consists of twenty-five persons, who elect the head chief from their own body.

The special purrah of each community investigates the offences committed in its district, sits in judgment on them, and sees that its sentences are carried out. It makes peace between the powerful families, and stops their wranglings.

The great purrah meets only on special occasions, and pronounces judgment on those who betray the mysteries and secrets of the order, or on those who show themselves disobedient to its mandates. But usually it puts an end to the feuds that often break out between two communities belonging to the confederacy. When these begin to fight, after a few months of mutual hostilities, one or other of the parties, when they have inflicted sufficient injury on each other, usually wants peace. The commune repairs secretly to the great purrah, and invites it to become the mediator and put an end to the strife.

Thereupon the great purrah meets in a neutral district, and when all are assembled announces to the communes at war that it cannot allow men who should live together as brothers, friends and good neighbours, to wage war, to waste each others' lands, to plunder and burn; that it is time to put an end to these disorders; that the great purrah will inquire into the cause of the strife; that it requires that this should cease and decrees that all hostilities be forthwith arrested.

A main feature of this arrangement is that, as soon as the great purrah assembles to put a stop to the feud, and until its decision is given, all the belligerents of the two districts at war are forbidden to shed a drop of blood; this always carries with it the penalty of death. Hence everybody is careful not to infringe this decree, and abstains from all hostilities.

The session of the High Court lasts one month, during which it collects all necessary information to ascertain which commune caused the provocation and the rupture. At the same time it summons as many of the society's fighting men as may be required to carry out the decision. When all the necessary particulars are brought in, and everything is duly weighed, it settles the question by condemning the guilty commune to a four days' sack.

The warriors who have to give effect to this decision are all chosen from the neutral districts; they set out by night from the place where the great purrah is assembled. All are disguised, the face being covered with an ugly mask (fig. 206), and armed with lighted torches and daggers. They divide into bands of forty, fifty or sixty, and all meet unexpectedly before dawn in the district that they have to pillage, proclaiming with fearful shouts the decision of the High Court. On their approach,

Fig. 207. Mask made of pieces of bark; Torres Straits
(British Museum).

men, women, children and old people, all take to flight, that is, take refuge in their houses, and should anyone be found in the fields, on the highway, or in any other place, he is either killed or carried off and no more is ever heard of him.

SECRET SOCIETIES AND MASKS

The booty obtained by such plundering is divided into two parts, one of which is given to the injured commune, the other to the great purrah, which shares it with the warriors that have executed its decree. This is the reward for their zeal, their obedience and loyalty.

If one of the families in a commune subject to the purrah becomes too powerful and too formidable, the great purrah meets, and nearly always condemns it to an unexpected sack, which is carried out by night and, as usual, by masked and disguised men. Should the heads of such a dangerous family offer any resistance, they are killed, or carried off, and conveyed to the depths of a sacred and lonely grove, where they are tried by the purrah for their insubordination; they are seldom heard of again.

Such, in part, is the constitution of this extraordinary

Fig. 208. Mask of palm bast, from Florida, Solomon Islands (Oxford Ethnographic Museum).

institution. Its existence is known; the display of its power is felt; it is dreaded; yet the veil covering its intentions, decisions and decrees is impenetrable, and not till he is about to be executed does the outlaw know that he has been condemned. The power and reputation of the purrah

SECRET SOCIETIES AND MASKS

is immense, not only in the homeland but also in the surrounding districts. It is reported to be in league with the spirits (instead of the devil).

According to the general belief the number of armed men who are members and at the disposal of the purrah exceeds 6,000. Moreover, the rules, the secrets and the mysteries of this society are strictly obeyed and observed by its numerous associated members, who understand and recognize each other by words and signs.

III. The Egbo

THE *Egbo* or *Esik* ("Tiger") Order in Calabar, near the Niger delta, is divided into eleven grades, of which the first three, Nyampa, Obpoko or "Brass," and Kakunde, are not open to slaves. Others are, or were, the Abungo, Makaira, Bambin-boko, etc. The usual way is for members to buy themselves into the higher grades in their turn. The money thus accruing is shared amongst the Nyampa or Yampai, who form the inner circle. The king himself assumes the presidency under the title of Cyamba. Each of the various grades has its Egbo-day, on which their Idem, or their ghostly representative, exercises absolute control, such as the Romans entrusted to the Dictator in critical times; nor does he exempt members of other grades of the Egbo Order, should he encounter them. The country is, so to say, in a permanent state of siege, which is necessitated by the excessive number of slaves and women, since the traditional customs of the olden times are constantly put aside and suspended by the Egbo-days, which regularly follow each other, and with which is connected the proclamation of martial law. As soon as an Egbo-day is announced, slaves, women and children take to flight in all directions,

SECRET SOCIETIES AND MASKS

as the emissary of the Idem, armed with his heavy lash, goes the rounds, and is not at all over-scrupulous in its application. A yellow flag on the king's dwelling signals the Brass Egbo-day, when only very few even of the freemen venture to show themselves outside their houses.

In the Egbo Order, whenever an accusation is pending and the culprit is to be punished, the Idem is summoned by secret ceremonies from his abode in the distant bush-land. Thereupon he appears in a fantastic disguise of mats and branches covering him from head to foot, and with a black vizor on his face. In the Kamerún the members of the Order themselves are linked together by a garb of leaves gathered up in a curious knot, so that they seem to move in a connected mass.

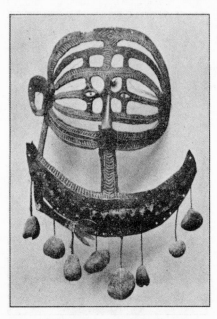

Fig. 209. Tortoise-shell mask from Torres Straits (Oxford Ethnographic Museum).

Every man, woman and child has the right to appeal to the Egbo for help against their masters or their neighbours. For this they have only to touch a member of the Order on the breast, or else beat the great Egbo drum. The person appealed to must at once summon a meeting at which the complaint is investigated, and, if found valid, the wrong is redressed. But if, on the con-

SECRET SOCIETIES AND MASKS

trary, it is found groundless, the plaintiff is punished. When the court returns a verdict of guilty, the officer on duty hastens, with his heavy scourge in his hand and surrounded by a noisy mob of Egbo brothers, directly to the condemned person's house, from which nobody must stir until the sentence is carried out; and as this usually involves the destruction of the whole house, all the inmates also must suffer more or less injury. While this is going on, and also as long as any Egbo session lasts, it would be death for anyone not taking part in the proceedings to be seen in the streets; nor can the business of everyday life be resumed until the Egbo drum announces the closure of the session. Members of the Order, when condemned, have the privilege of dying while intoxicated. People obliged to go on a journey usually place their effects under the protection of the Brass Egbo, and a piece of yellow cloth hoisted over the door suffices to safeguard the house from any injury. A man about to be initiated into the Brass grade has his whole body

Fig. 210. Feather Mask mounted in reed frame, Hawaii (British Museum).

rubbed with a yellow powder. In the Kamerún, a bunch of green leaves tied to a stake is the sign that the property is under the protection of the Egbo.

The Order of Free Egbos is said to have originated at the fairs which were held at a great palm-oil market in the interior, midway between Calabar and the Kamerún. As the place became the scene of much disorder, while the European trade made it necessary for the maintenance of public credit that all engagements should be strictly carried out, this institution was formed as a sort of Hanseatic Union under the most influential traders, for the mutual safeguarding of their interests. Later it acquired the political character of a *Vehmgericht*, or secret tribunal, by bringing within its sphere of action the whole police of the Calabars and the Kamerún. The kings always sought to secure for themselves the Grand-mastership of the Order, since otherwise their authority would sink to a mere shadow. European skippers have frequently found it to their advantage to be enrolled in the lower grades, in order thereby the more easily to recover their debts. A member of the Egbo has the right to claim as his own property the slave of his debtor, wherever he may find him, merely by fastening a yellow strip to his dress or loincloth. Even in the interior of the continent the standing of an Egbo is still respected and feared, and affords it a certain immunity from molestation, such as is absolutely needed for the extensive commercial speculations in Africa.

In the Kamerún, as a preliminary to their acceptance into the Free Egbos, the young men are sent for a protracted period to the Mokokos, a bush tribe in the interior; with these they live naked in the fields, and only now and then dart out, clad in green leaves, to have a

SECRET SOCIETIES AND MASKS

bath in the river. All women, and especially slaves, are prohibited, under heavy penalties, from approaching the forest where they reside. In the Kamerún, it is customary to pay particular honour to a visitor, above all if he be a European, by introducing the Egbo goat, which the people are otherwise seldom allowed to set eyes upon.

Holman reports that the whole of the Old Calabar district is subject to the rule of the so-called Egbo laws. These are promulgated at a secret Council, the Egbo Assembly, which is held in the "Palaver-house" erected for this special purpose. In virtue of his sovereign rights, the head-chief presides, under the title of *Cyamab*, over this assembly. Amongst the members of the Egbo there are different ranks, which must be acquired in their due order, one after the other. Holman quotes Englishmen who state that Europeans have bought themselves into the Egbo, and even into the Yampai, in order to be thus better able to get in their money. He gives the following as the names and prices of the different grades of Egbo:

1. Abungo	...			125 bars.
2. Aboko	...	...		75 bars.
3. Makairo	...	...	...	400 copper rods.
4. Bakimboko	...	...	...	100 bars.
5. Yampai	...	...	...	850 copper rods.

To these must be added rum, clothes, membo, etc. The Yampai is the only grade whose members are allowed to sit in Council. The sums paid for the various titles of the Egbo are distributed exclusively amongst the Yampai, who, however, are not limited to a single share, since every Yampai can multiply his title as often as he can purchase shares, and these give him a claim to the receipt of the corresponding quotas from the profits of the whole institution.

SECRET SOCIETIES AND MASKS

From all this we see that the secret society has grown out of the power of the spirits, the belief in their might, the spiritualistic idea. In the present aspect of the two latter forms one cannot but praise the institutions as now constituted. We must, however, urge that the power of the spirits, as it displays itself in the more primitive forms tending towards spiritualism, is anything but attractive. As the Australian, with the skull of the dead man, can do anything he likes, rob or murder, the same right and similar licence was accorded to primitive man. Not till the conditions become more developed, does the rude and crude power of the spirits assume the form and the character of a controlling and legal authority, of a dispenser of justice.

So it is not only in Africa, but also in the Eastern Archipelago, and in Melanesia.

In the Moluccas, if anyone wants to be received into the *Katean* Society, he is shoved at night into the Katean house through an opening in the form of a gaping crocodile's throat or a cassowary's beak, and then it is said of him that he has been swallowed by the *Setan-besaar*. Now, seated in dense darkness, he hears all kinds of strange noises, the clashing of arms and occasional gunshots. After passing several days in the house, during which the *Mauen* (priest) provides him with food and drink, he is secretly removed and conducted to a distant place where he passes a couple of months. Then he returns, apparently in a helpless state, to the bosom of his family, who had remained completely ignorant of his whereabouts—This is an excellent report, almost as clear as an African description.

If we look round for fully developed forms, we find in Oceania exactly the same societies as in Africa. The

SECRET SOCIETIES AND MASKS

facts connected with the spiritual powers stand out, if possible, even more clearly than on the continent. Important above all is the manifestation of the spiritual powers at the funeral feasts.

When a Maori chief gets killed, his friends plunder his wives and children. Others tell us that, on the death of a tribal chief, his neighbours assemble to pillage his possessions and appropriate everything they can lay their hands on.

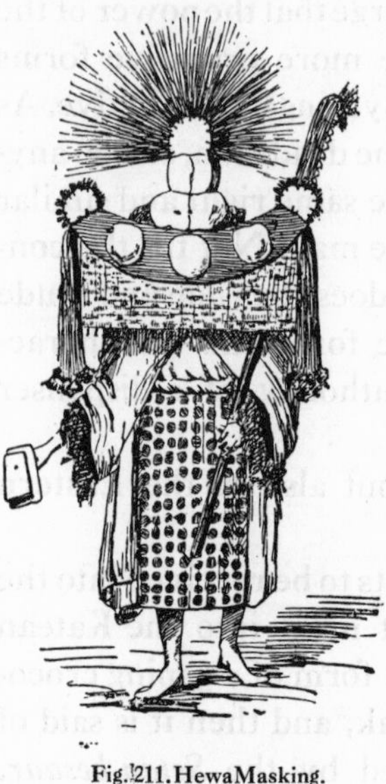

According to Forster, a relative of a deceased Tahitian disguises himself with the *hewa mask* (fig. 211), and sets out with a walking-stick on a wandering expedition, starting from the dead man's house and accompanied by two men painted black. Whoever meets him is greeted with a thrashing. Wherever he approaches, the islanders abandon their huts and betake themselves to a hasty flight in order to escape the blows. The death of a Tahitian chief is also followed by fighting, to the point of wounding or even killing. In Hawaii, the death is similarly followed by wild turmoil. Murder, robbery, arson, belong to the order of the day.

In Fiji, towards the tenth day after the burial feast, or perhaps a little earlier, the women arm themselves with sticks, rods and whips, and fall upon any of the men,

Fig. 211. Hewa Masking. Tahiti (after a drawing of Cook's Expedition).

SECRET SOCIETIES AND MASKS

except the highest chief, using their weapons unsparingly.

Here too, then, we have the same root-idea and customs as in the other islands. But here also, as elsewhere, the mask is intimately associated with these notions and observances. It is for the most part masked persons who indulge in these riotous doings, either after the death of another (hence as representatives of a freed soul prowling about), or else after their own decease, that is to say, as spiritualized beings. The mask, however, was assuredly not invented for the purpose of disguising its disorderly wearer. Such an assumption is excluded by its mystic and sacred character. Rather are we confronted with a form which is the most natural, the most original, and in its way the most primitive mask, one which must also have otherwise arisen in serious and intimate connexion with the spiritualistic idea. I refer to the skull-mask, for which see the chapter on skull-worship.

It is not to be supposed that all masks originated with the skull, although in the case of many peoples such an assumption may not be far from the truth. For the skulls of the departed are frequently preserved in an artificial way, used for spiritualistic purposes, decked with ornaments and applied to purposes which most vividly recall the customs of the New Pomeranians, their skull-masks, their Kinakinau, and the like. Hence, I will not assume that everywhere the mask has arisen in this way, although, on the other hand, it is an undeniable fact that wherever the mask at all appears, at least as a fresh, unmodified object, there too it is always to be brought into relation with manistic ideas.

Hence, the mask is not the image of the rioter, but a symbol of soul-worship, an object directly related to the ancestral effigies. This is revealed, not only by the significance of its application, but also by its very form, which has, for the most part, retained the character of a sacred object. There are the most divers types, the

Fig. 212. Mukish, masked mendicant, or Expeller of Spirits, from Angola (after M. Buchner).

most varied materials, as may be seen by reference to the illustrations. But so soon as the form or type is once adopted, there is no very great stretch of development from a quite primitive example made out of the bark of a tree to one daintily prepared with net and feather-work.

As the exercise of spirit-power has been transformed from its original brutal character to a relatively refined administration of justice, in the same way the application of the mask has been transformed from one extreme to the other. At first the masked person stalked in with tragic dignity and solemn awe; then the spectacle grew stale, and, with the waning of popular belief, even this outward expression of manism lost its serious aspect, till at last we see the masqueraders trooping through the streets amid the jeers of the spectators, developing at last into the universally despised buffoon, who now goes begging for what the original personator of the spirit-powers simply appropriated, that is, stole, in their name.

Nor does it all end with the buffoon. It passes to another sphere, to the bustling scene of the mimic arts, and becomes a stage mask. Of this I give an example from Africa.

IV. *The Stage Mask*

WE are indebted to Clapperton for a thorough description of a play amongst the Yorubas, one of the most interesting people in Africa, who live to the west of the Niger delta.

The place chosen for this pastime is the king's garden, facing the chief entrance, where a petitioner usually takes his seat. A temple stands on the left hand, and towards the south are two very large picturesque-looking granite blocks, and by their side an old withered tree. Eastwards are two beautiful shady trees, and on the north the king's residence, where he takes his seat as a spectator. In the centre of the open space are two clumps of fine trees, in one of which grows a tall fan-palm, towering high above the place, which may be from 700 to 800 yards square. Under these trees sat the players completely enveloped in sacks, and their heads most fantastically decorated with parti-coloured strips and shreds of silk and cotton.

SECRET SOCIETIES AND MASKS

The king's attendants take care that no spectator shall enter the enclosure, while the musicians keep up an incessant uproar with their drums, horns and pipes.

The first act consisted in the players dancing and jumping about in their sacks, and this they did in a remarkable way, considering that they could not see, or use their hands and feet freely.

In the second act the boa-constrictor was captured. First of all one of the sack-men came forward and knelt down on hands and feet; then appeared a large majestic figure with an indescribable head-dress and mask. It was quite pitch-black, and at times looked like a lion couching on the crest of a helmet, and again a black head with a large wig. At every turn it changed its form. The figure held a sword in its right hand, and, judging from its gorgeous dress and its action, it must have been the director of the performance. The players did not utter a word; and the manager, as I may call the big figure, went up to the man who lay in the sack, while another dancer was brought forward in his sack, and at a sign with the sword laid at the head or the feet of the other. Then he opened the ends of both sacks, whereupon the two persons crept into one of them. Now the manager gave such a tremendous flourish with his sword that I fully expected a head would fly off, as all the players had gathered about the two in one sack. But in a few minutes they were off, all but the manager, who made three or four thrusts with his sword, when the scene with the boa-constrictor began. The beast stretched his head out of the basket in which he lay, and tried to bite the manager, but at a sweep of the sword he turned his head on one side to avoid the blow. Then he crept slowly out of the basket, and imitated all the movements of a snake very naturally, espe-

Figs. 213, 214, 215. Dancing Mukish (after M. Buchner).

cially the opening and shutting of the mouth, which was probably done by the actor with his two hands. The snake was about fourteen feet long, and the skin was well imitated. After pursuing the manager for some time through the park, and trying to bite him, which he prevented with his sword, a signal was made to all the actors to come forward, and the manager made as if he meant to strike the snake's tail with his sword. Now the snake opened its jaws, coiled itself up, and seemed to be in great pain. When it was nearly dead, the actors took it on their shoulders, while it still kept opening its mouth and trying to bite, and carried it off in great triumph to the temple.

In the third act the white devil appeared. As the players withdrew to the background of the stage one remained behind, and as his sack slowly fell off, there first appeared a white head, at which all the people raised a great shout. Gradually the whole body became visible, and a white figure was seen, frightfully lean and perishing with cold. The figure constantly took snuff and rubbed its hands, and when it walked it did so in the most awkward way. It acted like the most timid of white men venturing for the first time barefooted on the ice.

The audience often asked us whether the performance was not first-rate, and begged me to look out and give heed to what was now coming on. I asked myself whether the caricature of a white man would give me as much pleasure as it would them, and certainly the actor played his part well. When it was over, all the actors went off to the temple. Between each act the king's women sang, and the assembly joined in the chorus.

America is not distinguished by such sharp definition in its manistic way of viewing things as is Africa, and to

SECRET SOCIETIES AND MASKS

some extent also Oceania. The secret societies of the North American Redskins, one of which I will describe in the next chapter in connexion with some drawings by the natives, are saturated with a spirit that is originally far removed from the primitive growth of manism. The *Midewiwin* are an association of the Chippeways, who live round about Lake Superior in Canada and the United States. Anybody can become a member of the club; but there are four grades, and promotion from one to the other is always gained by a further purchase, by gifts which are hung up on one, two, three or four posts in the sacred house, according to the grade, and shared amongst the members, and further by vapour baths and smoke offerings. At each initiation the bad *Manidos* (spirits) have to be vanquished, and in this the good Manidos help. The functions of the members of this society consist in divination, forecasting, medical practice and driving out devils.

CHAPTER XVI
THE MIDE

THE Ojibways (Chippeways), one of the largest of the North American nations, dwell round the shores of Lake Superior. Amongst them we find a peculiar class of people called *Mide*, who, as an exclusive association, trace their origin to the following myth:

When Minabozho, servant of Dzhe Manido, looked down on the earth, he noticed some human beings, the Anishinabegs, forefathers of the Ojibways. They inhabited the four quarters of the earth—the north-east, the south-east, the south-west and the north-west. He saw that they were very helpless, and he wanted to procure them remedies by which they would be cured of all ailments.

He kept hovering, full of thought, over the centre of the earth. While he was endeavouring to find out how he could put himself into communication with them, he heard something laughing, and perceived a black object on the surface of the water in the west. He could not recognize its form, and while he was attentively observing it, it slowly disappeared. Then it appeared in the north, and after a little while again vanished. Minabozho hoped it would again show itself on the surface of the water, and so it did, emerging in the east.

Then Minabozho wished he could draw near in order to speak with it. When it vanished from his gaze in the

THE MIDE

Fig. 216. A member of the Mide "practising," that is, occupied as a physician (after W. J. Hoffmann).

east, and afterwards reappeared in the south, Minabozho said:

"Come, then, to the centre of the earth, that I may observe thee."

Once more it vanished from his sight; and when Minabozho saw it again rising to the surface in the west he noticed that it was slowly drawing near to the centre of the earth. Then he came down and saw that it was the otter, which is now one of the sacred animals of the Midewiwin. Now Minabozho gave the otter admittance into the mysteries of the Midewiwin, and at the same time gave it the sacred rattle which is used for sick people, the sacred Mide-drum, which is used at sacred feasts, and tobacco, which is used at prayers and treaties of peace.

The place where Minabozho descended was an island in the middle of a great water, and therefore the Mide who is the most feared of all is called Minisinoshkwe ("He who lives on the island"). Now Minabozho built a Midewigan (sacred Mide-house), and took his drum, beat it, and sang a Mide lay in which he told the otter that Dzhe Manido had decided to help the Anishinabegs, so that they should have life, abundance of food and all necessary things.

Thereupon Minabozho took the otter with him to the Midewigan and confided to it the mysteries of the Mide-wiwin, and taking his Mide-bag shot the sacred Migis into its body to give it immortality and enable it to confide these secrets to his relations, the Anishinabegs. The Migis is a sacred symbol of the Midewiwin, and usually consists of a small white shell.

This myth is represented by the accompanying illustrations on Plate III, which at the same time

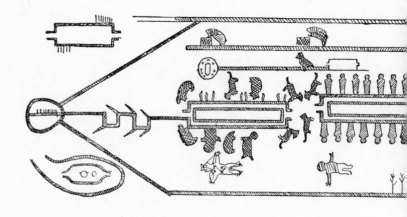

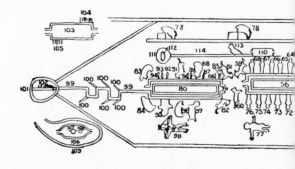

Native Representation of

A

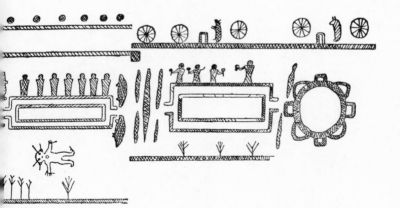

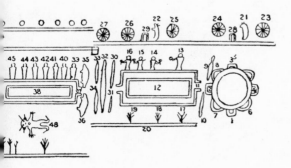

all its Rites and Symbols.

THE MIDE

offer perhaps the best elucidations of the Midewiwin ceremonies.

Plate II. The large circle on the right side indicates the earth on which Minabozho is looking down, while the otter appears to him at the squares in Nos. 1, 2, 3 and 4. The crescent-shaped appendages, Nos. 5, 6, 7 and 8, represent the four quarters of the earth which are inhabited by the Anishinabegs. Nos. 9 and 10 are two ot the numerous wicked Manidos, who are endeavouring to prevent the entrance into the sacred building and access to the mysteries of the Midewiwin. The longitudinal rectangles, 11 and 12, are sketches of the first grade of the society, and the inner parallel lines indicate the way that must be taken during the enrolment. The four human forms, 13, 14, 15 and 16, are the four officiating Mide priests whose services are always required at an admittance; each of them holds a rattle in his hand. Nos. 17, 18 and 19 represent cedar-trees, one of which is always planted at each corner of the Mide house. No. 20 indicates the earth.

The sketch of the bear, No. 21, represents the Makwa Manido, or Bear-spirit, to whom the candidate must pray and bring tobacco-offerings, with which the spirit compels the wicked Manidos to retire from the gate of the Midewigan, which is shown at No. 28. Nos 23. and 24 are raised drums which the candidate must beat while chanting his prayers.

When a candidate is admitted to a grade, and has prepared to pass on to the next, he gives three feasts and sings three prayers to the Makwa Manido, or Bearspirit (No. 22) in order to be permitted to enter that grade. The feasts and songs are shown by the three drums, Nos. 25, 26 and 27.

THE MIDE

Nos. 30, 31, 32, 33 and 34 are five snake-spirits, bad Manidos, who resist the progress of a Mide; but after the feasts and the prayers which are addressed to the Makwa Manido, the four little snake-spirits, which are stationed at the side of the path leading from one to the other grade, have to retire, while the large snake raises

Fig. 217. The entrance house or Midiwigan (after W. J. Hoffmann).

its body in the middle and thus forms an arch under which the candidate takes his way to the second grade.

Nos. 35, 36, 37 and 38 are four wicked Bear-spirits who guard the entrance and exit of the second grade, the doors of which are seen at Nos. 37 and 49. The form of this house (38) is like that of the foregoing. Nos. 39, 40, 41, 42, 43, 44 and 45 are Mide priests who assist at the second initiation. The number of priests at the entry feast is undetermined, but more are indicated at the second than at the first grade in order thereby to show its higher rank.

THE MIDE

When the Mide belongs to the second grade, he receives from Dzhe Manido supernatural power, as shown at No. 48. The lines running from the eyes upwards denote that he can see into the future; those which extend outwards from the ears, that he can hear what goes on afar off; those from the hands, that he can touch good or bad friends and foes, however far away they may be; and the lines drawn outwards from the feet indicate his capacity to give effect to his wishes or exercise his functions at any distance whatsoever. The little circle on the breast of the figure means that the Migis—life—has been shot into the body of a Mide of this second grade. The larger the spot, the greater the strength and influence thereby imparted to him.

Fig. 218. Ground plan of the Midiwigan (after W. J. Hoffmann).

No. 50 represents a Mitsha Mide, or wicked Mide, one who uses his strength for bad purposes. He has the power of assuming the form of any animal, and in this disguise of destroying the life of his victim, in order again to return to his human form and appear quite innocent. His services are sought by people who want to annihilate enemies or rivals who live far away. No. 50 shows a creature which has disguised itself as a bear, and the marks Nos. 51 and 52 represent the footsteps of a bear, which have been made by the being so disguised. Such traces are at times found near habitations where its selected victims dwell. The trees on each side of No. 50 denote a wood, the place to which wicked Mides and witches usually resort.

When a Mide of the second grade manages to become a member of the third, he again gives a feast to his teacher and the four officiating Mides, and prays to Manido for luck and success. No. 53 represents the candidate as a bear, no longer a wicked one, but one of the holy Manidos, of whom it is supposed that he was present at the entrance rites of the second grade. He is seated before his sacred drum, and when the fitting time comes the snake Manido (54), who has hitherto opposed his entry, coils himself up, and creeps under him into the door of the third grade (55 and 56), where he meets two of the four panther-spirits who are guardians of this grade (57 and 58). Nos. 61 to 76 show Mide spirits which dwell in the building of this grade, and the number of human forms, which is greater than that having reference to the second grade, imparts a correspondingly higher and more sacred character to the third.

When an Indian enters this grade he becomes very accomplished in his calling as a Mide. The power which he possessed in the second grade is enhanced. Hence, in No. 77, he is figured with outspread arms, while lines are drawn across his body and arms, which show that he is capable of bringing down from the invisible world the knowledge required to perform extraordinary exploits. Now he relies on the more prompt aid of the holy Manidos.

Nos. 59 and 60 are two of the four panther-spirits, who are the special guardians of the third grade. In order to enter the fourth and highest grade of the society a greater number of feasts is needed than before, and the candidate, who again represents the bear-spirit, again requires his sacred drum, as shown at No. 78, and chants still more prayers in order to secure the favour of the Dzhe Manido. This grade is watched by the greatest number and the most powerful of the wicked spirits, who make a final

THE MIDE

effort to bar a candidate from entering the door (79) which leads to the house of the fourth grade (80). The chief opponents are two panthers (81 and 82) and two bears (83 and 84), and these are vanquished by the aid of Dzhe Manido. Other wicked spirits also lurk about the building, which they often take possession of, and they are then in a position to offer prolonged resistance to the entrance of the candidate. The leaders of this group are bears (88 and 96), the panther (91), the lynx (97), and many others who are indicated at Nos. 85, 86, 87, 89, 90, 92, 93, 94 and 95.

The power with which a person may be endowed who belongs to the fourth grade is indicated by the sketch of a human being on whom are seen a number of spots, showing that his body is covered with the Migis or sacred shells. These spots show the places where the Mide priests have shot at the reception, and the lines connecting them point at the enhanced capacity of the different organs.

From the end of the fourth grade an angular footpath leading to the left denotes the way which must be taken by a Mide after he has acquired this exalted position. Now the course of his life is strewn with many dangers, which are shown by the right angles. Temptations present themselves which aim at leading him astray. The points at which he might possibly turn aside are shown by lines which branch off to the right and left (100). The egg-shaped figure (101) at the end of the path is called "end of the way," and means that here the life of the individual comes to a close.

The vertical strokes in the egg-shaped figure mean that the drawer of this illustration has been for fourteen years a member of the fourth grade of the Midewiwin. The sketch of the Midewigan (103) shows that he practises as a Mide, that is, has driven out demons, and the vertical strokes (104 and 105) mean that he was the high priest of the Midewiwin for thirteen years. The sketch of the Midewigan (106) with the circle (107) indicates the sacred stake, and (108) the stone on which the sick take their place when being treated. The path (109) denotes that the draughtsman also visits the sick who reside beyond the recognized jurisdiction of the society. Immediately above the fourth house is drawn the sketch of a Midewiwin (110), with a path (114) leading westwards to a circle (111) in which is a similar building whose longer diameter forms a right angle with the path. That is Dzhibai Midewigan or the spirits' house. No. 113 represents the Ko-ko-ko-o (owl), which goes from the Midewigan along the path of the dead to the land of the setting-sun, the abode of the dead.

Plate III. The four grades of the Midewiwin are also illustrated by the picture on Plate III, which, however, compared with the other, displays a higher artistic skill. The following is the interpretation of it given by the Ojibwas:

When Kitshi Manido decided to give the Midewiwin practices to the Anishinabegs, he took his Mide-drum and sang in order to summon the other Manidos to come and hear what he was now going to do. No. 1 shows Kitshi Manido's residence in heaven; No. 2 shows how the god beats the drum; No. 3 are little spots representing the Migis with which everything surrounding the god is covered. The Mide Manidos also come to him in the Midewigan (4); eleven of these are figured inside the building, while ten who are outside (5 to 14) descend on the earth laden with the means by which the Anishinabegs are to be shown the sacred customs. In the Mide-

PLATE III.

This Representation of the Mide, which for neatness leaves nothing to be desired, bears quite a different aspect from the figures of the same objects on Plate II. The explanation of the difference lies in the style of drawing, which is primitive on Plate II, while that of Plate III is influenced by European draughtsmanship.

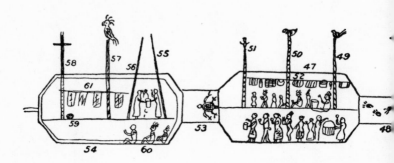

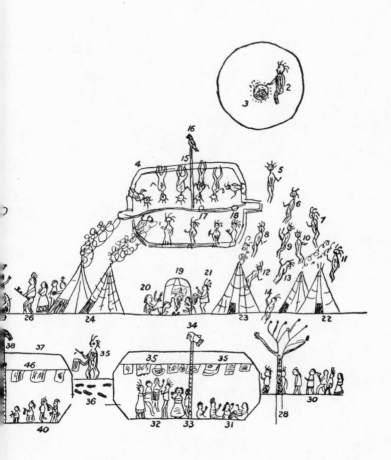

wigan is also to be seen the sacred stake (15) on which the Ko-ko-ko-o, the owl (16), has perched. The line which intersects the building from one side to the other denotes the footpath leading through it, while the two rings (17 and 18) on the right side of the stake point to the place where the gifts are laid down.

When an Indian is ready to undergo the initiation, he erects a wigwam (19) in which he takes steam baths for four days, one on each day. The four baths and the four days are indicated by a number of spots on the floor of the house, which at the same time denote stones. His teachers and the officiating priests of the society are present; one of them (20) is seen on the left side of the wigwam bringing a smoke-offering, and another on the right side beating the drum and singing. The four officiating priests are visible within the building on either side of the candidate. The wigwams (22, 23, 24, 25) denote the village houses.

On the evening of the day before the initiation the candidate (26) visits his teachers (27) in order to obtain from them instructions for the following day. The candidate is shown bringing his pipe with him, for the tobacco-offering is the most acceptable of all gifts. His relatives follow bearing presents, some of which are hung on the branches of the first Mide-tree (28) at the entrance of the first building. The teachers' wigwam is shown by No. 29, the two dark round spots representing two seats which are taken by the teacher and pupil. The figure, No. 27, has its left arm raised in order to point out that his lesson has reference to Kitshi Manido, while he holds the Mide-drum in his right hand. Next morning the Mide priests approach with the candidate at their head (30), enter the Midewigan, and the proceedings begin. No. 31 is the place of the sacred drum and of those who have been appointed to use the drums and the rattles, while No. 32 indicates the officiating priests. No. 33 is the stake of the grade, above which is the Ko-ko-ko-o, the owl (34). The line (35) running along the upper part of the enclosed space denotes the stake on which clothes, coverlets, kettles and the like are suspended. They represent the price which on the reception must be paid to the society.

When the candidate has succeeded in acquiring sufficient gifts as presents for the society of the second grade, he takes his drum and sings a song to the Kitshi Manido, thanking him for his favour (35). Kitshi Manido himself is the protector of the second grade, and his footsteps are shown at No. 36. No. 37 represents the interior of the second grade, and contains two sacred stakes, the first of which is the same as that of the first grade. A little branch at the top is used for hanging the tobacco-pouch after the ceremony. No. 40 denotes musicians and attendants; No. 41 the candidate on his knees, and 42, 43, 44, 45 the officiating priests surrounding him. The stake is hung with presents—clothes, garments and kettledrums.

When the candidate is ready to be received into the third grade (47), he personates Makwa Manibo, who is the patron of this grade, and whose spoor is seen at 48. The participators are visible in the interior, drum-beating and dancing. Three sacred stakes are seen with the owl on the first, while the second (50) has the likeness of an owl on the top of it, and the third (51) is crowned by an Indian. The rod (52) is also hung with presents.

The protector of the fourth grade is Makano, the turtle (53), which is gazing at the entrance to the fourth grade (54). In the fourth grade are set up four sacred stakes,

The towne of Pomeyok and true forme of their howses, covered and enclosed some w matts, and some w barcks of trees. All compassed abowt w smale poles stuck thick together in stead of a wall.

From the original water-colour drawing in the British Museum by John White, Governor of Virginia in 1587.

the first (55) painted white on the upper half and green on the lower; the second (56) similarly; the third red with a black spiral running from the top to the ground, ko-ko-ko-o, the owl, being perched on the top; the fourth (58) represents a cross. No. 59 denotes the site of the sacred stone; No. 60 the company, some of whom are seated at the wall, while others beat the drum. On the rod is shown apparel representing gifts for the society.

On the introduction of a candidate songs were sung, in

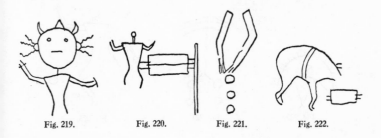

Fig. 219. Fig. 220. Fig. 221. Fig. 222.

which the god was thanked for having given to mortals the knowledge of medicinal plants, and also praying him to continue the tokens of his favour. These songs were scratched on birch-bark; but it is difficult at times to decipher their meaning, as each "writer" used his own signs.

In the following song, the teacher seems to be pleased that the candidate is prepared to undergo his initiation, and therefore tells him that the Mide Manido gives him a favourable answer:

(Fig. 219) *Listen, the spirit wishes to speak to us.* (The Mide-singer commands an immense power, as shown by the horns and the point on his head. The lines extending outwards from his ears mean hearing.)

THE MIDE

(Fig. 220) *Let me enter the sacred Camp* (house). (The Midewigan is traversed by a line to show that he is going through it.)

(Fig. 221) *I seize the remedy which imparts life to me.* (The circles denote sacred objects which are within reach of the speaker.)

(Fig. 222) *To thee I mean to give the remedy, and a hut besides!* (The Mide who personates the Makwa Manido is authorized to offer this privilege to the candidate.)

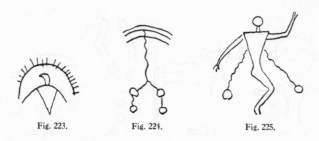

Fig. 223.   Fig. 224.   Fig. 225.

(Fig. 223) *I fly to my Camp!* (Here is represented the thunder-bird, who is a deity flying up to heaven. The short strokes denote the place of residence of the spirits or Manidos.)

(Fig. 224) *The spirit lets the remedy trickle down from heaven that we may collect it!* (The line which runs down from heaven and branches off to various points shows that the sacred remedies are found in several places.)

(Fig. 225) *I hold the remedy in my heart!* (The body [heart] of the singer is filled with knowledge, which has reference to the sacred medicine yielded to us by the earth.)

As already stated, the type of the ideas that lie at the base of these observances departs very essentially from

THE MIDE

the clear personations of spiritualism and spirit-power in the eastern manistic period. Assuredly the discrepancies are not alone due to the fact that the material has been contributed by American ethnologists, whereas all the other secret societies have been studied by European travellers. Nor do I find that the difference is owing to the circumstance that the American Indians have been influenced for centuries by Christian missionaries and thus deprived of the clearness of their conception in matters pertaining to the manistic view of the world. Nevertheless, a transient influence in this respect is not to be overlooked. *"The Great Spirit," and the "happy hunting-grounds"* are, to an appreciable extent, traceable to Christian influence and not exactly Indian notions. (See also fig. 280.)

Hence, faint and transient influences of this nature can certainly be pointed out. But they are not altogether sufficient to explain the other, the indigenous, type. That here other causes are at work is shown by one thing above all, namely, by the introduction of so many animal forms. Here, in fact, we have touched on the essential point. For while the African and Oceanic mythology and view of the world has, with its deeper manistic spirit, its cult of ancestors, thrown overboard as much as possible of the lumber of the previous period of animism and respect for animals, from all this the American has not yet shaken himself free. What this means I will endeavour to explain in the next chapter.

CHAPTER XVII
SACRED ANIMALS

SCARCELY one of all the problems in mythology has elicited so much general interest as the great mark of interrogation which in the ideal world of primitive man must be inserted between animalism and manism, between regard for animals and the contemplation of the human soul. I refer to the problem of sacred animals. The "transmigration of the soul" has been made the subject of a vast amount of fanciful speculation. It is a subject the first knowledge of which was acquired by European peoples and scholars from the Egyptians. Already in their time the Greek philosophers had cudgelled their brains and uttered many a preposterous word about the matter, for even learned Greeks have at times said more than they could answer for. So much, at any rate, is certain, that in no primitive people have we yet been able really to detect any clearly defined notions regarding transmigration through several animal forms. It is otherwise in Indian philosophy.

From the standpoint which I have established in the chapter on the animal stories of the Bushmen, that is, from the notion of animalism, looked at in anticipation of later developments, animal worship assumes a somewhat different aspect from what is commonly supposed.

People who esteem animals as themselves, who are ready here and there to attribute greater power to them than to themselves, must at any rate at the dawn of manism, when they begin to contemplate the soul, make some compromise with the animals. This compromise with the animal-souls, this merging of animalistic notions in the cult of the dead and in soul-worship, is the moving

Fig. 226. Tortoise-shell mask from Jervis, Torres Straits (British Museum).

power which has introduced the sacred animals into the sphere of mythology.

This is quite obvious. When man sets out to enlarge the range of influence of the dead, the activities of the souls of his departed relatives, to develop them into a vast system, then he must also raise the animals, whether friendly and neighbourly, or hostile and dreaded, to the level of such a broadened and more critical view.

It is indeed quite evident. When I have killed a man, and am now convinced that his soul will henceforth seek to be avenged, when I cherish such a notion, then the thought must also suggest itself to me that the animal that I have killed can likewise revenge itself.

Another thing is clear. Man seeks in every way to acquire supernatural faculties, seeks to get the better of

Fig. 227. Tortoise-shell mask from Hama, Torres Straits (British Museum). Seen from the side, as here, represents a kind of shark's head. Above (Fig. 228) a face. Is probably worn at the dances in the fishing season, when, no doubt, efforts are made to propitiate the sharks, who are so dangerous to the fisher-folk.

natural necessity, of nature's laws, seeks to become immune from chance by obtaining controlling power. As his garden suffers from too severe a drought, he tries to find out some rain-doctor. As the soul of his neighbour may bewitch him, he casts about for an amulet which is still more effective than his enemy's magic power. I think it should be in the same way self-evident that he takes pains somehow to acquire power over animal life, hence that, in times when he feels himself subordinate rather than superior to the animals, he flatters them for their favour, brings offerings and worships them.

Such a mental state may be shown in several ways. At the beginning of the great fishing seasons the South Sea Islanders organize dancing feasts, in which the action of these creatures is imitated. At the spring dances here and there masks are worn, the origin of which can be traced without difficulty. Amongst their number must, for instance, doubtless be mentioned figs. 226 and 227, of the latter of which I give further a view from above, which enables us distinctly to recognize the human face resting on it. As in these dances, so also in other ways is shown the interest in the matter taken by these remarkable fisherfolk. It will, perhaps, suffice to refer to the picture of a sea-god which is reproduced at fig. 229.

Fig. 228. The mask of Fig. 227 seen from above.

SACRED ANIMALS

With this illustration let us begin the consideration of the carvings, in which is best revealed the interest taken by primitive man in animals. This picture, with many others, might equally well find a place beside the figures which are reproduced in the chapter on the Bushman

Fig. 229. Melanesian Sea-God (after a native drawing in Codrington's Melanesians).

animal stories. Here we are presented with an embodiment of fish life fresh from nature. The ichthyologist will be able to identify the several fishes. Hence it is a reminiscence of the fresh young period of painting of which I have made mention in Chapter IX. With it are worthily associated the couple of fishes shown at fig. 230.

Both pictures show a remarkable peculiarity. In the representation the fishes stand in close relation with man. In fig. 229 they represent parts of a human body, the

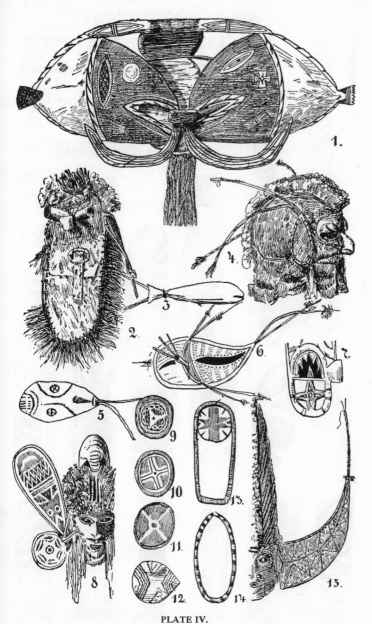

PLATE IV.

IV-VI. Fish ornaments on masks from New Mecklenburg and New Pomerania, New Ireland and New Britain, in the Museums of Berlin, Bremerhafen, Bremen, Cambridge (England), New York, Dresden, Jena, Stuttgart, Munich, Schwerin, etc.; all drawn from photographs. The figures 9 to 27 on Plate V are somewhat awkwardly drawn; figs. 9 to 11 being right ears, and 12 to 27 left ears.

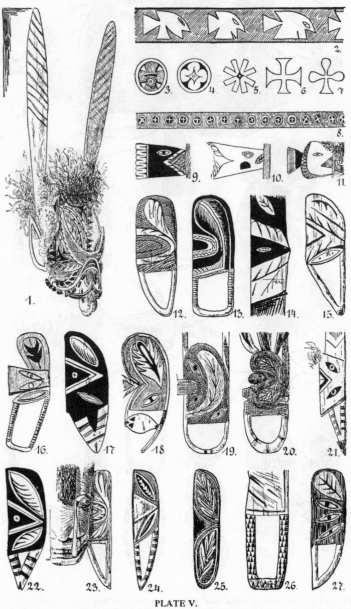

PLATE V.

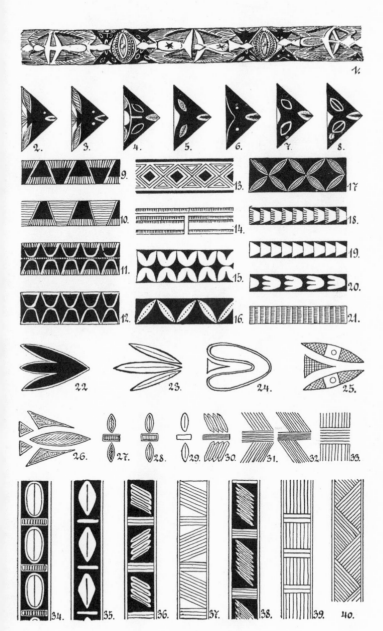

PLATE VI.

PLATE VI.

head, the hands, the feet, but in fig. 230 they are biting from right and left at the human face of the mask. What is figured in the latter we shall also observe in other pictures. What can be inferred from a study of this pictorial treatment of animals must also have a certain value in

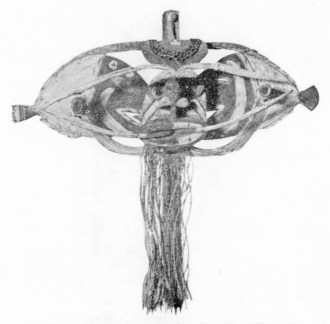

Fig. 230. Mask from New Mecklenburg (New York Natural History Museum). In the middle a face at which a fish on each side (right and left) is biting.

forming an opinion on the mythological way of viewing the world. *Verbum sap*.

Of the two charming little fishes, which in fig. 230 are hidden behind the human face, we can catch a back view by looking at the mask from behind, as on Plate IV, fig. 1.

SACRED ANIMALS

What we here observe, a little fish on each side of the mask, may also be noticed elsewhere. Fig. 231 in the text is prepared from a material of bark-cloth which is drawn over wooden sticks. That is an awkward medium for the modeller. Yet here also the fishes cannot escape

Fig. 231. Mask from New Pomerania (Pfeil Collection, Munich Ethnographic Museum). Bast material on stick frame Right and left (at a and b) a fish is figured.

notice. In fig. 5 of Plate IV I give a more detailed reproduction of these two. At fig. 8 of the same plate it will be recognized on the upper of the two ears, which are outspread like butterflies on the side here reproduced. It is a kind of flounder, with two eyes and a little open mouth. Figs. 9-27 represent ears all of the same pattern. It would be a pleasant Sunday afternoon's entertainment

SACRED ANIMALS

for the reader to set himself to solve the riddle of the ornaments of these ears. I will only betray the secret that they are all conventional fish forms.

For those who would like to prolong this Sunday afternoon's pastime I also give Plates V and VI, on which are introduced complete parts of masks and ornaments of plastic and pictorial art. On the first of these two plates the fish can be recognized in a corner to the left under the dolphin's wing which reaches like a fin over the eye. Figs. 2 to 7 on this plate show the gradual modifications of the fish to the form of a cross. In fig. 2 anyone will still easily detect the fish. But the lower and the left limbs of the cross are here already developed; here also the gaping jaw already serves to mark the division between the other two, that is, the upper and the right limbs. In fig. 3 the cross is completed, but the eye still lies outside the centre. In fig. 4 the centre is accentuated and the beginning of a further subdivision introduced.

Figs. 9 to 27 give us a further development, which, however, the reader will have much difficulty in following, especially as the artist—between ourselves, this time the author—has made a blunder. For in figs. 9, 10, 11 the worthy man has pictured right ears, but in 12 to 27 left ones, which increases the difficulty. Still one may perhaps succeed in detecting the several parts of the fish, such as the gills, eyes and mouth.

On the following Plate VI the forms take free play. Here a like development of the ornaments may be followed. Fig. 1 represents a decorative panel on which may be noticed six birds, two large eyes, and between the birds and the eyes eight little fishes. These eight little fishes I have disposed in a series on figs. 2 to 8, corresponding to the gradually conventionalized forms. If we are here sur-

Fig. 232. Ancestral effigy (?) from New Mecklenburg (Ethnographic Museum, Schwerin).

prised at the disappearance of the tail, in the next series, figs. 9 to 21, we find that the little tail alone is the motive of a striking ornamental development. In fig. 9 the tails are dovetailed; in fig. 11 they are arranged in two opposite rows; in fig. 18 they are displayed in a long chain.

This evolution of the fish is again exhibited by the forms brought together in the figs. 22 to the end. We need not suppose that such simple and primitive ornaments as figs. 32, 33, 39 and 40 are *necessarily* derived from the fish. They are merely to indicate how such simple lines may represent the final outcome of a figurative ornamental development. But with this I will now leave this subject, which doubtless many readers will

SACRED ANIMALS

have found wearisome enough, and confine myself to a consideration of the inferences to be drawn from the facts here displayed.

But the main point is that we have here a fishing people in whose life this species of animal possesses an extra-ordinary importance. This is shown, besides other ways, in the fact that the picture of the fish becomes a leading feature of pictorial representation. In this we have an evidence of deep spiritual interest. Something else, how-ever, is indicated by the ornamental evolution which we have just been considering. The evolution shows that the interest in the object itself has, in a measure, begun to wane. It is certain that the worthy New Mecklenburg people themselves are perhaps less in a position than we are to explain how the cross so often painted by them has originated.

As it is with these ornaments, so it is with the whole history of the sacred animals. As the people paint the conventional fish pictures without giving the matter much thought, in the same way they doubtless for the most part worship the animals themselves without quite under-standing precisely why they do so, how they have arrived at this animal-cult.

This lack of consciousness, of clearness, regarding their own conceptions, should become most apparent in a sphere of customs which science, adopting an American-Indian term, has comprised under the word *Totemism*.

What is Totemism?

An Indian tribe is divided into several groups or families, which are usually named after animals. Thus, a tribe may, for instance, have four families: a bear, a whale, a deer and a raven family. Each member must intermarry only with another family. The bear, for instance, must take to wife only a whale, deer or raven's daughter. That is a strict and sacred law.

Whence comes all this?

It is assuredly connected mainly with the origin of his name. In the early times men, doubtless, were not at all

Fig. 233. Body of a North-West American chief laid out with the whole paraphernalia of his totemistic system, masks, hats, clothes, etc. (after Niblack).

called by names. Why should they be? They roamed the land in little bands, probably even only in couples. With two, a simple "thou" suffices. Not till they became more numerous did they call themselves by names; and as that must, no doubt, have been in the animalistic period they called each other by animal names. And as, moreover, the law was soon enacted that no man should take a wife from his own group, it was self-evident that a fox should not marry a vixen.

With Totemism are connected other things which show still more clearly in what way the sacred character of

Fig. 234. Totemistic Play, or acting of the totemistic ancestral Saga, on the occasion of the burial of the chief laid out at Fig. 233 (after Niblack).

animals may arise. In totemistic families it may happen that people do not dare to taste the flesh of the animal whose name they bear, until they have first asked pardon for the crime of killing it, or even will not dare at all to kill and eat that animal. This is quite intelligible, since we know how superstitious people are regarding their names. What a multiplicity of notions are prevalent on the subject!

SACRED ANIMALS

That this Totemism should further assume specially animated forms amongst peoples who are in active association with animal life is also quite intelligible. Such people are found in North-West America, and farther on we shall have to relate many of their myths. In these

Fig. 235. Model of a Batta Coffin, Sumatra (Dresden Ethnographic Museum). The coffin in the form of a bird. The woman with the child is doubtless the effigy of the deceased. Compare figs 236 & 250.

we shall see how nearly all the individuals have animal names and animal forms, that the whole of their extensive solar mythology is clothed in animalistic garb. This is quite natural, since with them the whole of this mythical life is passed in a parade of masks and stage effects, all in animalistic dress (cf. figs. 233, 234).

But the sacred animals have been introduced not only by those of the chase and by Totemism. Intimately associated with the totemistic notions is always the thought that human beings can be changed into the animals whose names they bear, or that every animal of the name may harbour some dead member of the family, and we have

Fig. 236. Knyalon, a Dayak carving, Borneo (Vienna Ethnographic Museum). These carvings are used, i.e., set up and honoured both at the feast of the skull-dance—which is new—and at the feast of the dead. It represents a rhinoceros hornbill with enormously developed spiral horn. On the tail a soul with two animal figures, one of which seizes the stunted wing. In the bird's beak little objects of unknown import (Cf. Fig. 250).

Fig. 237. Kamerun Figure-head (Hamburg Ethnological Museum). On the shaft a man with two animals. In front, usually one, here two birds, the larger with a snake in its beak.

thus still to do with higher conceptions. For the bird, the most ideal of all the sacred animals, is not, as a rule, associated with Totemism.

I, half a child of nature myself, must loyally confess

that I regard the notions grouped round the bird as elevated and beautiful. For the root-idea is of this kind:

On the death of a man the bird killed and offered upon

Fig. 238. Decorative panel from New Mecklenburg, Pfeil collection in the Grand ducal Museum, Schwerin. A bird carrying four little creatures and with a snake in its beak.

his corpse bears his soul aloft, that is, to the after-world.

Is not that a beautiful idea?

Is there a man who, standing on the open ground and gazing at the course of a bird wheeling round, has not envied it as it soars higher and higher till out of sight? Is it not also, in its way, a beautiful thought when the Bagos, watching awe-stricken, a flight of birds

Fig. 239. Figure-head of a New Zealand boat, from an old woodcut. In front a large bird, behind a head with open mouth biting at a connecting bar. This bar, where it reaches the bird, has a kind of eye ornament, hence may have been conventionalized from the snake, so that we may have here an original motive like that in Fig. 245.

taking wing in the rainy season, exclaim: "There go our fathers away to a land which has no sickness and no floods, where the sun is always shining!"

SACRED ANIMALS

Such is the idea prevalent in a very wide domain of early civilization. It is not confined to the primitive races now surviving, since the ancient Germans also had a somewhat

Fig. 240. Figure-head of a boat from the Marquesas Islands (British Museum). In front a bird's head ; on its body is seated a big man whose legs are broken off, and before him a little mutilated figure.

similar notion, though I do not believe that they represented it in such a drastic way. For the West Africans

Fig. 241. Dance-rattle of the North-West Americans (Berlin Museum, after E. Seber). The rattle represents a raven with the sun drawn on its breast and a little object in its beak. On its back lies a man, at whose tongue a bird's head with a remarkable topknot is biting. According to Seler's apt remark this topknot is nothing else than the raven's tail projecting upwards and provided with a bird's head. The object in the raven's beak, which corresponds to the objects and snakes in the beaks of the birds on the foregoing pictures, should represent the fire, or rather the sun which according to the myth of these people is stolen by the raven. Compare the myths about the stealing of fire. The man I take to be the soul which the bird is carrying off to the next world, see Fig. 248, which is the same raven's rattle seen from below.

bind the bird to be sacrificed directly to the body of the man, while the South Sea Islanders bury him in a coffin which takes the form of the bird which is to bear the deceased aloft to the after-world (cf. fig. 234).

SACRED ANIMALS

This, I think, is likewise represented on the carving from New Mecklenburg at fig. 238. Here a bird has taken up little manikins in every possible part of its plumage, and stuck them fast to the feathers at the side, behind, and brushed forward away over the head, and I imagine that it is bearing them to the other world, in accordance with the original idea. The same must be the case with the carvings in fig. 236, and following fig. 236 is a carving which is set up at the Dayaks' feast of the dead. On the tail feathers of the bird the man is seated apparently with his totemistic animals. On the raven-rattles of North-West America, of which a few will also be here reproduced (figs. 241 to 249) is probably represented the same conveyance by an animal, the same journey to the next world. But we find here something more. If we look at them from below (figs. 248, 249), we are struck by a large face which the same ravens bear on their breasts. Prof. Seler, of Berlin, has quite correctly recognized the meaning of this face; it is the sun! But what, again, does this mean? The bird bears the soul aloft through the air up to the sun. Now we will pursue the soul on its way to the sun, on its path to the glorious day-star.

CHAPTER XVIII

THE TIWAH AND THE JOURNEY OF THE DEAD SOULS OF THE DAYAKS

IN the foregoing chapters I have mentioned many abodes, many destinies, many qualities of the souls of the dead. The remembrance of the relation to the name, to the kinship with animals, brings the disembodied spirit into an animal body. The soul of the person drowned in the river continues its existence in a water-spirit, and in the soughing of the topmost branches of the tree we hear the voice of the person buried between its roots. The bird of the dead bears the soul high up into the sky. And then again, on the other hand, the souls wander back to the homeland of the early generations of the tribe.

"The poor soul"—thus may our logically disciplined understanding exclaim—"the poor soul; she can herself no longer know what is really to become of her, and whither she has to betake herself after her human destiny is accomplished!"

It is true enough; there prevails an incredible confusion in the heads of the natives regarding the fate of the departed, if not always, at least very often.

Certainly, we have to distinguish between peoples of clear religious thought and those of vague mythological sentiment. There are also most assuredly differences between peoples in another respect, namely, whether they are or are not deeply interested in religious matters.

THE TIWAH

While, for instance, the warlike East Africans betray but very slight interest in such things, the heads of the West

Fig. 242. Dance-rattle of the North-West Americans, after Ed. Seler. Compare fig. 241. This time a frog also is seen in the mouth of the man on the raven's back.

Africans teem with all kinds of rational and irrational imaginings.

Amongst the peoples who are relatively clear-headed

Fig. 243. Dance-rattle of the North-West Americans, after E. Seler. Cf. fig. 241. Instead of the man here we have a skull, a proof that the man originally represents a dead person journeying to the next world. This time the raven's tail is in its right place. The reverse side is shown in fig. 249.

on religious subjects are the Dayaks of the island of Borneo, most ferocious of all head-hunters. With them the bewildering confusion of manistic ideas, intermingled with animistic memories, has developed into a system of notions which are, at least to some extent, clear and intelligible.

THE TIWAH

Hence, a picture from their daily life and view of the world will form an acceptable conclusion to the section

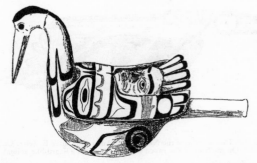

Fig. 244. Dance-rattle of the North-West Americans, after E. Seler. Compare fig. 241. Instead of the raven here we have a swan. Instead of the death's head of the previous figure we have now the face of a live person.

on manism and ancestor-worship. The material is very copious. Not only has Grabowsky given us a meritorious

Fig. 245. Dance-rattle of the North-West Americans, after E. Seler. Cf. fig. 241. On the back we have now a man who is biting at the tail of a snake, which in its turn is biting at the raven's head; the same motive is in fig. 239.

summary of the literature of the subject, but I have also obtained, through the help of a friend, a glance at a manuscript written on the spot, and this enables me to dash off a fairly finished sketch.

THE TIWAH

As amongst several other peoples, the perplexing number of theories regarding the future of the soul has led

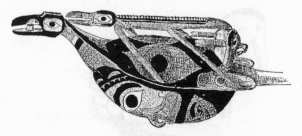

Fig. 246. Dance-rattle of the North-West Americans, after E. Seler. Cf. fig. 241. On the back of the raven we have this time a lizard-like animal.

the Dayaks to assume a considerable diversity of destinies for the spirits of the departed. As a distinct entity the soul of the living man is called *hambaruan*, and is able,

Fig. 247. Dance-rattle of the North-West Americans, after E. Seler. Cf. fig. 241. One must be struck by the great resemblance to fig. 245. Only instead of the snake we have now a quadruped which is not bitten by a man, nor on its part does it bite at the raven's head, but seizes the man with its mouth.

without his knowledge, to leave him and roam freely about independently of the body. But it may also be captured and carried off. Evil spirits may, perhaps, have induced it to leave the body, and then captured it. In

THE TIWAH

that case the man falls ill, and if the soul does not return he dies.

After death the soul divides into two parts—the soul's soul, and the soul's body. But the latter is again a compound being, consisting (1) of the soul's bony remains, (2) of the soul's hair-tips, and (3) of the soul's

Figs 248 and 249. The front side of the raven's rattle. Cf. figs. 241 and 243 after E. Seler. In each case the face represents the sun.

finger-nails. The soul's soul has a specially interesting fate. As soon as the soul's soul and the soul's body have separated after the man's death, the former tries to reach the *Levu-liau*. But as it cannot do so until the *tiwah*, or feast of the dead, is celebrated, it diverts itself meanwhile after its fashion. Its first business is to appear in dreams to the widow, or to the widower, or to the brother or the parents. It does this, however, not after the sensible manner of a kindly-disposed apparition of the deceased. Anything but that!

To the survivors the deceased appears as a cripple, a criminal, a craven; or it kills its relations, or it greatly enriches them, all in a dream, so that, on waking, the survivors wonder at the remarkable and quite new exhibition of the qualities of the deceased. Or, perhaps, sickness breaks out in the village, or a weird rattling is heard at night in the captured head of the departed, or stormy weather bursts over the land.

All these are achievements of the soul's soul.

When, however, the tiwah is celebrated, and especially

Fig. 250. Tempon-telon's Banama-tingang. Ship of the dead in the form of a bird, Grabowsky collection in the Berlin Museum. Compare also figs 235. and 236, and what is there stated.

when the banama-tingang is set up with appropriate rites, then the soul's soul, now freed and released, soars aloft to the Levu-liau independently of the soul of the body. That is a marvellous journey, a fearful and terrible quest of the after-world.

Already, before the tiwah is solemnized, the survivors have painted and set up a panel, which is from two to three yards long by half to one yard broad. On this board is figured Tempon-telon's ship, and that several times in various forms, each under a different name. Such a picture of a ship I reproduce from Grabowsky, who managed to secure a panel for the Berlin Museum.

THE TIWAH

The representations on the ships are usually the same. At the helm Tempon-telon himself is always figured, while in front is seen a perfectly fire-proof person who divides the air with a sharp cutting weapon, and from whom so much cold radiates that the souls on board the ship may be refreshed by it, when Tempon-telon kindles into too fervent heat. The ship itself is a bird, the *buceros*, or rhinoceros-hornbill, with a beak which, according to the Dayaks, excels that of all other birds in being able by its weight and its strength to disperse the dense clouds enveloping the sun.

In the ship, in this wonderful structure, the souls go in quest of the hereafter; and not only the souls themselves, but with them all the stores which are laid out at the tiwah, all the food and drink that are consumed at the tiwah, all the slaves and other poor wretches who on the occasion of this tiwah are openly or stealthily murdered and deprived of their heads.

A panel of this sort is accordingly set up at the tiwah, fowls are offered to it, and during the night their blood is sprinkled over the coffin containing the deceased. Then begins the tiwah, and aloft goes the banama-tingang, the ship of the dead.

Every twenty-four hours Tempon-telon hurries to the city of the souls. In the early morning he breaks away furiously, and sails so fast that, as Grabowsky says, those on board always come too late when they want to look and point at anything, because it is already far behind.

The road becomes constantly worse and more dangerous until they reach the fire-sea (in Grabowsky, fiery whirlpool). The journey becomes slower and slower. Slowly Tempon-telon and his crew impel the vessel forward until at last it reaches calmer regions, and now

THE TIWAH

again speeds more swiftly through the abode of all those who have on earth offended against the sacred ordinances, and have thus no right to dwell in the fields of the blessed. Then all at once the energy of the tingang relaxes, and a horrible stench pollutes the air. Still Tempon-telon holds himself erect; glowing flashes dart from his eyes and—the ship is saved; it floats over to the golden fields of the after life.* In this other world the soul lives a glorious life. Every pleasure is at its command; it enjoys all privileges; but, unfortunately, the Dayak knows nothing of eternity. Although the soul may reside in Elysium seven times longer than on this side, it must still at last once again return from the soul-land to the earth. It dies in the after life, and reappears on earth, passing into a fungus, a fruit, a leaf, grass, and the like. Should a man consume this grass, this leaf, and so on, then the efficacy of his father's or his mother's blessing is diffused in him, so that after a while he is presented with a little child. Then this child has the soul which was reborn in the grass or in the flower after the death in the after life.

But the soul does not always fare so well, for at times an animal browses on the herb with its indwelling soul, and then, of course, the little spirit passes into the animal. Now, if it happens luckily that a man consumes this animal, all is well, since then the little spirit again passes into a human body, and after a while reappears as its child. But should the animal die without having been eaten by a man, or should the herb wither away without being consumed by man or beast, then the poor soul must perish, die out for ever, being unable to be reborn.

* This section of the myth of the voyage of the souls, which deviates not a little from the earlier account, I have written down *verbatim* from my report.

THE TIWAH

In this view of the soul's journey we again meet all possible traces of the animalistic and manistic cosmic theories. Here we have the soul in the animal, the soul-bearing bird, the totemistic animals figured on the banama-tingang, the soul returning to its forbears, in fact everything neatly arranged. There is even something superadded—the fire-sea through which Tempon-telon makes his way with his spectral ship. I will ask the reader kindly to bear fixedly in his mind this ship of the souls, this fiery sea and this Tempon-telon. In the next chapters we shall often have to return to them, for these are indications of the third phase of cosmic thought of the solar mythology.

I have now referred in divers ways to the tiwah, the feast of the dead, by which the soul's soul acquires the freedom to escape with Tempon-telon's spectre ship to the life beyond.

The tiwah is not, indeed, celebrated immediately after a person's death. Not at all! It is often put off for a long, a very long time. For the means have to be collected to provide hundreds of people with food and drink, human heads have to be procured, and, lastly, the deceased requires an artistically-carved coffin.

Hence the dead man has first, amid the booming of the kettledrums to scare away the evil spirits, to be provisionally laid in a coffin and put aside on a hill situated far up on the river. Here he rests in solitude until the preparations for the feast of the dead are ready. And about this resting-place the soul hovers all the time, restlessly and anxiously on the wing. Meantime the relatives remain at home, troubled and hopelessly grieving, and ever on the watch lest the soul's soul should do them a mischief, "for the soul's soul shivers until it

THE TIWAH

can gaze in the glowing eyes of Tempon-telon. So they fear lest the soul's soul rob them of their fire. That would be very bad."

If the survivors are rich, the feast of the dead may soon be celebrated; if poor the family has long to pinch and save until the provisions for the feast are scraped together, and this often takes two or three years.

If the members of the family are brave, the required heads are soon procured. Should the men-folk fail, it may happen that the widow herself sets off to hunt up a head for her deceased husband. But should the family obtain no fresh heads, then old skulls have to be bought and hung up in the festive hall.

This festive hall, the balai, has also to be erected, and the musical instruments suspended in it: large copper kettledrums and high drums covered with goat or iguana skin. Every detail gives occasion for a little feast, for all kinds of ceremonies, and the recital of solemn incantations. The aged men who bring the instruments to the house flourish them thrice upstream, thrice downstream, saying the while:

"Quickly vanishes the history of the good name of the man who gives this feast [the deceased]. I have pointed out its way to the sun; it has vanished; so also may misfortune come to an end."

From that moment the drumming and uproar are kept up, day and night, to ward off the evil spirits, and to inform the soul's soul that its release is at hand.

Three days before the beginning of the tiwah proper, the coffin is brought in a boat from its temporary resting-place to the balai. The stake for the victims and all other ceremonial objects are set up, and at last the feast may begin.

THE TIWAH

First Day. Dispatch of the Soul's Soul

THE female relations of the deceased join with the other women invited to the feast in preparing the viands for the next day, while themselves consuming considerable portions of buffalo flesh and drinking copiously. All kinds of food are likewise offered to the friendly and invited souls.

At sunset the festal company all assemble in the balai, where the conductor of souls and the priestesses assume their functions. Now is got ready the spirit-gift, as entertainment for the spirit people assembled in the banamatingang. Grains of rice thrown seven times into the air become the souls of seven maidens, and rice thrown the eighth time becomes their apparel and adornments. These maidens go out in order to fetch helpful spirits and to purify the surroundings of the balai from foreign and malevolent packs of spirits. Then, also, the panel with the spirit-ships is animated by offerings of poultry.

Now the conductor of souls comes forward, holding in his hands the weapons which Tempon-telon wields in the pictures of the ships of the dead. He closes his eyes, and in a long drawn out and monotonous voice begins the first strophe of his magic song. He converses with the deceased and summons the departed relatives of the dead man. He mentions all the offerings that the survivors have made to give him a rich equipment of souls. For everything here exhibited, everything here offered, everything consumed during these days, has a soul, and the souls of the sacrificed men, the souls of the rice, the souls of the fowls and the clothes, the souls of all the treasures laid out, accompany the deceased on

THE TIWAH

the banama-tingang, "in order at sunrise to undertake jointly with Tempon-telon the voyage through the fire-sea into the golden splendour of the underground night."

The conductor of souls sings, and the *Blian*, the priestesses, reply. Once more shall the soul look round about it in its former home; once more shall it partake of the food, and then embark on Tempon-telon's ship.

Ullmann has vividly described this scene.

Still half-intoxicated, the conductor of souls begins his magic songs by which he believes that he has Tempon-telon entirely in his power. Thereby he becomes fearfully excited. He sees how Tempon-telon with the vessel, on board of which are the souls of the departed, gets nearer and nearer to the fire-sea. Now he strains every nerve; the muscles throb; he exhausts himself with violent movements; his features are convulsively distorted; he foams at his mouth; heavy drops of perspiration roll down his face, breast and arms; he shouts, yells and raves against himself, threatens and then again implores and promises Tempon-telon new offerings, . . . then suddenly exclaims, rejoicing:

"They are saved!—they are saved! They have passed the fire-sea! The souls are drawing near the city of souls!"

At this moment the sun rises through the morning mists, gunshots rattle, the whole people, whose excitement and rapture had towards the morning risen higher and higher with drink and song, now bursts into a tremendous uproar, a wild frenzy. The notion is that at this moment Tempon-telon's ship, with the soul's soul and the whole company, is mounting into heaven.*

* The conclusion I have modified from original communications.

THE TIWAH

Second Day. The Human Sacrifices

EITHER a stake is set up, at which the poor slaves purchased for this purpose suffer a miserable death, or else the wretched creatures are suddenly and stealthily dispatched so that they have no time even to utter a curse.

However agreeable it may be for the soul's soul to receive such a retinue, it is correspondingly unfortunate for it if before his death the victim can utter a curse against his murderers or the dead man.

For this reason it is very customary to send the slave destined for the sacrifice somewhere into the bush with strict orders to fetch perhaps some water, or certain flowers for the decoration, or a few lengths of rattan. Then the murderer, lying in ambush, strikes with the only too ready knife, and his head is rolling on the ground before he can utter a cry or a curse.

If, however, the victim is to die at the stake, by a peculiar ceremony "the soul is quickly brought out of his body." Some sand or rice is sprinkled on his head while an incantation is being sung, whereupon the body is regarded as deprived of its soul. But how if the poor fellow should swear or roar at the stake? Then the curse can no longer reach the next world. The howling can no longer injure the soul's soul of the deceased, since by the magic formula the soul was already extracted from the body, and in fact has already fulfilled its mission, that is to say, has started on its journey and carried up the soul's body of the deceased to Tempon-telon and to the ship of the dead behind the soul's soul, so that in the evening of the same day the soul's soul and the soul's body can again be united.

Frightful is the picture of this sacrifice.

THE TIWAH

The man is bound to the sacrificial stake, while the excited, bloodthirsty crew dance round him, each wounding him wherever he happens to hit. As they keep whirling about they grow more like furies, and foaming with rage they complete the barbarous rite. Their long hair flies dishevelled about their wild faces. With staring, bloodshot eyes they inflict stab after stab on the victim, and to his agonized groans or hopeless moaning the fiendish crew reply with wild shouts of jubilation; for they believe that the soul on high is all the happier the more each single victim suffers and the more victims there are to endure the cruel death.

At last the victim breaks down, to the last roaring and howling with pain.

At that moment the conductor springs upon the victim; the mandau flies through the air, falls like a flash on his neck, and his head rolls down on the ground.

With loud, yelling shouts of joy the priestesses daub the relatives of the deceased with the blood of the horribly mutilated victim.

This second day of the revels winds up with eating and drinking, copious drinking, until all, men and women, married and unmarried, old and young, lie promiscuously on the ground. . . . Let the curtain fall on the repulsive scene.

Now follows the real burial, either in a family grave, that is in a fenced structure enclosing many coffins, or else the body is burnt and the remains deposited in a little crematorium. There still follow several other rites, such as the general purification; for all who have taken part in these festivals are held to be more than usually under the power of the souls of the deceased, as long as they have about them any traces of the offerings and of the

THE TIWAH

sacrificial feasts. But before this general purification one more regular feast is given, and this is highly characteristic of the notions which to some extent lie at the base of the whole proceedings. On this day the widowers or widows, as the case may be, lay aside their mourning and preside themselves at the entertainment. Should the guests be unable to consume all the fare laid before them by the host, he rises at the end of the table and says: "If you have been unable to consume my buffaloes, swine, poultry and rice, then I have won and you have lost; you are weak, I am strong." Thereupon he drinks to his own health.

But should the company eat up everything, then one of the guests stands at the end of the table and says: "We have eaten everything; had more been there we should have eaten that also. You are weak, we are strong; you have lost, we have won." And he concludes with a toast to the achievements of the guests in eating and drinking.

Here is, at least, a little pleasantry in the course of a sanguinary and atrocious orgy. We feel relieved and breathe again, and look round for the meaning of what is decidedly the most interesting of the proceedings—the voyage in Tempon-telon's banama-tingang.

CHAPTER XIX
THE DOWNFALL OF THE GOD

TEMPON-TELON, the banama-tingang and the fire-sea have now to be more closely studied. For this I enlist quite a little army, a troop of gods, with whom to investigate the course of the banama-tingang. I call upon the noble host of solar gods for help. I will ask these gods themselves about their destinies, and from their own experiences obtain the materials for my comparative studies. I summon the solar gods from all parts of the world, and bring together all forms of the solar view of the world. Come hither, Maui, radiating a glowing warmth, deeply honoured lord of the Polynesian gods! Hither, Litaolane, from Africa, to tell us of thy fortunes; and come, knavish Yelkh, leaving the North-West American domain, for a while forego thy fooleries and try to make thyself clear and intelligible. As for Melanesian Quat and the genial Kamakayakau, you have surely no occasion to be ashamed of your legendary graces in the exalted company of the higher deities. Even though you may not be worshipped, you still remain the type of a sublime divinity.

'Twill be a noble train with which we advance to the encounter with Tempon-telon, verily the greatest and the mightiest mental visions that the fancy, the faith and the religion of natural man have ever evolved. In the forefront I place the Polynesian Maui.

THE DOWNFALL OF THE GOD

I. *Maui* (*New Zealand*)

MAUI had several brothers, but Maui-tiki is the one who performed the greatest exploits. When he was born, his mother, wrapping him in a lock of her hair, cast him into the sea; seaweed coiled round the little one, and he was swallowed by a fish.

The waves threw the fish on the shore, where flies and birds sucked and pecked at it till Tama-nui-ki-te-rangi cut him out of the fish, brought him home, hung him in the roof, and with the warmth of the fire brought him to life. In this way he came to the council chamber of the gods.

Maui sat in the garden of Hine-nui-te-Po on a hill and played the flute. The old woman said to her slave: "When you see a man walking about on his feet, capture him, he is a thief; if he comes on all fours, face and belly upwards, let him go in peace, that is an Atua (god)." Maui overhears it all, crawls in the way described into the Kumara-house of the old woman, eats his fill and goes off, too, with a basket of Kumara. The slaves let him go unhindered, for he goes on all fours. Next day the brothers want to know where he gets his booty. He tells them everything, but reverses the indications of the thief and of the Atua, and so advises them to go erect. Maui-mua, who now likewise goes to play the flute and to steal, is seized as a thief, since he walked erect, and squeezed so hard by the old woman between her thighs that he dies. That was the first death in the world.

Maui was vexed because the sun moved so fast, and thus the day was so short. So he found out the art of twisting flax into ropes. These he took with him and went away with his brothers. He wandered always by night, and cautiously hid himself during the day from

THE DOWNFALL OF THE GOD

the sun. This lasted so long that at last they came to the place where the sun rises in the East. Here they laid the snares in which the sun was taken. Maui-tiki struck it with the jaw-bone that he had received from his grandmother, wounded it and then let it go; so it was only able to creep slowly away.

Now he played many tricks, the most important of which was the theft of fire, which I will later inquire into. But after changing his brother-in-law, Irawaru, into a dog, he found he could not remain any longer in his village. Moreover, the father said that he would soon be destroyed through the grandmother, Hine-nui-te-Po, who flares up and gapes where heaven and earth meet. Hence Maui resolved to coerce her as he had coerced Tama-nui-te-Ra (the Sun). So he takes birds as his associates, but warns them against laughing when he creeps into the mouth of this monster, but they were to laugh when he came out. In the first case he would perish, but in the second Hine-nui-te-Po would die.

He puts his clothes off; the skin of his hips is beautiful, parti-coloured from the tattoo-marks which were cut by Uetonga's chisel. When he enters the throat of the old woman, the little bird, tiwakawaka, laughs out loud. Thereupon Hine-nui-te-Po wakes up and kills Maui. Had Maui's adventure succeeded, mankind would not now have to die.

II. *Kamakayakau* (*Ysabell Island, Melanesia*)

HE lived on the hills of Gayi. He mended his nets and looked down on the ocean. He saw it was very dark. His grandchildren went down to the sea to fish among the reefs, and Kamakayakau said to them:

"Go and fetch me some salt water up to this place,

that I may see whether its colour is the same as that of the ocean."

So spoke he to them. His grandchildren went off down to the shore and fished on the shore; they fished with nets. Afterwards they filled a pail with salt water and came up again and gave it to him. And he spoke to them:

"Give the pail of water here, and I will pour it down and see whether its blackness is the same as that of the sea water which I saw from above."

Thus spoke he. And he poured it down and saw that it was not of the same blackness as that which he had seen from above.

When it was morning, he took the pail of salt water and went away. He stuck in his ear a bit of obsidian and rambled on with it and came to the sea, and laid his pouch, his shield and club on the shore. He took the vessel in his hand and waded out into the water. He looked up at the hill where he dwelt and whence he came, and he could still perceive it. So then he swam still further out from the shore as long as he could see the hill Gayi. Then he dived down.

The surface of the sea heaved and bubbles rose up, and he heard how a kombini (*Polynemus paradiseus*) of huge size was coming towards him. The fish came and swallowed Kamakayakau and turned with him eastward to the sunrise, and moved on with him till he came to a shallow place where he touched ground, so that Kamakayakau noticed that evidently the shore was here.

"Here I am," said he to himself, and thought of the obsidian in his ear and felt for it. He found it and cut open the belly of the kombini and slipped out.

Then he saw a shining light. He sat down and reflected: "I wonder where I am," he thought. Then the Sun rose up all of a sudden, and threw itself from one side to the other. And the Sun said:

"Do not get in my way, else you must suddenly die. Get on my right side."

And he went on one side till the Sun had risen on high. Then he followed, and both climbed up skywards and thus came at last to the village of the Children of the Sun. The Sun spoke:

"Bide here."

So Kamakayakau stood by the Sun's children and grandchildren, but the Sun went on.

Kamakayakau stood still, and they asked him:

"Whence hast thou come hither?"

He spoke:

"From the earth. I dwelt in my place, and I dived into the salt water and a great fish swallowed me. And so I have come here to your good town."

So he and they lived together. They only ate raw food. Then he showed fire to the people up there, so that they were able to eat cooked food.

They warned him from entering a certain place, which was tabu. They went their way. While he is alone in the house he goes to the forbidden place. He lifts up a stone, and looks through the hole thus made in the sky down on the earth, and sees the hill of Gayi. Then he weeps; and even when they bring him food, that cannot console him. And they ask him, does he want to go to the earth? and he said he did.

Thereupon they put Kamakayakau in a house and gave him food and seeds of the pau. They fasten a reed to the top of the house and let him down. And they say to him that he is not to look out when birds and such beings who animate the air cry out. But when creatures

THE DOWNFALL OF THE GOD

of the earth are to be heard, then he should look out. They let him down by the reed, but when one is too short, then they tie another to it, and so on till Kamakaya-kau reaches his home on the hill.

III. *Mutuk (Badu Island, Torres Straits)*

ON Badu, an island in Torres Straits, a man named Mutuk lived a long time ago. He was once fishing on a reef, when the string of his hook got entangled. Thereupon he dived into the water to get it free. But a shark swimming by snapped him up and swallowed him without hurting him.

The shark swam northwards over the reef at Mangrove Island. Mutuk felt the warmth, and said to himself:

"Now we are in the warm water."

When the shark dived into deeper water, Mutuk felt the cold, and knew now that they had again plunged down. At last the shark swam to Boigu and got stranded with the ebb tide. Mutuk felt the glaring sun shining through the body of the fish, and knew that it lay high and dry. So he took a sharp mussel-shell, which he wore behind his ear, and hacked at the shark's body until he made a sufficient opening. Escaping from his strange prison, he noticed *that his hair had fallen off*.

IV. *North American Myths*
First Version (compare Fig. 251)

ONCE Yetl, the raven, let himself be swallowed by a whale. Inside the stomach he made himself comfortable, and kindled a little fire. The whale bade him take care not to injure his heart. But the raven could not resist the temptation and pecked at it.

THE DOWNFALL OF THE GOD

"Oh!" cried the whale, for it hurt him. He again requested the raven not to touch his heart. Yetl excused himself, pretending that he had knocked against it accidentally. But presently he again pecked at it, and this time bit quite hard.

Then the whale moved off. But now Yetl did not know how he was to get out again, for the creature's mouth shut tight. He thought:

"Oh, if the whale would only get stranded on a flat beach!"

Soon he heard the surf roaring and felt the whale's body beating against the stones on the beach. Then he was glad. Close by was a village, and children were playing with bows and arrows on the shore. When they saw the whale they at once ran home and called their parents, who thereupon went to strip off the blubber. While engaged at this work they heard some one inside the whale singing and shouting, but could not imagine who it could be. Then thought Yetl:

"Oh, if some one up there would only cut right down to me!"

Scarcely had he thought so when his wish was fulfilled. A man cut a hole in the stomach, and forthwith Yetl flew off, crying:

"Kola, Kola, Kola."

Second Version

ONCE Kaig, the Mink, went out to catch herrings with a huge herring-rake. But at the same time the whale was also herring-fishing, and chasing the fish from Kaig's boat. At this he was angry, and when the whale once rose to the surface to blow, Kaig called out:

"Fie! how you stink, whale!"

He repeated this four times, then the whale was en-

THE DOWNFALL OF THE GOD

raged and swallowed Kaig, boat and all! Every time the whale now rose to the surface, Kaig cried out from within:

"Know, you people, that the whale has devoured me!"

The fishers heard him, and told each other that Kaig was swallowed by the whale. The whale went on catching herrings, then Mink made a little fire in its stomach, and dried the herrings on a stand. Now, every time the whale rose, the fish fell down from the stand. At this he was very angry. *Moreover it was very hot in his stomach.* Kaig felt ill, and considered how he might get free again. He decided to kill the whale, and he cut through his throat. Then the whale died, and soon drifted near to a village on the shore. As soon as the inhabitants saw him, they cut him up, and lo! on their opening the stomach, out sprang Mink.

But, from the heat, he had lost all his hair in the whale's stomach.

Third Version

AFTER roaming about for some time, Kanigyilak came to a village, and was astonished to notice that no smoke rose from any one of the houses. He went into all of them, but saw nobody. At last, in the very last house, he found a man named Nauesta, and his grandchild, a little maiden, the only inhabitants of the village.

He asked:

"Where, then, are all your fellow-countrymen?"

"The monster, Tsekis, who lives in yonder sea, has killed them all. Whenever anyone went down to fetch water, he came and devoured him. We are the sole survivors."

He remained in the house with Nauesta and his grandchild. One day he spoke to the child:

"Go down to the sea and fetch me water."

THE DOWNFALL OF THE GOD

But the old man strongly objected, and would not suffer it. He exclaimed:

"No! she shall not and must not go! Tsekis shall not deprive me of the very last of my children, and he will certainly eat her if she goes."

But Kanigyilak tried to quiet him. He gave the child the bucket, tied round her the belt of the Sisiutl's skin, and bade her go. He followed her, saw how Tsekis rose to the surface and swallowed the poor child. Then Kanigyilak took a stick, and sang while beating time on a stone:

"Sisiutl! come to life and kill him; wake up and kill him!"

Scarcely had he ended his song when the monster came out of the deep and writhed in the agonies of death, vomiting forth the bones of all the people he had devoured. Then Kanigyilak shot him with his arrows. He put the bones together again, and sprinkled them with the water of life. Then they stood up and rubbed their eyes as if they had been asleep.

In connexion with the myths of North-West America, which I have just related, four illustrations have reference to kindred subjects. They are drawings by the natives. The Haidas, a North-West American tribe, are not whale-fishers, like the other peoples of this region, and they have never been known to kill a whale themselves, although occasionally a dead one drifts on to their coast. For this, however, they assign no natural cause, but connect the carcass with the whale myth, and say that Hooyeh (so the Jelkh, or Yetl, that is the raven, is called by the Haidas) has in an invisible way killed this whale and abandoned it to undertake some new adventure.

The manner of their fishing:

NORTH AMERICAN INDIANS FISHING

A shallow lagoon with a weir across it. The canoe is laden with fish, one man in it holding a landing-net, and other two crouching over a fire. Two men knee-deep spearing fish in the distance, and in the foreground a beach with flowers and shells.

From the original water-colour drawing in the British Museum by John White, Governor of Virginia in 1587.

THE DOWNFALL OF THE GOD

On the other hand, in explanation of fig. 252, they tell this story:

Years ago, the Haida Indians once went out seal-hunting. The weather was calm and the sea like a mirror. A grampus (a very large animal) always kept swimming on one side of a particular canoe. The young men amused

Fig. 251. The Raven in the Whale's stomach. Drawing by a Haida, in Niblack's work. Representation of the myth related on p. 277, as the first version of the North-West American legends of the downfall.

themselves by throwing stones from the boat's ballast at him, and hitting his fins with them. After a few rather hard hits, the creature turned round to the coast, where it ran aground on the beach. Presently, smoke was seen, and curiosity induced the Indians to try and find out the meaning of it.

But on reaching the shore they discovered, to their great astonishment, that, not the fish, but a large canoe lay there, and moreover that a man was cooking himself some food. He asked them why they had thrown stones at his canoe.

"You have broken it," he said; "now go to the woods and fetch some cedar planks to repair it."

THE DOWNFALL OF THE GOD

They did so, and when they were ready, the man said:
"Turn your backs to the water, and cover your heads
with your fur hoods; do not turn round until I call you."

They did so, and heard how the canoe was grinding

Fig. 252. Representation of the Skana myth, Drawing by a Haida in Niblack's book.

along the shore, as if it were being dragged down to the
surf. Then said the man:

"Now, turn round!"

They turned round and just saw the canoe as it topped
the first wave, and the man seated at the stern. But when
it came to the second wave, the boat foundered, and,
behold! on the off-side of the wave no canoe reappeared,
but a grampus. But the man was evidently a demon, a
skana, and had gone back into the creature's belly.

Owing to its interest I give a third picture (fig. 253)
representing the raven and the fisherman, of which it is
related that:

THE DOWNFALL OF THE GOD

Hooyeh, the raven, had the bad habit of descending into the ocean to look for the little fish of Houskana, the fisher, and steal both the fish and the bait (notice the similarity of the name of the wicked demon in the fish's stomach—skana, and of the name of this fisher—Houskana!) At last Houskana grew tired of this game, and in order to make sure as

Fig. 253. Myth of the Raven and Fisher, Haida Drawing in Niblack.

to who really was his enemy on the bed of the sea, instead of the usual hook he rigged up a magic one.

And thus the raven was taken. Now, when the fisher was taking home his tackle, the raven resisted by planting his feet and wings against the bottom of the canoe. But Houskana was stronger, and tore off the raven's beak, seized him, and brought him to the coast in order to find out who he really was. For no sooner was the beak torn off than the raven changed himself into a man who had his head covered with a fur cloak, so that only his eyes could be seen.

In vain the fisher tried to make the man show his face. But at last one of the young people took a handful of dirt and rubbed it in the raven's eyes. That did the business.

THE DOWNFALL OF THE GOD

He threw aside his cloak, and then every one saw that it was Hooyeh.

V. *Litaolane (Basuto Tribe, South-East Africa)*

WE are told that in the early times all mankind once perished. A monstrous animal, called Kammapa, devoured

Fig. 254. Picture of the cunning Raven, Haida Drawing in Niblack.

them all, big and little. He was a frightful beast. So enormous was the length of his body, that the keenest eye could scarcely see from one end to the other.

Only one woman still remained in the world; she had escaped Kammapa's savagery by carefully hiding from him. This woman conceived a son and brought him forth in an old stable. She was immensely surprised when, on a closer inspection of the child, she found that his neck was adorned with a magic ornamental necklace.

"As that is so," she said, "his name shall be Litaolane, the magician. Poor child! At what a time it is born! How will it be possible to escape from Kammapa? What use can his ornament be to him?"

THE DOWNFALL OF THE GOD

As she spoke, she spread out a little straw to prepare a crib for her child. When she returned to the stable she was struck dumb with surprise and terror at the child, who had already grown to the size of an adult man and spoke words full of wisdom. Litaolane went outside and was amazed at the solitude that prevailed around him.

"Mother," he asked, "where are the people? Is there no one except you and myself in the world?"

"My child," said the woman trembling, "only a short time ago the valleys and hills were covered with people; but a monster, whose voice makes the rocks tremble, has devoured them all."

"Where does this beast live?"

"There he is, not far from us."

Litaolane took a knife, and, deaf to the urgent entreaties of his mother, went to attack the devourer of the world. Kammapa opened his frightful throat and swallowed him. But the child of the woman was not dead. Armed with his knife, he entered the monster's stomach and cut up his entrails. Kammapa roared terribly, and fell to pieces.

Thereupon Litaolane began to carve himself a way out, but the point of his knife made thousands cry out who were buried alive with him. Countless voices were heard on all sides crying out to him:

"Take care; you are boring through us."

He succeeded in making an opening, through which the people of the world came with him out of Kammapa's belly.

In all these myths an important motive constantly returns, one which is very well known to us from the Biblical history. It is the story of Jonah, who was swal-

285

lowed by the fish and in the end cast up again. Naturally, the assumption at once suggests itself that the history of Jonah may have been spread over the world by the missionaries. This point might have to be more closely considered if the saga existed alone and independently in many places.

But such is not the case. We rather find the myth confined to a very well defined part of the earth, and deeply rooted in the imagination of primitive peoples. Moreover, it is not a question of detached and scattered fragments, as it were, of the Jewish stories of the Old Testament, but rather of a part of a whole, a section of an organic body of sagas standing in close connexion with large groups, large ideas, firmly established notions. And the sagas here under consideration are all solar myths, stories of the experiences and actions of the solar god.

In all the legends something definite is described—the history of the setting sun, that is, as it disappears and rises again. It is very characteristic that the insular and coast peoples let the sun be devoured by a fish, since for them the sun sinks under the sea, while, on the contrary, the Basutos, living on the mainland, instead of the fish make the monster Kammapa responsible for the disaster.

If we enter more into the details of the myth, there is, above all, much to be said of Maui. Here we have at the very beginning the history of the fish devouring Maui, how it is then hung before the fire, and how Maui is warmed by the heat of the fire. That is the warmth of the rising sun. Then, in the third version, we have again the same story of the setting and rising sun. One Maui, who, walking erect, gets crushed between the thighs of Hine-nui-te-Po, is the setting sun; the other, who, creep-

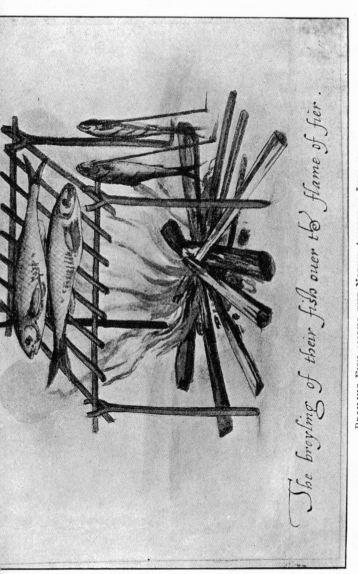

The broyling of their fish over the flame of fier.

BROILING FISH AMONG THE NORTH AMERICAN INDIANS

From the original water-colour drawing in the British Museum by John White, Governor of Virginia in 1587.

ing face upward, enters into the garden of the moon-goddess (Hina, moon) ruling the night (Po, or belto, night), is the rising sun.

Then Maui, wandering towards the rising of the sun, capturing it with cords and impeding its course, means the slow movement of the midday sun, whose leisurely course contrasts with the rapid movement at dawn.

The brief mention of the theft of fire I shall deal with in a separate chapter. Magnificent is the conclusion, the grand picture of the sunset where the gorgeously tattooed body of the god typifies the splendour of the setting sun; and then follows its disappearance in the throat of the night star.

The Kamakayakau myth presents in its way some charming details for observation. It is quite clear that during the night the fish swims eastwards, that in the morning, just as the belly of Kombini is cut open, the sun rises in the East, that it is expressly stated how the hero wanders along behind the sun. And where Kamakayakau is swallowed by Kombini, that is the night which swallows the sun.

Mutuk feels the glittering sun shine on the body of the shark. And farther on we discover in North-West America the cause of the hair falling off, that is, the heat of the sun.

In North-West America the raven is the sun-god, though he may also be represented by the mink. Valuable for the history of the evolution of the whole of this cycle of legends is an idea in the Kanagyilak myth, which it has in common with the Litaolane saga, namely, that all mankind has been devoured by the monster. This is unquestionably a manistic trait in the solar mythology, an element which again leads us directly back to the

THE DOWNFALL OF THE GOD

Tempon-telon legend. It may be again remarked that the radiant jewel of Litaolane should denote the rising sun.

This last manistic root-idea, now brought to light, recalls, as stated, the voyage of the banama-tingang. When we inquire into the essential features of this journey of the dead, we must be struck by the fact that Tempon-telon sets out in the morning with furious haste; crossing the fire-sea he slows down; then, suddenly, the glowing flashes radiate from his eyes; the last frightful obstacle has been overcome, and in majestic calm the ship glides over the golden fields of bliss.

But who knows what this means?

Quite evidently it is a solar journey. Was it not clearly stated beforehand that once every day Tempon-telon sails away to the waters of the world beyond? The furious ascent is the sunrise, the slow course on the fire-sea means the midday heat, and the flashing rays in Tempon-telon's eyes the sudden happy entrance on the golden stream of the land of the dead; all this denotes the beauty of the setting sun. Hence it is the opposite, or rather the supplementary, picture to everything related in the Jonah stories. Those stories describe the sunset, the course of the sun during the night till the dawn; the Tempon-telon voyage begins with the dawn, moves along its course by day, and ends with the evening glow.

Nor is this all. From the closeness with which they supplement each other, from their correspondence, from the intimate coherence which cannot be denied between Tempon-telon's manistic myth and Maui's solar myth, one fact speaks out: that the ancestral sagas, the manistic myths, by virtue of their origin, must be connected with the solar myths, and that a relation must thus exist

THE DOWNFALL OF THE GOD

between the solar sagas and this account of the voyage of the departed souls.

This is, indeed, further shown by the other fact that when the bodies of the monsters Tsekis and Kammapa are cut open, all mankind come out. Hence, in the soul-myth, the host of the dead goes down with the sun, while in the solar myth mankind rises with the sun.

And now comes the beautiful keystone which unites the foregoing material in a single whole. The Maui myth ends with the words:

"Had Maui's adventure succeeded, mankind need not have died to-day."

Before dealing further with the pleasant result here elicited, I shall introduce a few more solar myths.

CHAPTER XX
SHANGO, THE TYPICAL SUN-GOD

IN this chapter a study shall be made of a characteristic aspect of the Sun-God, as it has been displayed in Yorubaland, west of the Niger delta.

1

Shango is the second son of Yemaja (the Sea); his servant is Oshumare, the Rainbow, who has to draw water, from the earth up to his palace in the clouds. Ara, the Thunder-clap, is his messenger, whom he sends out with a loud noise. The little bird Papagori is sacred to Shango, and his worshippers profess to be able to understand its cry. He married three of his sisters, Oya (the Niger), Oshun and Oba (two rivers of the same name). All three constantly accompany their husband, Oya taking with her her messenger Afefe (the cool Wind), Oshun and Oba his bow and sword. Shango's slave, Biri (Darkness) goes in attendance. Shango's colours are red and white, and he is usually regarded as the god of thunder and lightning.

2

This demigod was born at Ife and ruled in the recently destroyed city of Ikoso. But others say that he was a god who came from Nupe. He had his palace of brass and kept a stable of 10,000 horses, which shows that he was at first only a mortal. Thence he went to live in heaven, where he rules in state, hunts, fishes, holds markets and wages war.

The abstract Shango is the grandson of Aganju (the Wilderness or the Firmament), a descendant of Okikishe.

SHANGO, THE TYPICAL SUN-GOD

His father is Orungan (Midday), his mother Yemaja or Iyemaja (Mother of Fishes), an unimportant river in Yoruba. His elder brother is Dada or Nature (from *da*, to create); his younger is the river Ogim; his friend and boon companion is Orishako (god of the farms); his slave is Biri (Darkness); his wives are the streams Oya (the Niger) Oshun and Obba; his priest is Magba (the Receiver). Shango's votaries wear his satchel because he is a friend of predatory war. Really he is the god of thunder, lightning and fire. He is also called Jacuta, or "Stone-hurler," and protects the good. But he is, above all, the protector of warriors, hunters and fishers.

3

Shango was at first a King who later became a god.

He was ruler of Oyo, capital of Yoruba. He was so cruel that chiefs and people sent him a calabash full of parrots' eggs, with the message that he was tired out with governing, and should go to sleep. The King called his followers together, but they failed him, and he had to save himself by flight. He left the city by night, accompanied only by one slave and one wife. Then he tried to reach Tapa beyond the Niger, his mother's native place. During the night his wife repented of her hasty action and also left him. Then he wandered about in the forest with his slave, seeking to find a way out of it, and at last Shango left the slave, with the words:

"Wait here till I return, and we will then try further for a way out."

The slave waited in vain for Shango. Then he went in search of him, and found that he had hanged himself. He found his way out of the wood, and reached Oyo, where he told the news.

Then a great terror fell on the chiefs and nobles. They went in search of the body but could not find it, but found a deep pit out of which the end of an iron chain protruded. They listened, and could hear Shango's voice in the pit, and then they built a small temple on the spot, and left a priest behind for the service of the new god.

In the city they reported:

"Shango is not dead; he is become an *Orisha*. He has descended into the earth and lives among the dead, with whom we have heard him conversing."

But when sceptics and scoffers said:

"Shango is dead, Shango has hanged himself," then the god himself came in a thunderstorm, and slew many of the unbelievers to show his power.

The place where Shango descended into the earth was called Kuso; soon a great city sprang up there. Many people went to live there.

4

Another myth makes Shango the son of Obatalla. He married Oya, Oshun and Oba, the three water-goddesses. As an earthly King he ruled at Oyo.

The myth relates that one day Shango received from his father a powerful charm. Whosoever ate of it was enabled to overcome all obstacles. Shango consumed the greater part and gave the rest to Oya, telling her to keep it for him. But when his back was turned she ate the rest herself. Next morning the chiefs and nobles assembled, as usual, to consult and advise. All spoke in their turn. But when Shango began to speak, flames burst from his mouth, and all were terribly frightened. Oya, too, belched forth flames when she began to scold the maids and women of the palace, so that every one ran off in great fright, and the palace was soon quite deserted.

Then Shango saw that, as a god, he was inferior to none, and called his three wives to him. He took a long iron chain in his hand, stamped with his feet on the ground which at once opened under him, and he descended into it with his wives. The earth closed again, but the end of the chain was left protruding from the ground.

Fig. 255. A small Shango Temple (private museum in Lyons). Shango and his wife. The head below seems to represent either the rising or the setting sun. The iron bars are emblems of Shango; the zigzag line represents the lightning.

5

After Shango with his three wives had descended into the ground, he often returned to the world. One day while he was scolding Oya down below, because she had stolen some of his medicines, she, being terrified at his

SHANGO, THE TYPICAL SUN-GOD

violence, ran off and took refuge with her brother, the sea-god Olokun.

When Shango heard where she was gone, he swore a great oath to beat her so that she would never forget the thrashing. Next morning he rose from below with the sun, and, following him in his course all the day, arrived with him in the evening at the place where the sea and sky join, and so he descended with him into the territory of his brother Olokun. The sun had unwittingly shown Shango the road across the sky to Olokun's palace, for Shango was careful to keep behind him all the time without being seen, and to hide when the sun looked round.

When Shango reached Olokun's palace, and saw Oya there, he made a great outcry and commotion. He rushed forward to seize her, but Olokun held him back, and while the two were struggling together Oya ran off to hide with her sister Olosa (the Lagoon).

When Olokun saw that Oya had gone, he released Shango, who, now more furious than ever, ran after his wife, threatening and cursing her. In his rage he tore up the trees by their roots as he ran along, tossing them to the right and left of the road. Oya, looking out from her sister's house, saw Shango coming along the banks of the lagoons, and well knowing that Olosa could not protect her, took to flight again and hurried along the shores to the place where the sun goes down.

As she was running, and Shango coming behind roaring and yelling, she rushed into a house by the wayside and claimed protection from the man whom she found there, whose name was Huisi. She implored him to defend her. Huisi asked what he, a man, could do against Shango. Then Oya gave him to eat of the medicines she had stolen from her husband, and he, being thus made an *Orisha*, promised to protect her.

As Shango approached, Huisi ran down to the banks of the lagoon, and tearing up a great tree by the roots brandished it in the air against Shango. There being no other tree at hand, Shango seized Huisi's canoe and flourished it in the air like a club, and the two weapons, striking together, were shattered to pieces. Then the two *Orishas* wrestled together; flames burst from their mouths, and their feet tore great fissures in the earth as they dragged each other to and fro. The struggle lasted some time without either being able to gain the mastery, till at last Shango, filled with rage at being baffled and feeling his strength failing, stamped on the earth, which opened

Fig. 256. Effigy of Shango; Badagri, West Africa (Mission Museum, Basel).

under him, and descended into it, dragging Huisi down with him. At the commencement of the combat, Oya had fled to Lokoko (near Porto Novo); she remained there, and the people built a temple in her honour. Huisi, who had become a god by virtue of the medicine he had eaten, also had a temple erected in his honour on the spot where he had fought with Shango.

The powerful god who dwells in the radiant brazen

SHANGO, THE TYPICAL SUN-GOD

palace, who owns over 10,000 swift horses, the cruel ruler who destroys everything about him; the man who will not be hanged (compare also p. 409, *The Death-form of the Ganga Chitome*) without disappearing in the earth —he is a solar god. The radiant brazen palace is the splendid brightness of the day-star; the horses represent the swiftness of its course; the cruelty is the terrible power of the fiery orb of the tropics; he disappears in the earth, that is, the sun goes down.

Specially beautiful is the last part. Here Shango reveals himself unreservedly as the solar god. He descends with the sun and follows its course to the sea. At the place were the sun goes down, Huisi and Shango fall out. Flames burst from Shango's mouth, for the sky is suffused with red from the rays of the evening sun. Yet Shango feels his strength giving way; he stamps on the ground, and the solar orb goes down (See A. B. Ellis, *The Yoruba-Speaking Peoples*).

CHAPTER XXI
ON THE PATH OF THE SUN

AS determining features of the solar myths we have the following: the incident of the swallowing up on the horizon (sunset); the incident of the release (as sunrise); the combat and the wild action connected with the rising and the setting; lastly, the slow movement along its course at noon.

I now add, as a fourth characteristic peculiarity of the solar myth-building, the emphasis laid on the fixed routes, which indicate the course taken by the solar hero, especially at sunrise. These solar routes are constructed in the most attractive way in the islands lying south-east of New Guinea, that is, in Melanesia and in North-West America. Hence I call to my aid the solar god, Quat, who has not yet been treated in detail, as well as a few North-West American Sagas, which give expression to this peculiarity in a specially clear way.

I. *Myth of Quat (Banks' Islands)*

QUAT (Qat) was not without a beginning. His mother, whose name was Quatgoro or Iro Ul, was a stone that burst asunder and brought him forth. He had no father, and he was born on the road. He grew up and talked at once. He asked his mother what his name was, saying that if he had a father or an uncle on his mother's side one of them would name him; then he gave himself the name of Quat. He had brothers also. The first was Tangaro Gilagilaga, Tangaro the Wise, who understood all things and could instruct the rest. The second was Tangaro Lologong, Tangaro the Fool, who was ignorant of everything and behaved like a fool. The others were Tangaro Siria, Tangaro Nolas, Tangaro Nokalato, Tangaro Noav,

Fig. 257. Archery of the Aetas. Negritos, shooting from the boat at the fish in the water. From a photograph.

Tangaro Nopatau, Tangaro Noau, Tangaro Nomatig, Tangaro Novunue, Tangaro Novlog: eleven of them, all Tangaro, twelve in all with Quat. The names of the last nine are the names of leaves of trees and plants, such as Nettle-leaf, Bread-fruit-leaf, Coconut-leaf, Bamboo-leaf, Umbrella-palm-leaf, etc., added to the name Tangaro, which is, no doubt, the same with the Tagaro of the New Hebrides and the Tanaroa of the Polynesians.

ON THE PATH OF THE SUN

These all grew up as soon as they were born, and they took up their abode in the village, Alo Sepere, where their mother, turned into a stone, may yet be seen. There Quat began the work of creation; he made men, pigs, trees, rocks, as the fancy took him. But when he had made all sorts of things he still knew not how to make night, and, therefore, the whole day was light. Then said his brothers to him:

"Hallo! Quat, this is not at all pleasant; here is nothing but day; can't you do something for us?"

Then, wondering what he could do with the daylight, he heard that there was night at Vava, in the Torres Islands.

So he took a pig and tied it, and put it into his canoe and sailed over to Vava, where he bought night, *qong*, from I Qong (Night), who lived there. Others say that he paddled to the foot of the sky (the horizon) to buy darkness from Night, and that Night blackened his eyebrows, and showed him how people fell asleep of an evening, and how to make twilight of a morning. Quat returned to his brothers with the knowledge of night, and with a hen and other birds to give notice of the time for the return of night. So he bade them prepare themselves bed-places, and they plaited coco-nut fronds and spread them in the house. Then, for the first time, they saw the sun moving and sinking in the West, and called out to Quat that it was crawling away.

"It will soon be gone," said he, "and if you see a change on the face of the earth, that is night." Then he let the night come.

"What is this coming over the sea," they cried, "and covering the sky?"

"That is night," said he; "sit down on both sides of

the house, and when you feel something in your eyes, lie down and be quiet."

Presently it was dark, and their eyes began to blink.

"Quat, Quat, what is this? Shall we die?"

"Shut your eyes," he replied; "this is the beginning of sleep."

When the night had lasted long enough, the cock began to crow and the birds to twitter. Then Quat took a piece of red obsidian and cut the night asunder. The light over which the night had spread itself shone forth again, and Quat's brothers awoke. But he betook himself again to the work of creation.

II. *Myth of Quat (Banks' Islands)*

ANOTHER remarkable series of adventures were Quat's encounters with Quasavara (Qasavara). This was a *bui*, very strong, a great fighter, tyrant and cannibal, who dwelt in the island which was the home of Quat and his brothers.

Once, when Quasavara fell in with Quat and his brothers, he invited them to his village and made a fire in his oven for them. When it was evening he told them that they were to sleep by themselves in his *gamal;* but they, knowing that they would be killed, were exceedingly afraid. Night fell and they were very sleepy, and Quat called them to come to bed. He rapped asunder with his knuckles one of the rafters of the gamal, and they all got inside and slept. In the middle of the night Quasavara and his men took clubs and bows and came to kill Quat's party, but not finding them in the sleeping-places went back disappointed.

At the approach of day the cock crew, and Quat awoke his brothers, bidding them crawl out at once, lest they should be seen leaving the rafter by daylight. So they came out.

When it was full daylight, Quasavara and his men, running to the gamal, found Quat and his brothers chatting together.

"Where did you sleep?" asked they.

Fig. 258. Archery of the Aetas. Shooting from the boat at the fish in the water; Philippines. From a photograph.

All of them answered that they had slept in the place appointed for them. But Tangaro the Fool cried out:

"We slept in this rafter here," to the great indignation of his brothers.

Quasavara's party again, as the night drew on, took counsel how they might kill them in the rafter; but that night Quat rapped a side post with his knuckles; it opened and they slept within it. Quasavara's party came in the night and smashed the rafter, found no one there, and again retired.

Next morning again they came into the gamal, and

found Quat and his brothers sitting unconcerned; and again Tangaro the Fool confessed they had been sleeping in the side post.

Next night again Quat opened the great main post and they slept in it, and again Quasavara came and smashed the side post and found no one there. Tangaro the Fool again made known their retreat, though he had been warned and scolded by his brothers.

Quasavara now determined to try another course, and to kill them as they were sitting at a feast. That night Quat opened the ridge pole with a rap, and they all slept in it. Knowing what was intended, Quat made his preparations to save his brothers. He planted a Casuarina-tree, and gave them his instructions what they were to do.

"When they are getting the food ready," he said, "wash your hands with the salt-water in the bamboo water-vessels till they are empty; and then, when they are looking for salt-water, and wanting some one to go and fill the vessels, two of you are to offer to go; and two are to go at once; and when you get some way off, smash the bamboo vessels on the ground and climb up into the Casuarina-tree. All of you are to do this."

They all agreed and did as they were bid. When the oven was all covered in, Quasavara's men cried out:

"Hallo! there is no salt-water! Who will fetch some?"

"We two," said two of Quat's brothers; and they went, and smashed the water-vessels and climbed into the Casuarina-tree. Quasavara's men waited for them till they were tired, and then asked some others to go; two more of Quat's brothers went, and smashed the vessels and climbed into the tree. So it went on till all his brothers were in the tree, and Quat alone was left beside the oven with Quasavara and his men.

ON THE PATH OF THE SUN

Then as they opened the oven, Quat sat with a large handful of food-bags beside the oven, and as they were taking out the food, Quasavara struck at Quat with his

Fig. 259. Aeta Archery ; shooting at birds in the trees, Philippines.
From a photograph.

club and missed him. Quat leaped away from him to the other side of the oven, and, taking up food from within it, cried:

"This is for my brothers, this is for my comrades," and stowed it in the bags.

ON THE PATH OF THE SUN

Quasavara leapt across after him, struck at him, but missed him again; and Quat again jumped across, took up food with the same cry and stowed it in his bags. So it went on till all the food in the oven was taken and all the bags were full.

Then Quat rose and ran to his brothers and Quasavara after him, hitting at him with his club and missing him as he ran, chasing him till he reached his brothers. Then Quat climbed up the tree and Quasavara after him.

The brothers were gathered together on the tree top, and Quat climbed to them, and there they sat still, for they could climb no higher. Then Quasavara climbed close to them, and stretched out his club at arm's length to strike them. But Quat cried out:

"My Casuarina, grow higher."

So the Casuarina grew higher between Quat's party and Quasavara, and left him far below. But Quasavara climbed after them again, and again came close to them; and again Quat cried:

"Grow higher, my Casuarina!"

Again the tree grew higher, and carried Quat and his brothers away from Quasavara. So it went on till the tree reached the sky. Then said Quat:

"Bend down, my Casuarina!"

And the tree bent its top down to the earth, and they all, one after another, got down to the ground, and Quat the last of them. And as they reached the ground he held fast on to the top of the Casuarina, and waited before letting it go; and Quasavara followed down after them and reached the end.

Then cried Quat:

"Now I revenge myself!"

ON THE PATH OF THE SUN

"Ah, Quat!" cried Quasavara, "do me no harm; take me into your house and I will work for you."

"No, indeed," said Quat, "but I will revenge myself for the mischief you have done me."

So he let go the top of the Casuarina-tree, and the tree

Fig. 260. A Brazilian woman shooting with the bow in the air, from a Spanish woodcut. The position of the toes and the stretch of the string is wrong. In this position the bow would fall inevitably to the ground when the arrow was let fly. Compare this with fig. 261.

sprang back and flipped off Quasavara, and his head knocked against the sky, and he fell back upon the earth; and there he lay at length upon his face, and turned into a stone.

III. *Myth of Quat (Aurora Island)*

ONCE some women came down from heaven, who had wings like birds; and they came down to earth to bathe in the sea, and when they bathed they took off their wings. And as Quat was going about, he chanced to see them; and he took up one pair of wings, and went back into the village and buried them at the foot of the main pillar of his house. Then he went back again and watched the women. And when they had finished bathing they went and took up their wings and flew up to heaven; but one could not fly because Quat had stolen her wings, and she was crying.

So Quat went to her, and spoke deceitfully to her, and asked her:

"What are you crying for?"

She answered:

"They have taken away my wings."

Then Quat took her to his house and married her.

And Quat's mother took her and they went to work; and when the leaf of a yam touched her there were yams as if some one had already dug them up, and if a leaf of a banana touched her, just a single one, all the bananas were ripe at once. But when Quat's mother saw that things were so she scolded her; but Quat did not; he was gone shooting birds.

And when Quat's mother scolded her she went back into the village; and she sat beside the post of the house and cried. And as she cried her tears flowed down upon the ground and made a deep hole; and the tears dropped down and uncovered her wings, and washed the earth away from them so that she found them. Then she flew back again to heaven.

And when Quat was come home from shooting he saw that she was not there and scolded his mother. Then he killed a pig and fastened points to very many arrows, and climbed up on the top of his house and shot up to the sky. And when he saw that the arrow did not fall back, he shot again and hit the first arrow. And he shot many times and always hit, and the arrows reached down to the earth. And, behold, an aerial banyan root twined round the arrows, and Quat took a basket of pig's flesh in his hand and climbed up to heaven. And he found a person hoeing; and he found his wife. And he said to the person hoeing: "If you see a banyan root don't disturb it." But as the two went down by the banyan root and had not yet reached the ground, that person chopped the root off. So Quat was dashed down and died. But the woman flew back to heaven.

IV. *Myth of Quat (Banks' Island)*

THE saga relates that on Gaua Quat took his departure from the world. Where the large lake now lies in the middle of the island, there was formerly a large wooded plain.

Fig. 261. A Weddah shooting with a bow; Ceylon. From a photograph by E. Schmidt.

Here Quat made himself a boat from one of the largest trees. While he was building it he was often laughed at by his brothers. They asked him how he was going to take such a large canoe to the sea. His only answer always was they would see. When the boat was finished he took his wife and brothers on board, collected the living creatures of the island, especially those so small as the ducks, and betook himself with them to the canoe which he had provided with a deck. Then came a downpour. The large depression in the middle of the island was flooded with water which burst through the surrounding hills at the place where now the great waterfall of Gaua plunges down. The boat took its course through a channel to the sea and disappeared. The people think that with Quat the best was taken from the island, and still expect his return.

V. *Myth of the Torres Islands*

THEY were living in their place, and his companions made a garden and planted bananas in it. When the bananas bore fruit and ripened, Dilingavuv went every day and ate bananas in their garden, not eating on the ground, but climbing into the trees and eating. After a while he was discovered; one of the party went into the garden and saw him up in a banana-tree eating; so he ran and told the others. Said he: "You fellows, I have seen the one who steals and eats our bananas."

Then said Maraw-hihi:

"Hew out bows for us to go and shoot and kill him."

But they said:

"Maraw-hihi, no one will be able to shoot and kill him."

"I will shoot and kill him," said Maraw-hihi.

"It is wholly impossible," said they.

However, they hewed out bows, each for himself, and put points to their arrows, and when that was done, Maraw-hihi said:

"Let us go after him, one by one."

So one went first and came to the garden, and saw him sitting up in the banana-tree, and went on tip-toe towards him to shoot him. But Dilingavuv stretched out his arms like a bat, and the man was afraid and went back and told the others.

"It can't possibly be done," said they.

Then said Maraw-hihi that one must go again; and

another went, and the same thing happened again. Thus they all went in turn, and came back and disputed with Maraw-hihi, saying: "It can't possibly be done."

Then said Maraw-hihi:

"I shall do it myself; I shall shoot him and kill him."

And this Maraw-hihi, they say, was more clever than them all; and he went last and saw Dilingavuv sitting in

Fig. 262. A Bororo shooting with a bow, Brazil;
after Von den Steinen.

the banana-tree, and he stepped along on tip-toe under the banana; and when Dilingavuv stretched out his arms he was not frightened at him; but he shot him with a swift arrow of Casuarina wood, and hit him on the ear, and shot off his right ear; and he fell headlong to the ground. So Maraw-hihi ran and told his friends; but Dilingavuv got up from under the banana and went home to his mother. When he reached his mother's house he called to her within; and she said:

"What is it, my son?"

And he said:

"Give me an axe."

ON THE PATH OF THE SUN

And his mother said:

"What are you going to do with it?"

But he deceived her and did not tell her that Maraw-hihi had shot his ear off. Then he went and cut another ear for himself out of the root of a tree called "Raw"; and as he was chopping the raw root, he said:

"Chop in pieces; chop asunder!"

And Maraw-hihi had sent one of his men who went and listened, and heard him saying this:

"Chop in pieces; chop asunder!"

And he ran back and told Maraw-hihi that Dilingavuv was chopping himself out an ear in place of the other. After this, Maraw-hihi and his men made a feast and danced every day. And when Dilingavuv heard of it, he said:

"I will go and have my revenge."

So he gathered a great quantity of Tahitian chestnuts, and took fire, and collected stones, and took a dancing-cloak of leaves and went to them. But he did not go right up to them in the open, but stayed behind the village. Then he made up a fire and roasted his chestnuts, and heated the stones, and dug a very deep hole and covered over the mouth of it with the dancing-dress of leaves; and so he sat and watched them dancing. Before long, as they were dancing, one of them fell out to take breath; and when he saw Dilingavuv sitting and eating chestnuts, he called to him to give him one.

"Run over here," says Dilingavuv.

So he runs over to him and sits down on this dancing-dress; and as he throws himself down to sit, he goes clean down into the hole. And Dilingavuv played the same trick on all the company at that dance, and let them all down into that pit, and Maraw-hihi last of all. Then he took the stones that he had heated over the fire and threw them down into the hole to kill the men with heat; but as he threw them down Maraw-hihi said to his companions:

"Come round over to this side of the pit."

Fig. 263. An Aeta shooting with a bow.
From a photograph.

And they did so, and not one of them was killed.

But Dilingavuv went home thinking he had killed them all. Then Maraw-hihi said to his men:

"Do you know how we shall save our lives?" And they answered:

"We are all dead already."

311

"Not at all," said he; "I know very well that we shall not die."

Then Maraw-hihi cast up his eyes out of the mouth of the pit, and saw a banyan branch bending over the pit, and he said:

"Let us *ker galgalaput* at that banyan branch" (i.e., shoot one arrow after another, making each one strike and fix itself into the one before it).

And they did so; and the reed-shafts of the arrows they had shot reached down to them into the pit. Then said Maraw-hihi:

"Climb up along the shafts."

And they said to him:

"You first, and we after you."

So he climbed up on the line of arrows and got out of the pit; and so they all saved their lives.

VI. *Utahagi (Bantik in Celebes)*

UTAHAGI, daughter of Limumu-ut and of Toar, flew down from heaven with six other nymphs, who were her sisters and also beautiful women, to bathe in a spring of very clear and pure water. At that time there lived at Mandolang a certain Kasimbaha, a son of Mainola and of Linkanbene, the latter being a son of Limumu-ut and of Toar. Now when Kasimbaha perceived the nymphs in the air, he took them at first for white pigeons, but when they came to the spring and undressed, he saw to his great surprise that they were women. While they were bathing Kasimbaha took a blow-pipe, crept through the bush as near as possible to the spring, and drew to himself one of the light garments which gave the power of flight to the person wearing them. After bathing, all the maids put their clothes on again, and flew up home;

312

only one of them could not find hers, and so had to stay behind.

This was Utahagi, so called from a white hair which grew upon the crown of her head and had a special

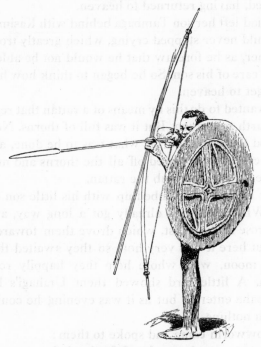

Fig. 264. Bow-shooting in Bogajim, New Guinea. From a photograph.

power. Kasimbaha took her to his home and made her his wife. Of this marriage was born a son named Tambaga, who afterwards married Matinimbang.

Some time later Utahagi told her husband the secret of the white hair, cautioning him to be very careful about it, since, if by any accident she were to lose it a great misfortune would happen. Now, whether these words

were not believed, or for some other unknown reason—
in short, so much is certain, that on his plucking it out
there arose a heavy storm accompanied by thunder and
lightning. After the tempest was over Utahagi had disappeared, having returned to heaven.

She had left her son Tambaga behind with Kasimbaha.
This child never stopped crying, which greatly troubled
his father, as he foresaw that he would not be able long
to take care of his son. So he began to think how he also
might get to heaven.

He wanted to do this by means of a rattan that reached
from earth to heaven. But it was full of thorns. Now, as
he stood there considering what was to be done, a field-
mouse came and gnawed off all the thorns and made it
possible for him to climb the rattan.

Now Kasimbaha climbed up with his little son on his
back. When they had already got a long way, a great
storm rose in the West, which drove them towards the
sun. But here it was very hot; so they awaited the rise
of the moon, with whose help they happily reached
heaven. A little bird showed them Utahagi's house.
Kasimbaha entered, but as it was evening he could distinguish nothing.

A glowworm came and spoke to them:

"I see at once that, unless I further help you, you will
not find Utahagi's residence, for in this house seven
rooms are occupied by seven sisters. So look well for the
door at which I shall stop, for it leads into your wife's
room."

Following this advice, he entered Utahagi's room, and
handed her her son Tambaga. She, however, reproached
him severely, attributing all the misfortunes that befell
him to his own fault.

ON THE PATH OF THE SUN

Utahagi's brother, who was also an *impong* (a demigod), said to the other celestials:

"What means this? As my sister's husband is not an impong, he cannot stay with us. But we will put him to the test, and serve up nine covered dishes, eight filled with rice and one with something else. If he uncovers the last first, then he is a mortal and no impong.

This time a fly came to Kasimbaha's aid, and advised him to watch its steps carefully. It said:

"The dishes into which I enter and out of which I come again, you may confidently open; but do not touch that into which I crawl but do not come out again."

As he did not touch the dish with the unclean contents, they were satisfied that he was no mortal's child, but an impong, and so he remained with his wife in heaven. But later he let his son Tambaga, by a long chain, down to the earth, and in this way Tambaga returned to his native place, Mandolang. From Tambaga and Matinimbang the Bantik people are sprung.

Fig. 265. An Aeta Archer, Philippines. From a photograph taken in the last position just before shooting.

315

ON THE PATH OF THE SUN

PROFESSOR FRANZ BOAS has collected such an extraordinary abundance of legends from this region, that I am easily able to choose from them divers variants of the incidents that we are here dealing with.

I. *The War with Heaven*
(*Fragment of a Saga*)

THE birds wanted to invade heaven and shot their arrows against the sky, in order to make a chain by which they might climb up. But not one of them was able to reach heaven. At last the bird Tcitu'c took his bow and arrows and he hit the sky. Then he made a chain of arrows which reached down to the earth, and all the animals climbed up by it. Later the chain broke, when only half of the animals had got safely down again.

II. *The Woodpecker and the Eagle*
(*The beginning slightly condensed*)

TEMETLEPSEM, the red-headed woodpecker, had a wife called Leqyiles. Tseskel, the Eagle, was the woodpecker's brother, and each of them had a son. The woodpecker taught his child to climb up the trees, the eagle taught his to fly up in wide circles. Lekyiap, the prairie wolf, lived with them in a village; he was a bad person, and was jealous at the cleverness of the sons of the woodpecker and the eagle. He considered how he might do them harm. By cunning and deceit he contrived to get possession of a beautiful waterfowl, which he caused to swim about before the two young men (*sic*) in order to tempt them to follow it. Then the bird began to swim farther and farther up the river. The youngsters were

316

ON THE PATH OF THE SUN

not able to get nearer, and so took to shooting but could not kill the bird. So it lured them farther and farther up the river, till at last they came to heaven. There they met one of the inhabitants of heaven who took them to his home.

When the woodpecker and the eagle missed their sons they were greatly troubled. They sent to all peoples and all lands in search of them; but they were not to be found. At last they heard from a man that their sons were in heaven. Then they wanted to get up into heaven in order to fetch back their sons. But they did not know how to get there.

They called a general council, at which they asked the animals how heaven could be reached. First of all

Fig. 266. A Weddah Archer, Ceylon. From a photograph by E. Schmidt.

they called on the pelican to try to fly to heaven. He flew up on high, but had to turn back without succeeding. Then they called on the mole to try to creep under the water and under the earth up on high; but he could not. Then they let the swallow fly up, but he also failed to reach heaven. Now the eagle himself flew aloft, but had also again to turn back without succeeding. Then one of the dwarfs who live by the wayside and are extremely strong made the attempt, but he also failed. Then as they did not at all know how to get up, Tamia, grandson of Leqyiles, stood up and spoke:

"Last night I dreamt how we might get there."

He brushed his hair back, dyed it a red colour, drew a red line from his forehead over his nose down to his chin, and began to sing while his grandmother beat time.

"I, Tamia, am not afraid to shoot up to heaven."

Then he aimed his bow high up at the entrance to heaven, and shot off an arrow, which sped and sped and at last hit heaven just under the entrance. He shot off a second arrow which hit the notch in the first, and so he continued until the arrows formed a long chain. In this his grandmother helped him by singing and beating time. When the chain was finished he wiped the red colour from his face, and painted his whole body white with burnt bones. Then he transformed the arrows into a broad way which led up to heaven.

Now all the people went up to heaven, fought with its inhabitants, overcame them and released the sons of the woodpecker and the eagle. Then they returned home. When all had got safely down again, they smashed the way by which they had gone up. They had not noticed that the snail had not yet come down; it had only reached the gate of heaven when the chain of arrows had already been broken up, and so had to let itself fall down. Then all its bones got broken, and ever since it has been very slow, etc.

ON THE PATH OF THE SUN

III. *The Tree-resin and the Sun*

LONG ago the tree-resin was a man called Momhanate, and he was blind. As he could not endure the heat of the sun he would go out at night to angle for red haddock. In the morning, when it dawned, his wife would call out:

Fig. 267. A Seri Archer, Central America. From a photograph by
W. J. McGee.

ON THE PATH OF THE SUN

"Come quickly home, the sun is rising."

Thus he always returned home before it got warm. But one day his wife slept too long, and on awaking she saw that it was bright daylight. Being frightened, she ran down to the beach and called out to her husband:

"Come quickly home, the sun is already high up in the sky."

He paddled as quick as he could, but it was too late! The sun shone so hot down upon him that he melted before he could get back. Then his two sons were sad, and said to each other:

"What shall we do? We must avenge our father."

And they decided to go up to heaven and kill the sun. They took their bows and arrows, and went to the place where the sun rises. Then they shot the sky, and the first arrow remained fixed in the sky. The second hit the first, and so they went on until a long chain was formed which reached from heaven down to the earth. Then the elder brother shook it to see if it was strong enough. He found that the chain was firm, and both brothers climbed up aloft. On reaching heaven they killed the sun with their arrows. Then they thought what they should now do. And the elder spoke:

"Let us now be the sun."

And he asked his younger brother whither he would go. He answered:

"I will go to the night, go you to the day;" and so it happened.

The younger brother became the moon, the elder the sun.

ON THE PATH OF THE SUN

IV. *The Mink Saga*

ONCE the people jeered at the Mink, and threw it in his teeth that he had no father or mother. Then he wept and said:

"The Sun is my father; I will go up to him."

Fig. 268. A Bororo Archer, Brazil. After Von den Steinen. The loincloth is wrong.

But the people laughed at him and said:

"How will you get there? The way to heaven is much too far."

Mink ran to his uncle, Yalamihomike, and asked him for his bow and his arrows. When he had got these he shot off the first arrow, which hit the sky, the house of the Sun. Then he shot off the second arrow, which hit the notch of the first and remained fixed in it. So he went on shooting until a chain was formed which reached from the sky down to the earth. He climbed up by it and arrived at the house of the Sun, and sat down before the door. Presently the slave of the Sun came to the door, and on seeing the youth sitting there he hastened back to his master and said: "Master, your child is seated outside."

Then the Sun was glad, and bade his slave to call Mink in. When he came in and sat down by the fire, the Aged One spoke:

"My heart rejoices that you are come, my son. It is a heavy load for me to bear the sun every day, for I am old and weak. Henceforth you shall bear it."

He bade Mink to bathe, and gave him his ear-ornament and his nose-plug of bright haliotis (ear-shell). His father impressed upon him not to go too swiftly, lest he should burn the earth. Next day he sent Mink out to bear the sun, and he sat before the house and watched his son, who followed his command and rose slowly up the sky. Towards noon many clouds gathered and obstructed Mink's way. He was impatient, thrust the clouds aside and began to move quickly. Then his nose-plug shone so bright and hot down on the earth that the stones burst asunder and the water began to boil. On seeing this, his father hurried forward, tore off his nose-plug and ear-ornament and hurled him into the sea. A woman who had gone out in her boat found Mink floating about in the sea. She took the little body into the boat, and said:

"The poor thing; it must long be dead."

Then Mink sprang up, rubbed his eyes and said:

"Oh! I believe I have long been asleep."

ON THE PATH OF THE SUN

V. *The Visit to Heaven*

ONCE Gamdigyetlneeq (The only Seeing Fire) wanted to ascend up to heaven. His friends did not think he would be able to do so, so he said:

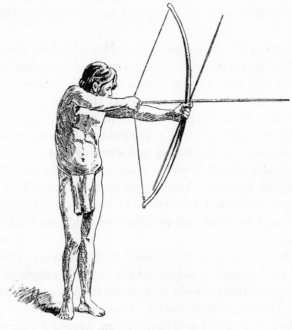

Fig. 269. A Khimila Archer, North Columbia.
From a photograph.

"When I reach heaven, you will see the sun standing still."

He went to a little sandbank in the vicinity of Meq-tlakqatla, and took with him his bow and his arrows and a strong rope. Then he shot an arrow towards the sky; he saw it flying and at last fix itself in the blue vault. He took a second arrow and aimed at the notch of the first. This he hit, and went on shooting until he formed a chain which nearly reached down to the earth. When he had shot off all his arrows he placed his bow at the foot of the chain, and then climbed up. On arriving at the house of the moon, he went to the door and cried out:

"I want to be made beautiful and healthy by Haiat-lilaqs."

Then the dwarfs called to him. He, however, took no notice of them, but went straight to the chief, going along by the east side of the house. He was received in a friendly way. Then the sun stood still, and the people knew that Gamdigyetlneeq was in heaven. The young man remained some time as the guest of Haiatlilaqs, who first cleansed him, bathing and washing him. After the bath, scales fell off from his body, and now he was clean and white as snow. After some time he wanted to get back to the earth. Even before he had said so Haiatlilaqs had heard his wish and promised to send him back. He spoke:

"Hear what you are to teach mankind when you get back to the earth. I rejoice at the sight of people in the world, else there would be nobody to pray and worship me. I require and delight in your homage. But if you continue to do evil I will destroy you. Man and wife must be faithful to each other; you must pray to me, and you must take no notice of the moon when you sit by the shore. I delight in your smoke. You must not play and riot in the evening. If you continue to do what I forbid, I will destroy you."

Then he sent the young chief back. He pushed aside a board right before their seat, and Gamdigyetlneeq saw the whole earth lying before him, and the chain of arrows by which he had climbed up. He climbed down again, and when he got to the bottom and took up his bow all the arrows fell down.　He went back to his home and taught the people what Haiatlilaqs had instructed him to say.

Fig. 270. East African Archer. After Glave.

All these myths represent the course of the sun, and indeed of the rising sun, as may be inferred from many circumstances. But we must regard as specially charac-teristic Quat and his history, where for the narrator of the myth the sun evidently rises on the dry land, since his mother is a stone which bursts asunder at sunrise. Now Quat buys the night, and indeed at Vavo, since for the Banks' Islanders this is the land, or at least the region, where the sun sets and it becomes dark. But when it has to become light again, Quat cuts the night in two with a piece of red obsidian. Those are the first red rays of the morning sun emerging from the darkness.

Now for Quasavara! He is a personification of the night as hostile to the day; he is the ruler of night. It is at night that he wants to destroy Quat, as by day he has evidently no power. Wonderfully pretty is always the indication of the going down of the sun. Quat's party slips inside one beam or another. Lastly there is the glorious picture of the course of the sun, how the tree grows and grows, until Quat and his brothers reach the lofty canopy of heaven; that is the rising sun escaping from the night.

The third myth of Quat and the sixth about Utahagi are very much alike. In both the road to the sun is described in the same way. This Quat myth also leads to an inquiry into all the "arrow myths" which now follow and flourish in great abundance, especially in North-West America. In the myth of the Torres Island the essential point is that Delingavuv should have his ear shot off, and that he should carve himself another, which is obviously an explanation of the waxing and waning moon. It is the moon as ruler of the night that entices Marawhihi into the pit (sunset). But the Sun-god knows how to help himself. Soon the arrows are shooting out of the pit into the air, that is, the rays of the rising sun are forcing a way for themselves.

In the North-West American myths we have the liveliest examples of sunrises. Here I have chosen a series in which the chain of arrows stands in the foreground, and in which some details must appear specially significant. When, for instance, the red-crested woodpecker takes to the chain of arrows, but then paints himself white with burnt bones, that can only be explained by the deep red of the rising sun and the dazzling white of the midday orb. In the opening of one such myth we read: "At that time the sky was near to the earth." That can mean nothing else but that the myths play about the horizon.

It is self-evident that these arrows mean the radiant rising sun. No doubt we hear nothing about arrows in Polynesia, but that is because the Polynesians fought only with spears; hence here we hear of spears which the gods and the heroes hurl at each other, and especially of Maui's spear, with which he kills the souls that fall into the net which he holds in his other hand. These are the destroying rays of the tropical sun, which again recur in Australia and in ancient Greece.

Above all in ancient Greece! Let us here linger for a moment.

Phaeton, being ridiculed by his friends, one day implored his mother Clymene to tell him whether Phœbus, the Sun-god, was really his father. Clymene assured him of the fact, whereupon he went off to seek his father. He sought and found him, and kept worrying him to let him for at least one day take charge of the solar chariot which rushes through the day. His father long refused to grant his request, but he had sworn by Styx, the river of Hades, to grant him whatever he asked, and so had reluctantly to lay the reins in the unskilled hands of his son.

The brazen gates fly open, and the steeds, radiant in their pride, stride onward before the glorious car. Soon, however, they feel they are no longer guided by the

ON THE PATH OF THE SUN

master's hand, grow restive and bolt. Now Phaeton, growing dizzy in the heights, tries to guide the horses earthwards. Then the springs dry up, the forest takes fire, the earth bursts asunder and the sun shines down into Tartarus.

Then Jupiter, with a thunder-bolt, strikes the rash youth from the chariot, and so the steeds are scattered.

Here we have the solar myth of the ancient Hellenes. Contrasted with that of the Mink, what a vast difference! On the one hand colossal greatness, on the other pleasant prattle! That is the outward impression; but within complete harmony. Both sagas even begin with the same motive, ridicule! The journey on high is the same; similarly stones burst asunder and the waters begin to boil; then, the most remarkable resemblance of all, the inexpert charioteer of the sun is hurled headlong down by an enraged deity. But while the Hellenic myth ends in a great tragedy, —Phaeton's sisters changed into alder-trees, his friend into a swan and his mother driven mad—the North-West American concludes with the Mink springing up, rubbing his eyes and exclaiming:

"Oh! I believe I have been long asleep."

That is the whole formal difference. The Greek legend winds up with a few grand touches, while the other, on the contrary, breaks off with a humorous pleasantry. But in saying this I by no means wish to imply that to the Greek myths compared with those of the so-called savages the phrase "far grander" once for all applies; assuredly not. I would ask the reader to compare the legend of Maui's stealing the fire with that of Prometheus. Surely neither of these is at all inferior to the other.

Now, one more point!

The Phaeton saga contains the words:

328

ON THE PATH OF THE SUN

"The sun shone in Tartarus." In Tartarus, that is the land of the dead. That reminds us of Tempon-telon, whom we left two chapters further back. Of Maui also it was said that his death brought death to all mankind. We heard further that with the sunrise the people once swallowed by the monsters Tsekis and Kammapa escaped from their bodies. The incident of the sun shining in Tartarus, in the land of the dead, through the descent of Phaeton, must have quite a special meaning.

What is it?

CHAPTER XXII
MANKIND ON THE PATH OF THE SUN

WHAT are we to understand by the incident in which mortals ascend with the rising sun out of the body of the monster, "Night?" Or by Tempon-telon who, with the ship of the souls, with the host of dead, sinks into the world beyond; there where heaven and earth meet, where the sun goes down, where the solar orb is swallowed up? Or when the sun shines out on the breast of a rattle representing a raven? (figs. 241 and following.)

In the Greek myth Phaeton's setting sun shines down into Tartarus, into the land of the dead.

Had Maui, the Sun-god, not died, neither would men have died.

By the place which Maui, when setting, had already passed on his way to Mauike, goes the way of the souls to the world beyond.

The chiefs of higher rank follow Maui into the sun. As Maui's right eye is the sun, so the left eyes of the chiefs shine as stars in the sky.

But here is the solution of the whole problem:

"The soul of the dead man follows the sun."

In Mangaya the greatest joy of the souls is to be able to follow the sun. In Puka-Puka also all who escape the wrath of Waeru hasten after the sun. But Waeru is none other than Hine-nui-te-Po, the Goddess of Night, who

MANKIND ON THE PATH OF THE SUN

swallows the solar orb. In Hawaii the souls are conducted to heaven by a god whose name is "The Eyeball of the Sun." In the Solomon Islands the souls of the departed follow the sun and descend with it into the ocean. In the New Hebrides also the afterworld lies in the West. Hence this is Tempon-telon's ship, the vessel of the sun, in which the dead arrive with the sun in the world beyond (compare also fig. 272).

And so we hear the same echo everywhere from the sphere of the old solar view of the universe—the souls follow the sun. In Australasia, Africa, America, everywhere, it is mentioned at least once; but still more frequently can it be inferred from the meaning and the form of the myths. For me the great problem of the solar myths is this:

Fig. 271. Bow-shooting on a bronze plate from Benin, Slave Coast, West Africa. Drawn from a photograph by von Luschan, and from the original in the Berlin Ethnological Museum.

"How did the solar mythology originate?"

When we now survey the various mythological epochs, the successive periods from animalism (the age of esteem for animals) and manism (the age when the power of

MANKIND ON THE PATH OF THE SUN

departed souls was dominant) to "Solar-ism," or the contemplation of the universe—*then we have before us the whole history of the faculty possessed by rude, primitive peoples for grasping and comprehending the cosmic world, as well as of the interest they take in it.* At first man knows only the beast. The changes around him, the problem of the changes in himself teach him to inquire into the potency of spirits, and especially to investigate the problem of death. But as the sphere of human interests has now been considerably enlarged; as man has meanwhile become an agriculturist, and has discovered the action of the sun on his crops, he naturally transfers his interest in the dead to the sky, to the solar orb.

But it would be a mistake, a mistake that has hitherto always been made, to suppose that the origin of solar worship is exclusively due to the action which by primitive peoples is attributed to the sun, that is to its influence on the growth of vegetation and on agriculture. Primitive peoples do not reason so logically as that. On the contrary, the first stimulus to solar worship, to "Solarism," to the contemplation of the sun, was most decidedly given *during the early migrations. When the peoples of the earth began to move in large groups over wide areas, when they had to find their bearings, to decide which direction to take, then they began for the first time to look around upon the world, and thus acquired an interest in the structure of the universe, in the sun, the moon and the stars.* For it is to be noticed that they did not confine their observations to the sun alone, but rather that the whole system of sun, moon and stars enters simultaneously and compendiously into their mythologies. That the sun takes the first place is obvious enough. We know, for instance, that in the South Sea whole migrations took place, the

Theire sitting at meate

A MEAL AMONG THE NORTH AMERICAN INDIANS. THE PLATTER CONTAINS MAIZE

From the original water-colour drawing in the British Museum by John White, Governor of Virginia in 1587.

sole object of which was to discover the Land of the Rising Sun.

In this connexion it must almost appear as self-evident that these peoples, these pronounced "Manists," these men learned in all things pertaining to the knowledge of spirits, should identify the destinies of human souls with those of the sun, that they should represent their dead as going down in company with the sun.

But I desire to do justice also to the other side, to the other theory regarding the origin of solar worship. I admit that in many places a relation may be pointed out between agriculture and the cult of the sun. But the understanding of the relation between sunshine and vegetation belongs to a later period. This later solarism, this conscious reference of good or bad harvests to the good or evil will of the Sungod is far more recent; between the two periods lies the great interval which separates rude from cultured peoples. *The earlier form of solarism still culminates in a solution of the spirit problem;* the later

Fig. 272. North-West American monument to the dead, erected at the house of the departed; after Niblach. On the broad part above is the image of the sun; below are totemistic figures. Formerly the remains of the cremated body were preserved in the broad upper part. The whole is a representation of the view that "The Soul follows the Sun."

was destined to mature for the first time the natural or scientific view. The earlier period is characterized by the story of the souls following the sun, and by human sacrifices. For it is quite natural that human sacrifices should be the most acceptable to the god who conducts the souls to the after-world, whose splendid ruddy glow at the rising and the setting presents the grandest phenomenon

333

MANKIND ON THE PATH OF THE SUN

in nature. The second period of the solar view of the world, which was taken by agriculturists who made deep furrows, and were no longer mere tillers of gardens and improvident gluttons who took no care for the morrow, but gorged as long as there was plenty, this second period is characterized by the sacred harvest-feasts, and further by regular well-constructed calendars.

In a work such as this, dealing with the childhood of mankind, we have to do with the views of the first period, and with these alone. The agriculturist of political economy, with his calendric lore and his harvest-feasts, belongs to the period of human development in which maturity begins. But here I will give a very interesting demonstration. I believe I have discovered a form of development in which the difference between these ways of viewing the universe is very distinctly marked. I refer to the civilization of ancient Mexico. I am led to the conviction that though the ancient Toltecs may have held to the second form of the solar way of viewing the universe, yet that the Aztecs, who in the time of Cortez were dominant in the Toltec territory and had arrived as conquerors not so very long before, were the true representatives of the second epoch of this period—hence that here a relapse had taken place. This I infer from the fact that the Aztecs were the first to introduce human sacrifices and all the notions and practices associated therewith.

Now let us return, after this digression, to our problem. We have to show that the manistic root-ideas, the thoughts prevalent in this period of man's view of the world which here interests us, are the really quickening and essential views. Accordingly I return to the saying: "The souls follow the sun."

MANKIND ON THE PATH OF THE SUN

Significant of the childlike but decisive views in this direction is the "materialization" of the course of the sun. As the spirit moves along the track after the sun, or as the sun itself is conceived as a manlike god, the lower consciousness of the people requires, so to say, firm ground for the migration of the dead. We have in fact seen how such firm paths are founded in the imagination of the people. Mink, Maraw-hihi, Quat and his brothers require strong trees, ladders of arrows, or the like, in order to move about above the sky. So also Kamakayakau, Kasimbaha and others climb back to the earth by means of cords, ropes of reeds, and spider's webs. So, too, the Maori dead descend by trailing plants down to the spirit-land, Havaiki.

Here is, in my opinion, the decisive turning-point for the whole problem. As the dead climb by means of trailers into the world beyond, so the story goes that once their forefathers climbed in the same way from Havaiki up to the earth. So simply are such difficulties always solved in the popular philosophies! They first of all settle to their own satisfaction how the souls, the ghosts, reach the next world. Then when they are asked what they really think about the origin of their forefathers, or of the first men, they simply reverse the process, and turn the migration of the departed to the world beyond into migration of their ancestors from the world beyond. Thus, for instance, the Kich people on the Nile relate how in the beginning men lived in heaven. Then some of them annoyed the deity, who sent them down to the earth by a long golden cord, whence those who mended their ways climbed back again. But a blue bird pecked at the cord until it was torn, whereby the connexion with heaven was broken off.

MANKIND ON THE PATH OF THE SUN

From Maui alone we might get a whole sackful of examples of the solar track becoming materialized. In the sling or hempen string with which he captures the sun in order to slacken its course we can recognize nothing but the path of the sun. By means of a string Maui holds the sun fast under the earth. Then again the case is reversed, and from Maui's hempen cords solar rays are made. Or Maui plants a vine by means of which one or other of his favourites climbs up to the sun, and so on.

The development of this solar track may be most amusingly followed, especially in Africa.

Amongst the Ga people of the Gold Coast west of Togoland a certain order of priests called *Gbalo* holds converse with the spirits, who for such interviews are usually seated on the top of the round huts. From this top hangs a string or a chain which the *Gbalo* keeps pulling until the spirit lets itself down. Römer mentions the specially interesting case of a string of bast which hung from the summit of the roof and the end of which came to rest on the back of a priestess; in this way the spirit descended, seized the priestess, that is, took possession of her, and spoke through her mouth.

Let us now follow among various tribes the degraded forms of this materialized embodiment of the sun-path of the souls, that is, the string or cord used by them.

The Isupus wear certain magic rings called "lobo," which have the faculty of bringing the wearer into relation with certain spirits. The Okomfus (the Gangas of the Ga people) wear a white coral chain round their necks, the object of which is that the deity may come down and enter it.

With this string, which the priests often coil round themselves in order to induce their ancestors or some deity to descend upon them, or else to send petitions up to the spirits, we have come upon one of the most efficacious and powerful amulets, that is, religious appliances, any-where to be found amongst primitive peoples, and not amongst them alone.

Once a Belgian friend of mine at the head of an expedi-tion entered a Ngombe village rather late in the evening, and was not a little surprised to see the inhabitants gathered on a neighbouring hill, all painted white, all staring at the sun which was about to set. In front of the whole assembly a body lay on the ground, and the moment the sun began to sink the ganga (chief) sprang at the dead man with a long red-coloured cord, which, quick as lightning, he threw round its forehead, and then round three young women, the wives of the deceased, who were squatting close by. While the sun kept sinking all sat there in eager expectation, the three women pale as ashes with excitement. But as nothing happened, on the disappearance of the sun all stood up; the ganga undid the cord from the forehead of the body and cut it into three lengths; while on their part each of the three women tied a piece round her forehead, and then all went down to the village.

To the question as to the meaning of the ceremony the people gave evasive answers. But on returning to the place three months later, the explorer noticed that the women were still wearing the string, and he was told that they must do so as long as their husband's body lay above ground. It would also be their duty during that interval to bring him food and drink every evening at sunset, and, moreover, give him the opportunity of letting them know his pleasure, which he could do only so long as these women wore the cords round their head. At the burial the cords would be thrown into the grave with him.

Now, although the natives gave no explanation of the ceremony, after all that we have so far observed it will scarcely be very difficult for us to divine the meaning of it all. It is certain that with the string it was intended to give the spirit an opportunity of entering the bodies of the women; hence, that in the string we have to recognize a materialized sun-path reduced to its primal element.

With this are associated an endless number of other examples. *The string coiled round the head occurs as a sign of mourning amongst all peoples holding the old solar view of the world.* Hence, when we anywhere meet the mourning string, this will afford us an interesting insight into the mythological notions of the people in question.

With the string by which the spirit descends from above on the conjurers of spirits is associated a great body of incidental but still not uninteresting phenomena. We have, first and foremost, all amulets in general, by means of which petitions are sent to the upper world and questions addressed to the dead. Not a few of these are attached first to the wooden effigy of the departed, and then to the person's own body. There are, further, the strings by means of which vows are similarly fastened to the votary's body.

Here is also a little example from Borneo, which has only recently come to my knowledge. The Dayak who has to send a message to the land of the dead ties to the carving of Tempon-telon's ship a cord, and to the cord a shell, a bit of wood or the like, to which he has first whispered something, or bespattered and sprinkled it with the blood of a fowl. The cord must be attached at sunset, and if the supplicant expects an answer he will

FIG. 273. THE JUJU NKALI FEAST

From a native drawing; details and sketches of the masks by Keil, the missionary.
Compare also the Juju Nkali picture, see Fig. 281

MANKIND ON THE PATH OF THE SUN

untie the string at the approach of dawn and attach himself to the carving. Now he is convinced that he will dream the answer the next night. But should this not happen, he believes that the spirit to whom he has dispatched the message for some reason is angry with him, and must first be appeased by offerings.

But of special interest in this connexion is a ceremony of the Bagos, which has been related to me by the missionary Keil, and which in former times was performed once a year, but which only very old people could now describe.

Formerly a spider-feast was held once a year, or once every other year, by the Bagos who live in North-West Africa. For this purpose the members of a priestly society prepared as many carved masks as there were dead to mourn for. Then one fine day this band would come suddenly dancing into the village towards evening with fearful howls and cries, and constantly yelling out the words, "Juju Nkali; Juju Nkali."

Then all took refuge in their houses. But some one, usually a slave or an old man, was seized and carried off to the bush by the masqueraders. What here befell him nobody could tell, but it is certain that a few days later the masked band returned to the village with a finger, a toe or a bit of skin, or some other part of the slave, fastened to a pole. This pole was then brought before every house occupied by a young man who wanted to be received into this priestly association. The sequel of this was that all these young people went off to the forest, singing and playing music, seeking thereby to drown their own fear. So, at least, said Herr Keil's informer.

Then, a few weeks later, once more was heard the howl-

Fig. 274. The Solar pole, with two dancers; seen from the east.
Native drawing in Dorsey's book.

ing and roaring of the masqueraders, who were this time followed by the novices of the society, painted white. These carried first a shrouded object, and then one and all a string coiled several times round their necks. Now the company advanced into the middle of the village. The maskers dragged forward a long post or pole, to the top of which each of the young men attached the free end of the string, the other end of which was twined round his neck. Thereupon the maskers took the shrouded object and fixed it on the top of the pole (fig. 273).

This object was nothing less than the now more or less decayed head of the victim who had been seized on the first day of the maskers' appearance. But it was stuck round with feathers, so that it looked like a hedgehog. A fire was kindled in the midst of them and the maskers began a furious dance, wildly yelling:

"Juju Nkali; Juju Nkali!"

This was kept up till it was assumed that the young men were dead. Then the strings were coiled tight round the pole, and pole and young men all carried off to the forest. It was then explained that the spider had seized the souls of the young men; but that would not matter, since the priests had the pole with the strings, and the souls of the young men continued to live on in the strings.

And sure enough, after one or two years, the young men again made their appearance, and now they were hailed as quite distinguished persons.

The drawing here given of the Juju Nkali feast is made from a sketch in the missionary Keil's diary. This sketch was based on drawings by the natives. In the next chapter on the spider myths I shall be able to give the sequel to this remarkable narrative. But let us here first rapidly dispose of one more episode.

MANKIND ON THE PATH OF THE SUN
Solar Dance of the Sioux

A PARTICULARLY marked veneration for the sun, for the Sun-god, Wakantanka, is to this day still found amongst the Dakotas, one of those tribes which still live

Fig. 275. A Dakota at the Sun-dance, a buffalo's skull on his back.
From a drawing by the Indian, Bush Otter.

within the sphere of influence of the old Mexican civilization, and have consequently borrowed many of their religious and cosmic notions from the more advanced southern peoples. But in this homage paid to the sun we have, in any case, to recognize an outcome of the later and more developed form of the solar view of the world, for this homage culminates in offerings to obtain the favour of bountiful harvests, fruitful seasons and the like.

344

MANKIND ON THE PATH OF THE SUN

When the Dakotas suffer too severely from hunger in winter, or else when they want to get the better of some enemy, one and another of them will say:

"Well! I will pray to Wakantanka in summer."

From that moment the man in question will be regarded

Fig. 276. Dakota at the Sun-dance, between four stakes.
From a drawing by the Indian, Bush Otter.

with a kind of awe and reverence as a saintly person. They bend humbly round him, avoid strife in his presence, and when it comes to a conflict he holds himself aloof as a being exalted above all earthly contentions.

Summer draws near. Messengers repair to the surrounding villages and invite the people to the sacred feast of self-sacrifice. Now they come from all quarters; deadly enemies may meet, but at the feast all are good neighbours. The sanctity of the rite imposes absolute peace on all.

One evening, by moonlight, a band of chosen men sets out to look for a tree-stem which may serve as a sacred post for the sun. By moonlight the first man strikes his axe into the stem, the second draws it out; stroke follows stroke till the giant is felled. Then they drag it to the place appointed for the feast, and make fast to the top a brush-wood figure of what they are praying for.

On the place of the feast, round which the tents of the

Fig. 277. Dakota hoisted up at the Solar Stake.
From a drawing by the Dakota, Bush Otter, after Dorsey.

tribe and of the visitors have already been pitched in a wide circle, a separate tent has been erected between the centre and the east side. Here the little band that have vowed to make the self-sacrifice prepare for the sacred offering by the customary abstinence from tobacco-

346

MANKIND ON THE PATH OF THE SUN

smoking and dancing. The stake is raised in the centre, and round it runs an embowered path, and between the stake and the path the gruesome solemnity takes place.

All preliminaries have now been carried out. The evening before the men have ridden the *Uncita* on the open space round the embowered path. During the night the candidates have completed their equipment, painted themselves artistically, put on a red tunic and a buffalo hide, and stuck the eagle feathers in their hair. But above all they have procured a new pipe, finely ornamented and filled with the sacred herb.

The ceremony begins with sunrise. From the tent where the preparations have been made they step across the open space to the covered path. Along the way posts

Fig. 278. The man in the moon. Drawing by a Haida in Niblach's work. Once Koong, the Moon, with his beams drew up a man with all his buckets and a bush which he wanted to hold on by. All this can now be seen in the moon. When the man upsets his bucket it rains.

have been erected, and on these the offerers have hung the gifts, such as tobacco-pouches and cloth, which after the feast go to the poor. In the covered way follow processions with dancing and singing. Those who are willing to offer themselves afterwards have raised their hands, turning the palms towards the sacred orb.

When the sacred orb stands over the stake, then the barbarous sacrifice is made (fig. 274). They now offer their blood in fulfilment of their vows. Some simply cut strips of flesh from their bodies. Others make holes under the sinews of the back, and by means of a thong suspend a buffalo's skull from the loop and dance about thus weighted (fig. 275). But others again pierce both breast and back, pass thongs under the skin and bind them to four posts (fig. 276). They also dance thus half-suspended in the air. But many are not satisfied with this swaying about and tearing of the skin. They also have the skin of the back cut loose and bits of stick passed through, to which thongs are fastened. Then by means of these thongs they have themselves hoisted up upon the solar stake, and there they hang high in the air until the strips of skin and little shreds of flesh give way (fig. 277). Often the poor fellows have long to dance and hang before the end comes. Frequently heavy buffalo skulls are hung on to them in order the sooner to end their agony. But at times it has also happened that a friend, thinking that the brave fellow was suffering too much, would present him with a horse, so as to hang only from its body, whereby his flesh would get torn the sooner and thus put an end to the torture.

Such was the sacred sun dance of the Dakotas.

I say "was," because it exists no longer. In the year 1883 the United States Government forbade the continuance of this ceremony.

It was; but the remembrance of the cords by which voluntary victims were suspended on the solar stake will survive in the world's history; for they represent one of the most interesting materializations of the path of the sun, that path of the sun by which the dead migrate to the next world, the path by which here brave men, so to say, offer themselves to the sun so that it may shine favourably on the fields of the tribe.

CHAPTER XXIII
THE CUNNING SPIDER

PEOPLE who, like the West African Negroes, are fond of "spinning yarns" may often pick up a myth the inner meaning of which has been forgotten, and, through their sheer delight in story-telling, will concoct from originally significant materials pleasant and entertaining fables which are entirely destitute of any deep mythological character. To me it seems that such a process of recasting has taken place on the Upper Guinea Coast, say, between Senegambia and the Niger delta. Here a remarkable group of legends has crystallized round the figure of *Nany* or *Anasi*, that is, the Spider. Many of these still bear the traces of their mythological origin, while many others betray the characteristic qualities of fanciful stories due to the lively humour of the narrator. As a good many of these may be described as really delightful "fairy tales," I may here reproduce a few of them.

I. *Spider Stories: Accra (Gold Coast)*

THE Negroes have traditions of a certain *Nany*, his artful ways and roguish tricks. Nany might justly be called the "Eulenspiegel" (Merry-Andrew) of the blacks. The Negroes have little to do except sleep by day, and come together by moonlight, squatting pretty much in a cluster before their doors. Then the old people tell the young ones the stories about Nany. These take a rare delight

THE CUNNING SPIDER

in his pranks and tricks, and wish for nothing more eagerly than the opportunity of imitating his waggeries. Of all this a few instances may here be given.

A huge black spider, called Nany, made the first men by the command of God, or rather, as the Negro puts it, Nany had to provide the raw material out of which man was made. Nany was delighted and spun material for a multitude of men, until he could do no more. Then Nany expected some thanks from the men for all the trouble he had with them. But they ran away, and a deity instructed them as to what they should do and not do.

Nany now made one more man from the little material that was left over. He was smaller than the previous lot, and Nany brought him up himself, educated and gave him his own name, Nany. This is the hero that the traditions are concerned with; how he could not live in the world without work, and so took to cheating others; how he was able to befool the deity when he had to offer him a fowl. His mother showed him how he might eat the flesh, and then put the feathers and bones together and so reproduce the form of the fowl again.

If he had to give an egg, she taught him how he was to make a hole in it, drink up the contents, fill it with earth or sand and then close up the hole again, with the assurance that he would thereby acquire even greater merit, because he was bringing such a large and heavy egg. And they relate many more such things.

THE CUNNING SPIDER

II. *Spider Stories: Accra*

WHEN the Negroes relate the following tale they imitate everything in the narrative. If Nany goes from one place to another, the speaker, too, makes a few strides. If Nany has eaten anything to his taste, cried, laughed, drunk, danced and so on, the narrator mimics it all. In the narration and representation of the following story several blacks are required, each of whom has to play a part.

Once the crops failed and there was a great hunger in the land, so that a bean cost an egg. Now Nany was aware that his neighbour had still a considerable store of beans. He was a sportsman, and when he went out in the morning he left orders that his children were to lay the beans in the sun and carefully turn them over to prevent any worms from getting at them; but they were to eat none of them till he came back, when he would share out the portions.

When the shooter was away, Nany turned up, greeted the children, and they did likewise. Nany had daubed his whole body with pitch or gum and asked leave to execute a dance before them, as he had invented a new one. The children very readily consented, and Nany began dancing and waltzing among the beans, so that many adhered to his body. When the game was over Nany showed his hands to the children, saying:

"You see plainly that I am taking nothing with me."

"No," answered the childen; after which he picked the beans from his body and gave them to his wife.

On the shooter's return the children told him that Nany had been to see them, and they showed him the dance which they had been watching. Eventually the

THE CUNNING SPIDER

shooter noticed that his beans grew less, and suspected Nany. One morning he went out and hid in the bush near his house. Then he saw how Nany stole his beans in the way described above. Thereupon he pounced upon Nany, cut off both his hands and let him go. Nany went home and hid the hands under his loincloth. He began to scold his wives for not serving the food at once, and said that in future he would no longer supply his wives, but only feed his children, at the same time ordering his children to be brought to his house and take their meals with him.

The women agreed to this and each brought her child to Nany's hut. Thereupon he shut the door, came to the children, thrust his mutilated arms in their face and threatened he would cut off their hands in the same way if they did not say they had been thoroughly well fed. The children promised to do so, and for two days remained silent. But on the third day they complained about the matter to their mothers, who took Nany by surprise and saw that he had no hands.

So they all now decided to leave Nany and look for other husbands. They all ran off, but the artful Nany got before them, hid in a bush and began to hew wood. The women as they went by greeted him without seeing who he was. Nany changed his voice, thanked them for their greeting and asked where they intended going. The women briefly related the incidents and their resolution. They also asked him whether he did not want a wife. Nany answered:

"Friends, if you take my advice you will turn back and go to your husband. I had twenty wives, but dismissed nineteen of them, finding one enough in these hard times."

Fig. 279. Prayer to the Rising Sun; Pueblo Indians, North America; after Matilda Stephenson.

THE CUNNING SPIDER

The women took their leave and went on. Nany again ran before them and gave out that he had fifty wives and sent off forty-nine. The same thing happened a third time, and then he said he had a hundred wives and sent ninety-nine away.

Thereupon the women consulted together and decided at last to ask the deity for advice. This Nany also overheard, and spoke in the bush, where he lay hid, just like the deity. The end of it all was that the women went back to their husband's house.

But he was here also before them, and would not let them again enter his hut until they had consented to grant Nany advantageous conditions.

III. *Spider Story: Accra*

"SHALL I tell you a story or not?"

"We are ready to answer."*

Was that not a great famine when there was nothing to eat, not a mouthful, and the hens and the cock, in desperate straits, discovered one more nut on the dunghill, and our Spider-man and Spider-son, driven by want, also went about looking for nuts? Then after a long search Spider-son had discovered and cracked a nut, when the kernel dropped into a rat-hole. Spiderkin ran after to fetch it out, and, before he was aware of it, found himself in the underworld surrounded by three ghostly dwarfs—a red, a white, and a black.

Their hair fell down over the face, their fingernails had

---

* These tales are usually related to the people assembled in the market-place by a story-teller who goes his rounds. He always puts questions, to which the audience seated round about answers in chorus and in the sense already indicated by the form of the question. The first two lines of the present narrative represent the ever-recurring first question and the first answer in such entertainments.

THE CUNNING SPIDER

become claws, and they had never yet washed themselves. Little Spider was shocked, but when they inquired what business he had there, he told his tale. Thereupon the spirits fetched a fine large yam, but bade him put the skin only on the fire and throw the yam itself on the dunghill. Little Spider did so and found the skin the best eating. When he had eaten and was quite satisfied, the spirits gave him a whole load of yam roots and taught him this little song:

The narrator sings:

> White Spirit, hoho!
> Red Spirit, hoho!
> Black Spirit, hoho!

The audience sing:

> If my head o'ertops it,
> What then will happen?
> The head away he throws;
> The foot away he throws;
> The head away he throws;
> Thou, thou offendest the great gods.

Then they conducted Little Spider back again, but bade him never to sing the song and teach it to nobody, and always to eat the yams in the prescribed way. Little Spider did so, and at home there was great rejoicing over the yams. When that load was consumed, Little Spider fetched a second, and so on.

Now, however, Spider-man wanted to know whence Little Spider brought the yams. But he dreaded his father's temper, and persistently refused all information.

Then his father, when it came once more to another, a fifth, expedition, got up in the night, took Little Spider's sack, pulled out the clothes, put ashes in, and moreover made a little hole at the bottom of the sack. Thus he

THE CUNNING SPIDER

found the spoor of the ashes along the way, and next time made up his mind to go.

At sight of the three spirits, he began to bully them:

"Ho! what sort of manners are these? You dirty, lubberly fellows, come here and let me cut your hair and wash you."

And in this way he went on squabbling with them, until they asked what he actually wanted, and gave him some yams to cook. He, however, did nothing as he was told, but put the yams in the pot and threw away the skins. But the roots did not get soft; so the spirits rallied him for a fool, and told him to do it differently, whereupon the yams became eatable.

Finally, they taught him this song:

> White Spirit, hoho!
> Red Spirit, hoho!
> Black Spirit, hoho!
>
> If the head should o'ertop it
> What will happen?
> The head away he throws;
> The foot away he throws;
> The head away he throws;
> Thou, thou offendest the great gods!

But as they were still bidding him neither to sing nor to teach it to anyone, and had not yet quite done speaking, Spider-man began to sing. Being taken to task for this, he said he was singing one of his native songs. But he had scarcely gone a little farther when he began again. But suddenly something falls from above; Spider-man is dashed down. Here lies his head, here a hand, there a foot; Spider-man is dead. But he still goes on singing. Then says the White Spirit to the others:

"He is a poor knave; let us make him alive again."

THE CUNNING SPIDER

Then the spirits took pity on him, made him alive again, and once more threatened him. But scarcely had he come to himself when he began to sing again. Then they gave him a sound thrashing and let him go empty-handed.

So he came home in shame and disgrace, and there the conduct of Father-Spider was condemned, and that of Little Spider became the rule, namely:

"When you come to a strange town you must not abuse the customs of the inhabitants, but conform to them."

IV. *Spider Story: Accra*

ONCE it happened that Spider tilled a piece of land for the reigning King, for which he was to receive an ox in payment, since already in those days, as at present, the principle ruled that, "for nothing there is nothing but death." Spider was a rogue, and he remembered that "eating for oneself makes fat." He accordingly took careful steps to prevent any uninvited guests from being present at the coming feast. Hence, he drove the fatted beast to a lonely place, where the preparations could be made and the feast itself pass off without danger of disturbance from intruders. But lo! As he was about to lay the horned animal on the ground and deal it the death-stroke, there appeared a many-eyed monster. Spider was startled at the strange sight, let the beast go and took to flight.

But being called back and encouraged by the many-eyed creature, Spider returned and was compelled by him to kill the ox and prepare the meal. Spider obeyed the orders loyally, whether willingly or not; he had just got ready one part of the entertainment, and was already inhaling the warm fragrance of the smoking viands with

THE CUNNING SPIDER

inward relish, when the many-eyed beast shouted the word, "Tamoku," at which Spider sank dead on the ground. Then the murderer fell at once on the food and devoured what had been prepared and served up by the other's toil and culinary art. But after finishing the repast the many-eyed monster, by another magic word, called back to life the inanimate Spider.

So it happened the second and the third time—Spider cooking, hoping, and sinking into the night of death. Then at last the ill-used spider complained of his sufferings to a little old woman who, being experienced in such magic tricks, was able to give counsel and help. She knew of a counter-spell against the death-bringing "Tamoku," and told Spider to cry out, "Tomodso," as soon as the many-eyed uttered the fatal "Tamoku" at the festive table.

Spider did as the old woman bade him, and behold! "Tamoku" had no longer its usual efficacy. On the contrary, at the sound of the magic word, "Tomodso," the many-eyed monster fell dead, as if struck by a flash of lightning.

Now Spider fell to vigorously, and tried his best to indemnify himself for the privations he had hitherto endured. After doing full justice to the fare, he took the lifeless beast and laid it on the fire. Then its flesh took on such a beautiful white colour from the roasting that Spider was seized with the fancy to taste it. But, alas! that same moment his tongue became so thick and so long that he could not bear it.

'What shall I do?" asked the now big-tongued Spider.

He reflected long over the matter; and see, this time also his artfulness did not leave him in the lurch. As the King's messenger or herald, he summoned all the people

Fig. 280. Iroquois display of thanks towards the Great Spirit. After Erminnie A. Smith. This drawing should show us how the Solar ceremonies appeared before the Christian period, that is, before the Indians had introduced the "Great Spirit" into their religion.

THE CUNNING SPIDER

and proclaimed a pretended royal decree to the effect that everybody was to repair to the sea and there take a bath in the waves. But before doing this each person had to lay his tongue on the beach, and after the bath take it up again.

They went in company with the King's herald to the appointed place the lagoon. All laid their tongues on the bank and took to the water. While they were all thus busy with themselves and their washing, Spider seized his favourable opportunity to bring off a stroke of genius. He let his eyes range over the row of tongues, on the look out for the finest, daintiest and most delicate. As such he recognized that of the pig, which he selected and appropriated to himself without more ado, and thereby became a liar and a thief. In its place he put his own big and shapeless tongue. Then he went off as if nothing further had happened.

When all was over the bathers came out of the water and groped about for their tongues. All found their own except the pig, for whom nothing remained in the end save the long thick one. This he had to take "for better for worse," thinking to himself that "an ugly tongue is better than no tongue at all," although it looked as if henceforth he would have to feed only on muck. The pig went off and has done so to this day.

Moral: "What one loses, another gains."

Or: "If you have anything you won't share with your like, then you must share it with the beasts."

THE CUNNING SPIDER

V. *A Spider Story: Temne*

THE Spider proposed to the Wild-Goat that they should go hunting together. She was willing, and Spider brought a noose with him. In the wood Spider found a stone which had grown a beard, ("This is really the goat's net") and exclaimed: "O wonder! a stone with a beard."

Scarcely had Spider said this when he fell down and lay there, and did not wake till the evening. This was what led to his deceitful conduct towards his comrade whom he afterwards ensnared.

So he again invited the Wild-Goat to accompany him to the hunt, and as they drew near the same place he told her to go a little ahead and wait for him while he relieved himself. When they again came to the stone, Spider said: "Now come on."

But the Wild-Goat replied: "See how the stone has got a beard!"

Scarcely was the remark made when down fell the Wild-Goat, and Spider took her up, brought her home and devoured her with his children.

When the Wild-Goat was devoured, Spider invited the Trak-an (a species of antelope) to the hunt. Near the stone he again requested the Trak-an to go on as far as the stone as he wanted to make water. When he rejoined the Trak-an at the appointed place, she said: "Look, Spider, how the stone has got a beard!"

The Trak-an fell down; Spider picked her up and brought her home, where he and his children consumed her flesh.

Spider did the same with the Antelope. But when he went to work with the Wild-Ox in the same way, the Fillentamba was surprised, as it had well noticed that

THE CUNNING SPIDER

the animals who went out hunting with Spider never returned. So Fillentamba followed unseen and witnessed the scene at the stone, how the Wild-Ox said: "See what a beard the stone has got!" how Spider and his children divided the animal and brought it home. Fillentamba also ran home and told it to all his comrades.

Then Spider also invited Fillentamba to the hunt. Fillentamba consented, and as usual Spider sent him ahead. But when Spider came to the stone Fillentamba did not utter the magic word. Spider tried to induce him to say it, but he avoided the charmed response. Then at last both together said the word, and both fell down senseless. It was in the morning, and they woke again in the evening. As soon as he was awake Spider again endeavoured to lead the conversation up to the same subject. Thereupon Fillentamba asked:

"What shall I say?"

Spider replied: "Say, the stone has got a beard."

Scarcely had Spider uttered the word when down he fell. But Fillentamba did not repeat it after him. He ran home and warned everybody not to utter the word at the stone, for if they did they would fall into the hands of Spider, who would devour them.

VI. *A Spider Story: Temne*

A KING was careful about his cows. Spider saw them, and noticing a particularly large one, invited Tamba (a mystic personage) to join him in eating it. Tamba was willing enough, but did not know how it was to be managed. But Spider said he knew, and off they went together to where the herd was grazing. Here they met the ant-eater, who was just digging a hole in the ground. Spider said to him that it would be a bad business for

THE CUNNING SPIDER

him if any of the King's cows trod in the hole. Then the ant-eater was frightened, and began to fill up the hole again. But as he was tired he soon fell asleep. Thereupon Spider caught the big cow and led her into the hole, and then went back to the town. Meanwhile the King said to his people that it was getting dark, and they should look after the cows. They went out to bring them in. But one of them they found in the hole, with only her head looking out. Then they ran off to the King and told him that one of the cows was in a pit and dying. Then the King called his people together to get the cow out.

Here the myth relates in detail the palaver which the King held when they came upon the cow. The ant-eater was summoned and examined, Spider throwing in a word between, and the sentence was:

"As the ant-eater has killed the King's cow, let himself be killed."

For it was conclusive that the ant-eater had dug the pit.

The ant-eater was buried in the pit in which the cow had died. In return for the pains he had taken to find out the murderer of the cow, Spider received one of the legs. When all had gone back to the town, Spider fetched Tamba, who was to help him in searching for the ant-eater, digging him out and taking him home. With Tamba he shared the flesh, which was all consumed in a moon.

Now one evening, when the King's people had gone to bed, the two repaired to the place where they found the King's cattle tethered. Then Spider took his medicine, stroked a big cow and said: "Cow, break wind; Cow, break wind!"

The cow did so, and both slipped into the belly of the animal! Spider showed Tamba the heart, and warned him from cutting there. Then Spider cut out pieces of flesh,

THE CUNNING SPIDER

and Tamba put them into the basket they had brought with them. Then Spider again called upon the cow to break wind, and thus they again got out of her body. Four days they lived on the flesh, and then they both again went off for the same purpose.

As before, they got into the cow. But this time Tamba cut and severed the heart-strings, so that the cow fell dead to the ground. Now they did not know what to do. Tamba got into the rectum, and the King's people reported the death of the cow.

When the men began to cut up the beast, Spider cried out: "Be careful not to hurt me!"

The people were frightened and reported it to the King, who came himself and bade them to go on cutting in the same place. But Spider had crept to another place. When the people at last reached him they drew him out with his basket. Then he was bound and was to be beaten for having killed the best of the King's cattle, but Spider cried out:

"I and Tamba were together; I and Tamba were together."

"Who is Tamba?" they asked.

"I don't know whence he came," said Spider.

The King did not believe him, Tamba being all the time in the rectum. This the people cut out in order to clean it in the river, and when they shook out its contents Tamba also tumbled out and climbed unnoticed on to the other bank. Now he complained that the people with their spurting had covered him with cowdung. So the King, to appease him, presented him with a new dress.

Now, however, Spider maintained at the palaver that Tamba had really taken part in the theft. Thereupon his wife was called in order to question her, and she certainly

THE CUNNING SPIDER

admitted that Tamba had not been at home since yesterday morning. He, however, was able to justify himself
by pointing out that had he been present, he, too, must
have been found in the cow.

Then sentence was pronounced on Spider, who was
bound to a palm-tree and "dusted" with palm-branches;
and that is how he has got so many legs. When he had
been thrashed enough, the King let him off. After all this
he fell ill, but recovered, and now had many legs. Then
he ran away to the woods.

VII. *A Spider Story: Nigerland*

SOME Asbon people brought a horse of the Asbon breed
to sell it. But the price being very high this was not so
easy. The owner of the horse said: "This horse of mine
is not to be bought with money, but only with the hand
of a woman."

People came, questioned the owner and said to him:
"What is the price of your horse?"

He replied: "As to the price of my horse, I have to
say that it can be bought only with the hand of a woman."

The people said: "Ho, ho! The price of this horse of
yours is too high. Who is going to buy it?"

A young fellow came along, questioned the owner and
said: "What does it cost?"

He told him it could only be bought with the hand of
a woman.

The young fellow said: "Many thanks; I cannot buy
the horse," and went off.

And another youth, his comrade, came; he knew that
his mother would do anything for him that he wished.
He came, questioned the owner and said: "How much
for the horse?"

THE CUNNING SPIDER

He answered: "If you could go and cut off your mother's hand and bring it to me, I would give you the horse."

The youth said: "All right."

Then he went to his mother to ask her, and said: "Ah, my mother! Buy me this horse with your hand."

She said: "All right; go and fetch a knife and cut it off."

The youth went, brought a knife, and cut off his mother's hand and gave it to the owner of the horse. The owner gave him the horse, and the youth immediately let it loose.

Three days after, he said to his mother: "I want to see the place where the land of the world comes to an end."

His mother said: "All right"; and his father also. All said: "All right; may God bring you safe back."

The boy said to his horse: "Look at me; with my mother's hand I have bought thee. Carry me to the place where the world's end is."

He got everything ready, put on the saddle, mounted the horse and rode off.

As he trotted along, he met his friend Spider, who asked him: "Ah, child, whither goest thou?"

He answered: "I want to see the world's end."

Spider said: "May I follow you?"

He said: "Follow me."

Spider took his seat on a twig or leaf of a tree.

In this way the two jogged along, farther and farther, till they came to a place where there was no more land. Here they saw in the distance a woman who was a witch. They saw her, but she did not see them and did something unseemly. The young man and Spider came to her place and greeted her. She accepted the greeting and said to them: "Is it well with you, my children?"

They said: "Quite well."

She said to them: "Come, let us go to my house."

THE CUNNING SPIDER

They said: "We are willing."

They travelled on to where were neither land nor trees, nothing but wind, nothing but water, nothing but a dark place. They alighted at the witch's house. In the evening she looked for the cock, to kill him; but he ran out and hid in the grass. She searched and searched, but could not find him. She cooked the meal, brought it to the youth and Spider, and said to them: "There is my food; eat!"

They said: "All right."

The youth said: "I don't like this food."

Spider said: "There is no help for it; let us eat."

They sat down and ate.

Spider had an iron stick. When they had eaten the meal and were done, they went to sleep. In the middle of the night the witch took a knife and sharpened it. The cock crowed and said,

"Look out; she is coming; get ready."

The youth understood the language of the cock.

The witch said: "Where is the cock? I have looked for him all day long but cannot find him."

She looked under the bed; stretched her hand under it and felt for him, but could not find him. She sat up again, again took the knife, and while she was sharpening it she sang: "Just eat flesh! just eat flesh!"

Again the cock crew and said: "Look, there she comes."

The woman, that is the witch, understood the language of the cock. Thrice the cock crew before it began to dawn. She greeted the youth and asked: "Have you slept well?"

Then she questioned them saying: "Did you notice yesterday that I did something unseemly?"

Spider answered and said: "I saw it."

THE CUNNING SPIDER

The witch was ashamed, went and looked for the cock and said: "If I don't kill this youth and the Spider they will bring the news to their country."

She looked for the cock, caught and killed him, then cooked and brought him to the Spider and the youth. When they had eaten and gone to bed, Spider said to the youth: "Be on your guard to-night."

The youth said: "All right."

Spider took his iron stick and laid it close by his side. After he had slept a little, he got up, took his stick, and so took his seat in the night by the entrance. The woman got ready; she came to kill the youth and Spider and eat them. She sharpened her knife as she sang: "Do thou eat flesh! Do thou eat flesh!"

Spider was on the alert and said: "Look, there she comes!"

He took his iron stick and placed himself near the entrance. The witch came softly, softly by. Spider took the iron stick. The witch thrust her head into the room. Spider broke her head with the iron stick.

But the witch went back to her room and licked off the blood from her whole body. After waiting a little, she said: "Now they are asleep."

She sharpened her knife as before; she came gently, gently along; then Spider heard her. She put her head into the room; Spider broke her head with the iron stick. The witch returned to her room and, as before, licked up the blood.

Three times the two contended in this way, the witch and Spider all the night long until the day dawned. Then said Spider to his friend: "Look out, this woman is a witch; all night long I have been breaking her head."

The youth said: "Is that so?"

Spider said: "Yes, it is true."

THE CUNNING SPIDER

The youth said: "Let us get ready; in the morning we will go back to our country."

Spider said: "All right."

The woman came and said to them: "Have you slept well?"

Spider answered: "Quite well."

After greeting her they said to her: "To-day we shall go back to our country."

She said: "All right."

The youth took razors and tied them to the horse's tail. His whole tail was nothing but razors. The youth put on the saddle, made everything ready and mounted the horse. They went off.

The woman changed herself into a witch. She wanted to get hold of the young man. She kept trying to seize the horse's tail, but the razors cut through her hands. She stopped and licked up the blood. Again she came along like the wind and said: "Stop before the mouth of this fire. I shall catch and eat you."

The youth and Spider hastened and came to a place of hot water, which was boiling hard. The youth said to his horse: "Rescue me from this hot water, for I have bought you with my mother's hand."

The horse made a mighty leap, and so in one bound cleared the whole hot-water lake. Spider sat up, but both he and his leaf-horse fell into the water. The youth turned quickly back and drew them out.

The witch came alone to the hot water. She came and overtook them. She grasped at the tail of the youth's horse, but when the razors gashed her she let it go, stopped and licked up the blood. The youth and Spider both ran on and came to a fire, which poured down like water.

THE CUNNING SPIDER

The witch said to them: "Stop there; I shall overtake and eat you."

The youth said: "Save me from this fire. With my mother's hand I have bought thee."

The youth applied the whip; the steed galloped on and cleared the whole lake. Spider he took with him.

When they had got over the lake, the woman came along like the wind. She crossed the fiery lake, overtook the youth and Spider and grasped at the horse's tail. But the razors again gashed her hands. She halted and licked up the blood.

The youth and Spider galloped on and came to a lake of cold water. Then said the youth to his horse: "Save me from this water; with my mother's hand I have bought thee."

And when he lashed the horse and took up Spider, they crossed over the lake.

The witch said to herself: "Why should I worry myself any longer? It will be better for me to go home."

She said: "I shall never catch them."

She went back to her town.

After crossing the first and the second lake, the youth and Spider came to a place where was land once more, and so they journeyed on dry ground.

Spider went to the place which he liked best.

The youth also came to his town, and went to his mother's house. When his father and his mother and his sisters and brothers saw him, they were greatly delighted; for their son had really come back from the world's end.

Thus it is, and it is finished. The history of the horse of the Asbon breed, of the youth, of Spider, and also of the witch has come to an end.

THE CUNNING SPIDER

As the spider stories are told to-day, they should be regarded as nothing more than pleasant little popular tales. As such they are at once characterized by the whole artless way in which they are set forth, especially the last story in which, as in most of the others, Spider figures as an artful young person.

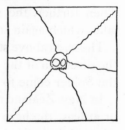

Fig. 281. The Juju Nkali; a native drawing. This is intended to represent the Spider-god and the Juju Nkali pole. Compare fig. 273. Juju Nkali is supposed to dwell as a spider in the sun. To make it clearer, the Bagos point to a spider in its web and to the radiant midday sun.

It is a somewhat different matter when we consider the origin of these narratives. Then we are confronted above all things with the incident of the swallowing and next with that of the nocturnal conflict, as distinctive indications. When Spider breaks the witch's head at night-time, when her blood flows round about, we are decidedly reminded of Maui, who contends with the fire-god, or with other solar deities, who rise out of a blood-bath in the morning. And to all this is added the incident in the Hausa variant last produced, where Spider journeys to the horizon, which is the land of darkness (the night or the underworld). During this night, and indeed usually towards dawn, the cock crows, always a sign of the victory of the sun in the East.

To elucidate fig. 281 and the Juju Nkali: the picture of the spider's web and of the sun with its rays.

371

THE CUNNING SPIDER

Then further, the sun, or the spider, crosses the fiery lake, which again suggests the sunrise.

These, as above stated, are late survivals, which betray the direction of the earlier origins. But how exactly does the Spider come to represent the sun?

In New Zealand there is a sun-god who is also a spider, or at least the hero climbs by a spider's thread up to the sun and from the sun down again.

Then we again have the sun which guides the souls to the next world, the sun being this time represented as a thievish witch in the middle of a spider's web in which it captures the souls of mortals who thereupon die. This last is a myth of the Bagos (West Africa) related to me by the missionary Keil. It solves the whole problem. The pictures are not unlike:

In the form of rays the sun emits its sea of light; in the form of rays the spider, too, weaves its web. Thus the slender threads of the spider become solar rays and the sun becomes the spider which in artful ways ensnares the souls of mortals.

The solar myth, however, became a nursery tale. Reflect a little whether you, too, may not perhaps remember some German story which had its origin in the solar mythology! With this we conclude.

So is it, and now it is ended, as the African story-teller would say.

CHAPTER XXIV
ORIGIN OF THE WORLD, FALL OF THE SKY, THE FLOOD

RIGHTLY understood, the development of the solar mythology amongst primitive peoples inplies a certain scientific inquiry or interpretation of outward phenomena. The whole of this mythology suggests theories. In the opinion of these men all changes in nature are dependent, not, indeed, on fixed natural laws but on the action of certain deities. Now, when we hear that these rude tribes, too, have their sagas, that is, notions regarding the origin of the world, and so on, we may at once take it for granted that everything turns on assumptions which stand in some definite relation to the solar myths. This is specially the case when we hear of sundry downfalls of the sky.

Of the comparatively few African creation stories we shall first endeavour to understand a great Yoruba myth, and then a few lesser ones. Afterwards we shall seek for parallels in other lands.

The Yoruba Creation Myth

THE Yorubas have two celestial gods, Olorun and Obatala. Olorun is the Sky-god, who is too far away, too indifferent and too great to trouble himself about mortals. His name means "Owner of the Sky"; but A. B. Ellis has not noticed that he is also called "Owner of the Sun," since "orun" means both sky and sun. Olorun has no priests; of him no image is made, nor are there any temples of Olorun. Only rarely, when all the other gods have refused their aid, is he invoked by the Yorubas. One may say that Olorun lives more in familiar expressions than in myths or worship, just like "Heaven," the name of which we also often use, perhaps misuse or misapply. Nor is he all-powerful, since a proverb says: "A man cannot cause rain to fall, and Olorun cannot give you a child."

For this is one of Obatala's functions, as each god has his own duties.

Obatala is the chief god of the Yorubas. The name means "Lord of the White Cloth," white being the colour sacred to him. White are his temples, his images, his amulets; his priests, attendants and worshippers always wear white clothes. Obatala, say the priests, was made by Olorun, who handed over to him the world and the firmament, while he himself withdrew. Hence, if Obatala is also a sky-god, he is still a more anthropomorphic conception than Olorun. According to a myth which, however, does not appear to be general, Obatala made the first man and woman out of clay, and all are agreed that he sends the children.

Odudua or Odua is the chief goddess of the Yorubas. She is "The mother who receives."

Her name comes from *do*, that is, "to be black," and *dudo* means "black." The Negroes consider a black skin a great beauty and far superior to one of the ordinary cigar-colour. Odudua is always represented as a woman sitting down and nursing a child. She is the wife of Obatala, but she was coeval with Olorun, and not made by him as was her husband. Other natives, however, believe that she had her birth in Ife; but this is altogether

ORIGIN OF THE WORLD

a secondary myth. Odudua represents the earth, and is married to the anthropomorphic sky-god. Obatala and Odudua, or Heaven and Earth, resemble, say the priests, two large closed calabashes which, when once shut, can never be opened. This is symbolized in the temples by two whitened saucer-shaped calabashes, placed tightly one over the other, and so presenting the appearance of a flattened sphere. The upper one represents the vault of heaven, and the lower one the earth which is closely joined to it at the horizon.

According to a widespread myth Odudua is blind. In the beginning of the world she and Obatala were shut up in darkness in a large closed calabash, Obatala being in the upper part and Odudua in the lower.

The myth does not state how they came to be in this situation, but can only tell us that they long remained there, cramped, hungry and uncomfortable. Then Odu-

Fig. 282. Warrior of the Molucca Islands, with wooden shield; the shield as shown from one side. After Kukenthal.

dua began complaining, blaming her husband for the confinement; and a violent quarrel ensued, in the course of which, in a frenzy of rage, Obatala tore out her eyes because she would not bridle her tongue. Then Odudua cursed him, saying: "Naught shalt thou eat but snails in future." This is the reason why snails are now offered to Obatala.

As the myth does not make Odudua recover her sight

ORIGIN OF THE WORLD

she must be supposed to have remained sightless, but no native regards her as being blind.

Odudua is, moreover, the Goddess of Love, and many stories are told of her adventures and amours. Her chief temple is in Ado, the principal town of the State of the same name situated about fifteen miles to the north of Badagri. The selection of the place is explained by a long story of Odudua's love for a hunter. Before leaving him she promised good fortune to him and all others who might come and dwell in the favoured spot where she had passed so many happy hours.

Before this *liaison* with the hunter, Odudua had presented her husband with a boy named Aganju and a girl called Yemaja. The name Aganju means uninhabited tract of country, wilderness, plain, but according to Burton, the sky; and Yemaja, "Mother of Fish." The offspring of the union of Heaven and Earth may thus be said to represent Land and Water. Yemaja is the goddess of brooks and streams, and presides over ordeals by water. She is represented by a female figure, yellow in colour, wearing blue beads and white garments. The worship of Aganju seems to have fallen into disuse; but he was formerly worshipped in an open space before the King's residence in Oyo.

Yemaja married her brother Aganju, and bore a son named Orungan. This name is compounded of *orun*, sky, and *gan* (from *ga*), to be high, and appears to mean: "In the Heights of the Sky." It seems to represent the open space between the sky and the earth. The offspring of Land and Water would thus be what we call the Atmosphere. Orungan loved his mother passionately, but once they had a quarrel and she ran away.* Orungan rushed

* Story condensed.

ORIGIN OF THE WORLD

after her, and was just stretching out his hand to seize her when she fell backwards to the ground.

Then her body immediately began to swell in a fearful manner; two streams of water gushed from her breasts and her abdomen burst open. The streams joined and formed a lagoon. From her disruptured body sprang fifteen deities:

DADO. God of Vegetables.

SHANGO. God of Lightning.

OGUN. God of Iron and War.

OLOKUN. God of the Sea.

OLOSO. Goddess of the Lagoon Olosa.

OYA. Goddess of the River Niger.

OSHUN. Goddess of the River Oshun.

OBA. Goddess of the River Oba.

ORISHA OKO. God of Agriculture.

OSHOSI. God of Hunters.

Fig. 283. Dayak with widened wooden shield, tarche; Borneo. From a photograph by Kukenthal.

OKE. God of Mountains.

AJE SHALUGA. God of Wealth.

SHANKPANNA. God of Small-pox.

ORUN. The Sun.

OSHU. The Moon.

To commemorate this event, a town which was given the name of Ife (distension, enlargement or swelling up), was built on the spot where Yemaja's body burst open. The place where her body fell used to be shown, and

377

probably still is; but the town was destroyed in 1882 by the Ibadans.

It is noteworthy that not all the gods sprang from Yemaja's body.

In what cycle of ideas, in what notions has this creation story originated?

If we consider that the assignment of these definite functions and spheres of activity is due to some particular faculty for composing myths existing within the single area of Yoruba; that it is thus less a question of the kind of gods than of the structure and salient features of the myths themselves; and that in this very area of Yoruba we have recognized the great significance of Shango—of Shango the Sun-god—it will not be difficult herein to detect three important ideas which recur in other mythological areas. These should be compared with the Yoruba myth, since they afford a clue to our answer to the question: "What is the origin of the creation story?" Here we have three points: (1) The position of Obatala and Odudua, lying one beneath the other in the closed calabash; (2) the pursuit by Orungan; (3) the backward fall of Yemaja on the ground.

For the pursuit of Yemaja by Orungan Yoruba itself presents a parallel case. In the same furious way Oya is pursued by Shango. Here also the sun has a direct relation to the myths of the theft of fire, and hence to the myth according to which Maui, for instance, is pursued by the underground god. This idea thus leads us to the group of solar myths.

Once we arrive at the conjecture that here, too, the sequence of the solar myths has to be investigated, it is no longer difficult to discover the answer to our question. In the Kammapa story the people also lie at first squeezed closely together in Kammapa's belly, so closely that the sword of Hubuane or Litaolane as he frees himself—that is, the rays of the rising sun—has to be carefully used in forcing a way through, since he does not wish to hurt the thousands of them.

That is the first point. Obatala and Odudua are in the

Fig. 284. Warrior of Wetter Island, Banda Sea; after Jacobsen. The position of the shield, front view, below has been corrected from the original. Jacobsen's treatment is wrong.

calabash similarly pressed close together one on the other. That is, the sky lies in the darkness on the earth. Then Obatala tears out Odudua's eyes. That is the sun rises on high.

Thus in the closely pressed position of Obatala and Odudua is represented the darkness of night, and then the rising sun follows logically. The same idea is presented

ORIGIN OF THE WORLD

by an Akwapim saga, according to which in the olden time the sky was much nearer the earth than at present. When anyone wanted to fish he had only to thrust a stick into the *Nyankupong*—the embodiment of Nyam, the sky—and lo! out came fish, and they fell like rain-drops, only larger, on the earth. After such a rain of fish, the fisher had nothing more to do but pick them up. But what happened? A woman once was pounding *fufu* in a mortar but could not manage very well, as there was not room enough over her. So she said to Nyankupong: "Just lift yourself a little, I have not room enough for a fufu pestle."

Nyankupong obeyed, and asked: "So far?"

"No," said she, "still farther."

So he did three times; at last she bade him stop. In this way it came about that Nyankupong got so far from the surface of the earth that, when anyone calls, he hardly hears any longer, and as to the fish, they are now very scarce. But for that woman the people would still be able to get fish for nothing.

The Ova-Herero relate how many, many years ago, owing to the increasing godlessness of men, the "Great" in heaven (Eyuru) caused the sky to fall down on the earth, in consequence of which nearly all lost their lives; a few only survived. These few, who had remained alive, finding the sky weighing very heavy on the earth, in their distress took a black sheep and offered it to the Great in heaven. Then these decided to spare the last men, and drew the sky back again, and so they keep it to the present day. But since that time nobody can any longer ascend into heaven. For the Great in heaven have appointed guards who have to keep watch where heaven and earth join together. These sentinels are huge one-eyed giants.

ORIGIN OF THE WORLD

Thus the great giants keep watch where Heaven and Earth are united, that is, where the sun rises and sets. And as they are one-eyed, no doubt their relation to the solar myth is at once recognized. To meet them thus

Fig. 285. Archer, Aru Islands, south-west of New Guinea; with bow shield. From an original sketch.

again in the myth of day and night in this region (Damaraland) is singularly attractive.

The Kangas and Loangos have likewise a tradition about a collapse of the sky, which brought about a universal destruction of mankind. But when they had all been killed the deity created new men.

Let us now turn to Oceania, and examine the creation story of these natives.

In contrast to Africa, Oceania presents sublime, magnificent, all-penetrating, all-embracing cosmogonies. These

ORIGIN OF THE WORLD

I cannot here analyse, but will confine myself to discussing some parts of them—the more important. Let us open the inquiry by recalling the two chief features of the Yoruba myth—the closely-pressed position of Obatala and Odudua, and Yemaja's fall to the ground.

As the two gods, Obatala and Odudua, lie squeezed together in the calabash Obatala tears out his consort's eyes, that is the sun rises on high, the sky is lifted, it is daylight. So, too, in the beginning Tangaroa lay in the egg. He bursts the shell and there is day. Thus the egg is identical with the calabash. The process of daybreak presents itself in the same form in the mythologies of Oceania and Africa. Why the egg should be specially appropriate for this particular myth I need scarcely stop to inquire.

In Africa we passed from this version to the myth of the lifting of the sky. In New Zealand Rangi and Papa—Heaven and Earth—lie at first closely pressed one on the other; their children are enveloped in darkness, and consult how to remedy matters. Tamakanenga (others say Maui) proposes to kill the parents. But Tane-matua, god of the woods, advises only to separate them. This proposal is accepted, and Tane thrusts head and feet against his mother, raises his father with his back, and so heaven and earth get separated.

That Tane-matua, god of the trees, is the separator, is peculiarly interesting, because the height of the trees and the bushes plays a special part in the myths of the other islands, and also because the Wakamba myth relates how the sun having come too near to a tree the sky was lifted higher up.

So also in Rarotonga we learn how the sky lay so near the earth that the people could only crawl about. Then

a man propped it up by jerks, first to the height of the
teve-plant (four feet), then up to that of the kauariki-tree
(a sycamore), then to the tops of the mountains, and then
to the present height of the sky. Ellis found the same

Fig. 286. Warriors with bow shield, Angriffs-
hafen, German New Guinea; after Finsch.
Below is the shield showing the inner side.
After the original.

myth in Tahiti, where the man was the god Rua. In Samoa
also the plants lift up the sky.

In Samoa Turner discovered a version of the myth which
is strikingly like that of Akwapim. In the beginning the
sky lay close down on the earth. Then came a man to a

woman asking for a drink of water. He said he also wanted to lift the sky higher up.

"Lift it first on high," said she.

He did so.

"Is it enough?"he asked.

"No, still a little higher!"

Then the man raised it still higher.

The Motu islanders also report that in the beginning the sky lay on the earth. But a man who was angry at the wrangling of his wives cut through the reed that kept the sky and the earth together, so that the former rose higher, the latter sank down. In the Gilbert Islands the god Rigi has raised the sky on high in order to make existence possible for men and animals.

From a general survey of the whole, it results that in the myths concerning the origin and the destruction of the world, we should see nothing more than variants of those ideas with which we have long been familiar from the solar mythology. The sunrise becomes changed to a story of the origin of the world, so that the origin of the world is nothing more than the first sunrise. On the other hand, the sunset is in like manner introduced as a single great event, as a first great going down of the sun in the remote past.

When we have once advanced to a recognition of this view, we get puzzled when we hear of other similar great events which are described as historical. If the origin of the world is nothing more than the first sunrise, and the famous widespread saga of the collapse of the sky merely a very intelligible interpretation of the sunset incident, then we should be fully justified in doubting whether the widespread deluge myth is really to be re-garded as a historic reminiscence, and to be forthwith brought into association with the Biblical tradition. The doubts are indeed justified. When we consider the deluge myth in connexion with the other solar myths, we are struck by its harmony with this group. In North-West America, when Yely the Raven has stolen the sun from his uncle, he (the uncle) lets the water rise so high that the Raven is nearly drowned and has to hold on by his claws to the vault of heaven. That is a decided sunrise myth, in which the flood means nothing more than the sea in which the sun rises or sets. We shall hear the same, as already said, about Maui in the next chapter.

This experience already makes us cautious. It teaches us how dangerous it is to bring narratives from Holy Writ into association with the sagas of primitive peoples.

So we come to the last chapter on solar myths.

Now for the theft of fire!

CHAPTER XXV
THE THEFT OF FIRE

PRETTY well amongst all peoples who have views about the solar world we meet with the Prometheus saga, a myth which ascribes the acquisition of fire to some god or other. Here follow a few examples.

I. *Polynesian Version: Mangala Island*
(after Gill)

IN the underworld (Avaiki) a famous son, Maui, was born to Ro and his wife Buataranga. In his early youth Maui was stationed as one of the guards of our upper world where mortals live.

Like the other inhabitants of the world, he lived on uncooked food. Once his mother Buataranga visited her son; but she always ate alone from a basket which she had brought with her from the underworld. One day as she slept Maui peeped into her basket and discovered cooked food. On tasting it, he found that it was far superior to the raw food to which he was accustomed. This food came from the underworld, consequently the secret of fire must be there. To the underworld, the home of his parents, he wanted to descend and acquire this knowledge, so that henceforth he might always enjoy the luxury of cooked food.

Next day when Buataranga got ready to descend into Avaiki (the nether world), Maui followed her unnoticed through the bush. This was not difficult, because she

THE THEFT OF FIRE

always came and went by the same way. Spying through the tall sedge he saw his mother stopping before a black rock, which she thus addressed:

> Buataranga, advance with thy body through this cleft,
> To her like unto the rainbow must obedience be,
> As two dark clouds disappear before the dawn,
> Open, open my way to the underworld, you fierce ones.

At these words the rock opened and Buataranga stepped down. Maui carefully noticed these magic words, and without delay took the road to Tane, owner of some wonderful pigeons, and urgently begged him to let him have one. But Maui did not like the pigeon offered to him, and at once returned it to the owner. A better pigeon was then produced for the exacting borrower; but this, too, was declined. None would satisfy Maui except *Akaotu*, or "Fearless," a red pigeon specially valued by Tane. She was so tame that she knew her name, and whithersoever she might fly was always sure to return to her master. Tane, who was most reluctant to part with his darling, exacted from Maui the promise that he would let him have the pigeon back uninjured.

Now Maui, taking his red pigeon with him, wafted himself through the air to the place where his mother had gone down. At the magic words which he had overheard, to his great joy, the rock parted, and letting the pigeon down he descended. Some assure us that Maui changed himself into a stinging fly, got on to the pigeon's back and so passed through. When the two fierce demons mounting guard at the cleft saw that they had been outwitted by a stranger, they grasped in a rage at the pigeon in order to destroy her. But, luckily for the borrower, they only got hold of the tail, while the pigeon, losing her beautiful tail, continued her way to the shades. Maui was much troubled at the mishap which had befallen his friend Tane's beloved bird.

On reaching the underworld Maui looked about for his mother's house. It was the first his eyes fell on, and he was guided to it by the sound of the beating of garments. The red pigeon alighted on a bakery opposite the open hut, in which Buataranga was busy beating the bark cloth. She stopped and gazed in amazement at the red bird conjecturing that it was a visitor from the upper world, as none of the pigeons in the kingdom of the shades were red. Buataranga said to the bird:

"Hast thou not come hither from the light of day?"

The pigeon nodded assent.

"Art thou not my son Maui?" further asked the old woman.

Again the pigeon nodded.

Thereupon Buataranga entered her dwelling and the bird flew to a bread-fruit tree. Maui again assumed his own human form and went to embrace his mother, who asked him how he had descended to the underworld, and what was the object of his visit. Maui admitted that he had come to discover the secret of fire.

Buataranga said: "This secret is kept by the Fire-god Mauike. When I want to cook, I ask your father Bu to request Mauike to let him have a bit of burning wood."

Maui asked where the Fire-god was. His mother pointed out the direction and told him the place was called *Areava*, or "House of the banana trees." She bade Maui to be careful, "for the Fire-god is a terrible fellow of a very irritable disposition."

Maui went fearlessly to the Fire-god's house, guided by a column of smoke curling up. Mauike, who was just then busy cooking some food, interrupted his work and

THE THEFT OF FIRE

asked what the stranger wanted. Maui replied: "A fire-brand." This was given, and Maui took it to a stream that flowed by the bread-fruit tree and there extinguished it. Then he came back to Mauike and got a second fire-brand, which he likewise quenched in the river. When the fire-brand was for the third time asked of the Fire-god, he was beside himself with rage. He heaped together the ashes of his oven and gave some to the daring Maui on a piece of dry wood. These glowing embers found their way to the stream, as the burning logs had already done.

Maui thought, quite rightly, that a fire-brand would be of little use to him, if he could not get at the secret of kindling a fire. The brand might get extinguished, and then how again make the fire? Hence his intention was

Fig. 287. Warrior of Alor Island, Banda Sea; after Jacobsen. The shield, drawn from the original, shows the side with the bearing strap.

to get up a quarrel with the Fire-god, and by superior force compel him to reveal the priceless secret which till then was known only to him. On the other hand, the Fire-god, trusting to his own wonderful strength, determined to destroy the impudent fellow who wanted to get at his secret. For the fourth time Maui requested fire from the enraged Fire-god. Mauike ordered him to be off, else as a punishment he would be chucked into the air, for Maui was small of stature. But he now replied

THE THEFT OF FIRE

that nothing would give him greater pleasure than to measure his strength with the Fire-god's.

Mauike went to his dwelling to buckle on his fighting belt, but on his return he saw that Maui had expanded to an enormous size. Still, without being discouraged at the sight, Mauike grasped him boldly with both hands and hurled him as high as a coco-nut tree. Maui was crafty enough to make himself so light in falling that he was not the least hurt by the shock. Enraged that his antagonist still breathed, Mauike, collecting his whole strength, hurled him much higher than the tallest coco-nut tree that ever grew. Nevertheless Maui remained unhurt by the fall, while Mauike lay there gasping for breath.

Now it was Maui's turn. Seizing the Fire-god, he threw him to a giddy height and then caught him like a ball with both hands. Without letting Mauike touch the ground, he tossed him a second time into the air and again caught him with his hands, assuring him that this was only preparatory to a last toss that would seal his fate. Then Mauike, out of breath and completely exhausted, implored Maui to stop and spare his life and he should have anything he wanted.

Being now reduced to a pitiful state, Mauike had to stop and recover his breath. Maui said:

"Only on one condition will I spare you; reveal to me the secret of fire. Where does it lie concealed? How is it produced?"

Mauike gladly promised to tell him all that he knew himself, and led him to the interior of his wonderful dwelling. Here in one corner lay a heap of coco-nut fibre; in another bundles of sticks of inflammable wood, the *au, oronga, tauinu*, and especially the *ava* or banana.

THE THEFT OF FIRE

These sticks were all dry and ready for use. In the centre of the room lay two other smaller sticks side by side. One of these the Fire-god gave to Maui, bidding him hold it tight while he himself rubbed the other hard against it, the Fire-god singing the while:

> Give, O give me thine hidden fire,
> Thou Banana-tree!
> Perfect the charm;
> Address a prayer to the [Spirit of the]
> Banana-tree.
> Kindle a fire for Mauike
> From the splinters of the Banana-tree!

During this song Maui saw, to his great joy, how from the fine dust produced by the friction of one stick against the other a light smoke arose. As they continued to rub, the smoke became stronger, and, fanned by the Fire-god's breath, a slight flame broke out, which was kept up and increased by the fine coco-nut fibre. Then

Fig. 288. Warrior of Letti Island, Banda Sea, with Asiatic shield, after Jacobsen.

Mauike brought the various bundles of sticks to his aid, and soon to Maui's amazement, a bright flame blazed up.

The great secret of the fire was secured. Still the conqueror decided all the same to have his revenge, because he had been annoyed and thrown into the air, and so he set fire to his vanquished opponent's dwelling. In a short time the whole of the underworld was in flames, which consumed the Fire-god and all his belongings. The rocks themselves cracked and burst asunder from the heat, and from that came the old saying: The rocks burn in Orovaru (in the Shades).

Before leaving Spirit-land, Maui carefully took posses-sion of the two fire-sticks which were once the property of Mauike, and hastened to the bread-fruit tree, where the red pigeon "Fearless" was quietly awaiting his return. His chief anxiety was how to get the bird's tail in proper condition, so as to avoid Tane's anger. There was no time to be lost, for the flames were spreading with furious rapidity. He again got on the pigeon, which, taking his fire-sticks one in each claw, flew to the lower entrance of the cleft in the rocks. On his once more uttering the words he had learnt from Buataranga, the rocks parted and he got safely back to the upper world. Thanks to the efforts of his mother, the pigeon met with no opposition from the grim guards of the way to the shades. When they again returned to daylight, the pigeon put on a long tail, alighting in a carefully secluded valley which since then has been called *Rupe-tau*, "the Pigeon's Resting-place." Maui again assumed his original human form, and hastened to take back Tane's beloved pigeon.

Crossing the chief valley Keia, he saw that the flames had got ahead of him, and at Teao had found a passage which since then has remained open. The Kings Rangi and Mokoiro trembled for their land, for it looked as if everything must be destroyed by the all-devouring flames. To protect Mangaia from further devastation, they applied all their strength and at last succeeded in stamping out the fire. From that time Rangi took the name of "Moist-eye" in memory of his troubles, and thenceforth Mokoiro was always called *Auai* or "Smoke."

THE THEFT OF FIRE

The natives of Mangaia made use of the brand in order to produce fire and cook their food. But after some time the fire went out, and as they were not in possession of

Fig. 289. Warrior with Asiatic shield, Solor Island, Banda Sea. From a model figure of natural size in the Royal Museum, Leiden.

the secret they were unable to make any new fire. Maui alone was never without fire in his home, a circumstance which caused universal surprise. Manifold were the inquiries into the reason thereof, and at last, being filled with pity for the inhabitants of the world, he communicated to them the wonderful secret that the fire was concealed in certain woods, in the *hibiscus*, the *Urtica argentea*, the *tauinu*, and the banana, and that this fire could be extracted by using the fire-sticks which he made; lastly, he made them intone the Fire-god's song, in order to make the use of the fire-sticks effective.

Since that memorable day all the inhabitants of this upper world have successfully used the fire-sticks and enjoyed the luxury of light and of cooked food.

II. *Myth of Nias Island, West Coast Sumatra (after Bastian)*

SADAWA, one of Balugu Luomewona's concubines, wanted her son Bela also to be let down to the earth, as Sirao had sent down all the other first inhabitants. She fastened him to a long thin chain, which was so violently shaken by the wind that it broke. So Bela fell headlong down, and alighted on a tall tree. Hence he had to seek his residence in high trees, and feed with the wild animals of the woods.

At present the priests alone still see the Bela people, whereas formerly not only did all men see them, but both men and Belas paid each other mutual visits in order to fetch fire from each other, as the Nias islanders still do to this day.

Now, when a son of *Hia* ("men") once went to a Bela woman to fetch fire, she had none at the moment, because it had gone out. She was able, however, like all the Belas, to make fire by friction, an art which they most carefully kept from men, regarding it as a private secret.

Hence the Bela woman, while she was making the fire, wanted to cover the son of Hia with a cloth. But he

THE THEFT OF FIRE

said to her: "Through this cloth I can see; put a basket over me."

Now, however, it was too evident that he could also see through the basket. The rogue asked her just to throw another basket over him.

So she did, and struck fire under the belief that he could not now see it.

But the man who came to fetch fire had gained his object; he had plainly seen how she came by the fire, and laughed at her.

Thus did men learn the art of kindling fire.

III. *Saga of the Catlo' ltq, N.W. America (after Boas)*

A MAN had a daughter who possessed a wonderful bow and arrow, with which she was able to bring down

Fig. 290. Warrior of Solor Island. Back view of fig. 289.

everything she wanted. But she was lazy and was constantly sleeping. At this her father was angry and said:

"Do not be always sleeping, but take thy bow and shoot at the navel of the ocean, so that we may get fire."

The navel of the ocean was a vast whirlpool in which sticks for making fire by friction were drifting about. At that time men were still without fire.

Now the maiden seized her bow, shot into the navel

395

THE THEFT OF FIRE

of the ocean, and the material for fire-rubbing sprang ashore.

Then the old man was glad. He kindled a large fire; and, as he wanted to keep it to himself, he built a house with a door which snapped up and down like jaws and killed everybody that wanted to get in.

But the people knew that he was in possession of the fire, and the stag determined to steal it for them. He took resinous wood, split it up and stuck the splinters in his hair. Then he lashed two boats together, covered them with planks, danced and sang on them, and so came to the old man's house. He sang:

"O, I go and will fetch the fire."

The old man's daughter heard him singing, and said to her father: "O, let the stranger come into the house; he sings and dances so beautifully."

The stag landed and drew near to the door, singing and dancing, and at the same time sprang to the door and made as if he wanted to enter the house. Then the door snapped to, without, however, touching him. But while it was again opening, he sprang quickly into the house. Here he seated himself at the fire, as if he wanted to dry himself, and continued singing. At the same time he let his head bend forward over the fire, so that he became quite sooty, and at last the splinters in his hair took fire. Then he sprang out, ran off and brought the fire to the people.

THE THEFT OF FIRE
IV. *A Story from Bogachim*

(Private communication from A. Hoffmann)

FORMERLY only one old woman in Bogachim had a knowledge of fire. She alone cooked all the food, and carefully kept the secret of fire. In the village there were some inquisitive young fellows who would have gladly found out the old woman's secret.

One day they hid themselves and waited till the old woman left her hut. Then they hastily entered, but could discover nothing remarkable except a large pot. In their curiosity they lifted the cover, but were tremendously startled when out of the pot rose the moon, bearer of the fire. They snatched at the fiery orb, but the moon mounted through the roof of the hut and alighted on a coco-nut tree.

Here one of the young fellows again caught hold of it, without, however, being able to keep it. The moon rose higher and higher, and at last remained hanging in the sky.

The youth who had caught the moon the second time had dirty hands, and their impression is still seen in the moon (compare also fig. 278, the explanation of which is afforded by a North-West American interpretation of the spots in the moon).

Our question is, what is meant by these remarkable myths? Are they really concerned with a history of the origin of fire? Have we here really an account of how the aborigines explain to themselves historically the acquisition of the fire-sticks?

Assuredly not!

Without going further, we can recognize the meaning of the stories about fire-stealing from the conclusion of the Maui myth, as it is related by the Maori. They tell us that the sun had risen for the first time, when Maui

THE THEFT OF FIRE

had escaped from the pursuing Fire-god to the upper world with the fire-making instruments in his hand. Hence we are here dealing with a solar myth, a myth which, so to speak, supplements the sunset myths, those in which the sun is swallowed up. For when Maui disappears in the throat of Hine-nui-te-Po, and she has closed her maw, then we have the first sunset.

The myths concerned with fire-stealing are, perhaps, the most beautiful of all solar myths, for in them the sunrise is always described most realistically. Consider the glowing fire which flares up behind Maui as he escapes from the nether world; but no! here I am even less accurate than the myth itself, which says that the flames got ahead of him. This is far more correct, for the morning red flames forth, before the sun itself, high up in the sky. Moreover, there is yet another variant of this myth which is almost still more beautiful. According to it, Maui likewise obtains a brand from the Fire-god, who extracts a nail from it, which the crafty Maui at once quenches in the stream. The god gives him a second, a third, a fourth, and Maui extinguishes one flame after the other. At last the Fire-god has given him twenty brands, in each of which was a nail, that is, the ten fingernails and the ten toes. It is the same image that the ancient Greeks employed when they spoke of the rosy-fingered dawn. They are the beams of the rising sun.

In another way the following myths are highly significant. When the implement for making fire by friction lies in the navel of the ocean, that is as much as to say that the sun rises from the ocean. But here, in North-West America, I can also point to a peculiarity of the solar mythology which has already been frequently referred to, and with which we are quite familiar. In this region many of the

THE THEFT OF FIRE

fire-stealing myths begin with the words: "The ghosts, the spirits of the departed, possessed the fire."

Naturally this again means nothing more than that, as the souls of the departed follow to the land of the sun, the departed are thus, so to say, the possessors of the sun, the sun must have been stolen by the departed.

And such, too, is always the trend of these myths. Sagas, which begin in the way just described, always wind up with the fire being wrested from the spirits.

An analogous idea also underlies the Nias myth, which is introduced with the explanation that the Bela people had come down from heaven by a long thin chain. Now we know well enough what such chains mean. Here we have once more a solar ray, and in the Belas the child-

Fig. 291. Dancer with dancing shield, Hawaii; after Cook.

ren of the sun. From the Belas, however, the fire is pilfered, and this again means nothing more than that the sun rises.

In this way fire is in divers manners brought into close association with the solar mythology. Hence we have here to do, not so much with an explanation of the origin of fire, as with an explanation of the circumstance that fire is sacred for all peoples who hold the solar view of the world. From these Sagas we get nothing but an elucidation of the fire-worship. But to this subject we shall now devote a separate brief chapter.

CHAPTER XXVI
FIRE-WORSHIP

IF the foregoing cycle of myths concerned with the theft of fire already shows that between fire-worship and the worship of the sun there must exist a certain relation, this relation must above all things be inferred from the somewhat marked fire-worship which is not rarely met with amongst those peoples who live within the exclusive sphere of the solar view of the world.

Altars of perpetual fire, the fire sacred to Vesta, the fire maidens of Peru, and so on, are symbols of this phenomenon. There is always a more or less pronounced system of sun-worship which underlies the vestal fires. I shall, as usual, present a few examples, not forgetting to put in the foreground the specially instructive fire-dances of the Navajos north of Mexico.

The Dsilyidje Oacal feast is kept in winter, when thunder and lightning are silent. Perhaps a member of the tribe may say he feels ill. Perhaps he says so without really being ill. That does not matter at all. The main point is that he will now pay for the feast, the essence of which consists in prayers for bountiful harvests and fertilizing rains.

Now the man or the woman having thus complained of feeling unwell, is ordered to the sweating-house to be taken in hand by a well-ordered "Board of Health" for body and soul.

FIRE-WORSHIP

Messengers are sent out, who are called Akaninili, and are clothed like the mythical Dsilyi Neyani. In their hands they carry the white flour which they strew along the path. It is the white colour that indicates the course of the sun. On their skins and forearms is drawn on a black ground the white zigzag line of the god of thunder-storms and of swiftness. Tufts of feathers adorn their limbs, and an ornamental feather-staff rests in their left hand. In a word, to judge from the illustration, the young fellows look quite ravishing. The messengers make a long round and invite the other tribes as guests.

Fig. 292. The messengers, Akaninili; after Dr Matthews.

The festive night has arrived. A brushwood hedge forms a wide circle round the festal place, in the middle of which rests a huge pile of wood, immense stakes brought hither with much labour. This is the great hearth which throughout the night is to illumine with its flames the eleven scenes which will be presented between sunset and sunrise.

The sun has set. A troop of the people belonging to the performing band appears in the enclosure. They wear close-fitting tights; their loose hair flows freely down; they are daubed over and over with white earth; in their hands they wield the staff, which is about the length of an arm and covered with feathers at the thickened top end.

With grotesque bounds they approach the fire. The blazing flames are already flaring up, crackling at a white

401

FIRE-WORSHIP

heat in all directions. The white figures move from east by south to west, by north back to east, and so on, springing round about the sea of fire. They leap as Indians always dance, with a sort of clumsy constraint, half crawling, half creeping. Their efforts are aimed at bringing the feather covering at the thickened end of the staff near enough to the fire to singe the feathers. The white glow blazes out against the white figures; it is dangerous to come too near the hearth; many wriggle like snakes along the ground, creeping nearer to the fire.

At last the little tuft takes fire. Hallo!

Now comes a little artistic piece. In their hand they had a feathery ring, which they quickly slip over the thick end as soon as the first feathery covering is burnt.

For the spectators it is evident that the white jumpers can work magic; else where could the new feather-tuft come from?

After hailing the appearance of this second feather-ball with jubilation, they shout wildly, and with mad bounds break through the enclosure.

Interesting also is the next of the eleven dances; for are we not familiar enough with the meaning of the arrow in the solar mythology? The two lads who now come forward are clothed almost like the Akaninili, that is, in the garb which the butterfly-gods once fashioned for the founder of the Dsilyi ceremony. They lack, however, the feather-staff and the flour-bag, instead of which they carry a long-feathered arrow. Each of them holds his arrow high up, shows how far he will swallow it, that is from the point to where the feathers begin; and then bends backwards and swallows the arrow a length of about eight inches. This exploit does not take very long. After a few steps to the right, a few to the left, and a few shuffling strides

Fig. 293. The First Fire-dance after Sunset. From Matthews.

he carefully draws the arrow out again without hurting himself. Therewith the arrow is in a measure consecrated, and the dancer goes off to the real or imaginary sick

Fig. 294. The Dancer holds the large feathered arrow high up.

Fig. 295. The Dancer swallows the arrow; after Matthews.

person, and with the tip of the arrow touches his arms, hands, soles of his feet, etc.

After some more dancing the ceremony of the sunrise is performed as the eighth in the series. It opens with the appearance of sixteen men who carry the image of the sun in a basket. They group themselves round a staff,

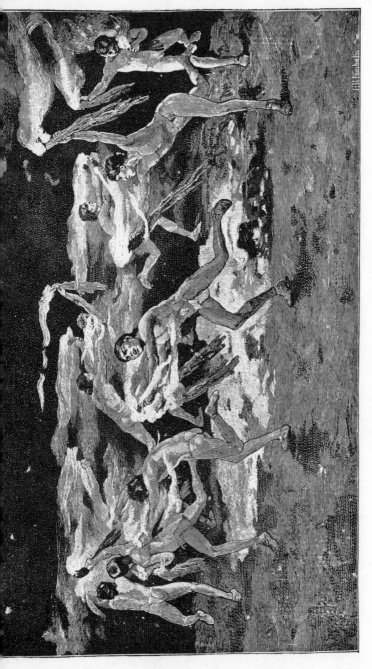

Fig. 296. The Last Fire-dance before Sunrise; after Matthews.

singing and dancing, and then spring asunder, and behold, the sun now rises on the staff, the image of the sun. The image in majestic calm wavers aloft over the staff before all eyes; for a few minutes remains hovering above the dancers, and then sinks down again.

Twice the sun rises thus, and then a fresh dance begins. The band not only shows that it holds sway over the sun, but it now wishes also to indicate that it possesses the power and the fertilizing energy of the sun. From a root which they plant in the ground before all eyes, and which discloses nothing more than the bud of a little green shoot, they conjure up a large plant with great flowering stems. But even so they are not satisfied. Yet again they group themselves round the plant, and when they again separate, the petals have fallen and the shrub bears splendid fruits, which are now gathered with much rejoicing.

Towards sunrise the sacred ceremonies of the night draw to a solemn close. The huge pile of timber is nearly burnt out; the men daubed in white again come forward, this time provided with a piece of bark from a cedar-tree, which they light at the dying flames of the hearth. Then they begin again to spring in a wild chase round the fireplace, always striving to get as near as possible to the man in front flourishing the brand. Or else during the dance they throw sparks, smoke and flames about their own bodies; they leap through the last glowing embers; they seem bathed in fire. This also they can do without getting burnt, as the white coating, the daubing with earth, protects them from the flames.

With this impressive dance the sacred night ceremony comes to an end. At sunrise the brushwood enclosure, which before had only one entrance from the east, is now open at four points—east, west, south and north.

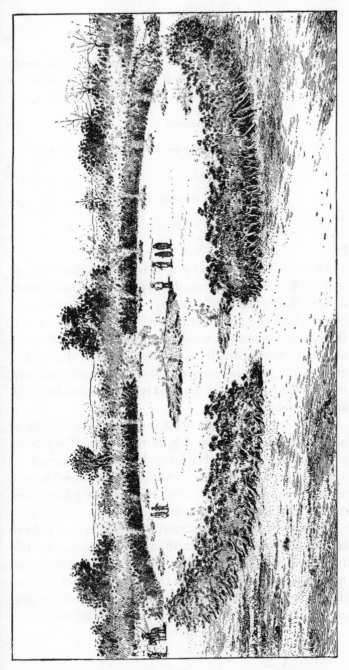

Fig. 297. The brushwood enclosure at sunrise opened to the four quarters; after Matthews.

FIRE-WORSHIP

During the night they have sung many beautiful songs.
Before the sun rose there still echoed joyful strains:

> Lullaby! Lullaby!
> The day is breaking!
> Lullaby!
> Now appears the youth of daylight!
> Lullaby!
> Now it is day!
> Lullaby!
> Now appears the maid of daylight!
> Lullaby!
> Round about is day!
> Lullaby! Lullaby!

That this peculiar feast is a solar feast is shown by so
many indications that I need scarcely enter into further
details. Only a few special points may here be dwelt upon.
We see how the people at the staff raise up the sun, and
thus declare what the whole is meant to show. We see,
above all, how beneath the uplifted image of the sun the
growth of a plant is represented; and we have been told
that the main purpose of the feast is to obtain rich harvests
and fertilizing rain.

Thus everything is grouped round the fire, which is
nothing else but the solar orb on the earth. If we compare our fig. 297, the brushwood enclosure opened at
dawn to the four quarters, with the conventional representation of the sun (fig. 298), this will be better seen
than by any graphic descriptions.

But fire-worship also presents itself elsewhere as a glori-
fication of the sun on the earth, in close association with
the questions of everyday life. Let us take, for instance,
the cult of Ganga Chitome in the old kingdom of Kongo.
He was a priest who had to keep up the sacred fire day
and night. At the beginning of a new year all the fami-

FIRE-WORSHIP

lies put out their fire, and brought fresh fire from Ganga Chitome. This fire was expected to shine favourably on their fields, the health of the household and the well-being of their cattle. Hence, to the holy fire-priest were brought the first-fruits of the field, the firstlings of the herds.

Fire-worship is clearly characterized by this. The worship which could not be paid to the sun as a far off luminary was offered to its representative, the fire, on earth. But one point should be laid stress upon. We find fire-worship chiefly amongst peoples of the second period of the more developed solar view of the world; that is, amongst agricultural peoples who associated with the

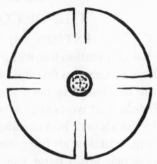

Fig. 298. Picture of the Sun on a clay vessel of the Pueblos. In a Private Collection.

sacred orb not so much the manistic views regarding the departed souls in the wake of the sun, as the idea of the day-star diffusing the fertilizing rains.

Hence, during times of drought, the Bakongo also petition the Mokisso (that is, the departed soul) of Chitome, for rain. And since the Ganga Chitome represents the sun, he may not die in the usual way; when he feels his end approaching he hangs himself by a cord.

Thus, in fire-worship, we once again come upon the sacred string, which forms the course of the sun followed by the departed souls.

CHAPTER XXVII

THE DISCOVERY OF FIRE

UNQUESTIONABLY the history of discovery and civilization knows no people who do not understand how to keep up fire and how to make use of it. Although the fact has long been contested, it is now fully established. But we cannot so readily reply in the affirmative to the second, and certainly the equally important question, whether all the peoples of the earth know how to produce fire. I have weighty reasons for thinking that such is not at all the case.

With this subject I connect the mythological chapters; but in the present chapter I leave the sphere of mythological conceptions, and shall here endeavour to analyse the characteristic elements of material development. But I must start with the preliminary statement that "all mankind have a knowledge of fire."

It is this possession that distinguishes the development even of the very lowest peoples from that of animals. There are animals who build themselves houses, who clothe themselves, who rear live-stock, till the land, and have established orderly government; but there are no animals who keep up fire, who understand how to use it constantly. On the social ladder of our culture the acquisition and employment of fire mark the first of the three rungs—Fire Age, Steam Age, Electric Age.

Human civilizations have been classified according to

THE DISCOVERY OF FIRE

the use of iron, of bronze and of stone, and thus we distinguish a Stone Age, a Bronze Age and an Iron Age. But a time will come when, with more justice, greater stress will be laid on the pre-Fire Period, the Fire Period, the Steam Period, the Electric Period, and who knows what beyond? For the utilization of these natural forces means a great deal for general culture, more than the employment of raw materials, such as stone and iron.

With fire, man acquired a never-failing working power.

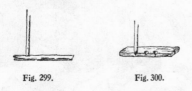

Fig. 299.   Fig. 300.

299. Firestick from Australia.
300. Firestick from the East Indian Archipelago; after Pleyte.

Flesh need no longer be pounded, it can now be roasted. Pots can be fired, iron smelted, people can warm themselves, and so on.

When, however, we consider fire as this great factor, we must frankly admit that we are no longer acquainted with peoples of the lowest imaginable development. Nevertheless, and this is of infinite importance, there still survive for us some transitional forms between the period before the production of fire and the period of the sedulous maintenance of fire.

As it was very important for me to acquire as accurate a knowledge of these relations as was possible, I have thoroughly surveyed the subject, making many inquiries, until I have at last succeeded in finding some definite standpoints from which to show *that within recent times*

411

THE DISCOVERY OF FIRE

there have been peoples who did not know how to produce fire itself, and that these peoples rather concentrated their whole art in keeping up the fire. Proof is thereby afforded that, prior to the period of fire-making, there was a period of the maintenance of fire casually obtained. In the year

Fig. 301. Two Barotse fire-drilling, South Central Africa. From a photograph.

1897, A. Hoffmann wrote to me about the natives of German New Guinea Coast:

"When I came to New Guinea in 1892 the people on the coast were already generally using Swedish matches. To my question, how they formerly made fire, I received the constant answer: "We never let the fire go out." In the upland villages, which still have but little intercourse with the coast, the people even at present anxiously guard the fire. But should the whole village be left without fire, people are sent to the neighbouring village to fetch some. There is a species of wood which

THE DISCOVERY OF FIRE

is hard to light, but keeps aglow for a long time. Such glowing wood the native always puts on his fireplace. When he wants to cook or warm himself he takes some dry leaves and withered brushwood and thrusts into the heap the glowing wood which he has first fanned to a fresh flame by vigorously twirling it to and fro. When the native goes to the fields or on a journey, he always takes a piece of glowing wood with him. On the camping grounds in the woods, as well as on the banks of the streams and in the fields, trees are often met with which keep slowly smouldering, and have been set on fire by the natives in order always to have fire at hand."

Fig. 302. A Chimila of North Columbia fire-drilling, From a photograph.

If we have here an area where fire is artificially maintained, I can supplement it with yet another.

Guy Burrows informs me that the bush people on the Upper Welle keep the fire alive by preserving it in large trees, which keep aglow for months together. Such is, likewise, the case with the Negritos squatting or rather wandering about—for they are never sedentary—on the headwaters of the Chwapa in the interior of Congoland. The Mongos, who have here formed their settlements in the primeval forests towards the South-east, stood for a long time on friendly terms with these pygmies, who, in return for their game, received from the Mongos garden produce, pots, arrow-heads and *fire-brands*. The Negritos had become so completely habituated to this barter trade that they allowed their smouldering trees to go out. But then came troublous times, days of hostilities and bitter feuds. The little folks struggled and fought to the death

Fig. 303. Fire-driller, North-East Australia.

Fig. 304. Fire-driller, South-East Australia.

—for fire. At that time the poor fellows must have been sorely distressed, being often driven to feed on raw flesh, till one day they fell upon a village, made off with the fire and retreated to their inaccessible woodlands. Since then they are seldom seen. But the main point is that in several places they have again lit up their smouldering trees, so to speak, their "fire-stations." My informant says that it is very dangerous to approach such trees, for there is always a look-out in the vicinity, and the pygmies would not take it as a joke if they saw these fire-stations threatened.

Hence, it is certain that we have here to do with peoples

THE DISCOVERY OF FIRE

who do not understand how to make fire, their whole art consisting in keeping it alive.

Von den Steinen has already rightly pointed out that the knowledge or recognition of the value of the possession of fire must be older than the simplest fire-producing implements that we are acquainted with. Wherever a prairie fire sprang up the people may have eagerly

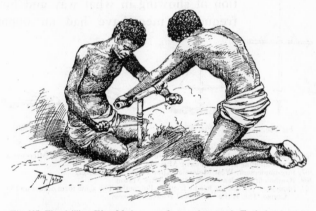

Fig. 305. Fire-drilling, West Madagascar; from a photograph. Typical string-drill.

sought for its charred victims, just as rats, birds and small game overtaken by the conflagration are now scented out by wild animals. Mankind may have thus learnt how to roast animals, and, as a matter of fact, the roasting can be shown to be older than the boiling process. Opportunities for observing the outburst of fire would appear not to have been so very rare. We need not refer to lightning alone. We are told that in the island of Buru, Malaysia, the kinar-tree (*Kleinhovia hospita L.*), in exceptionally dry years, easily sets fire to its branches by friction without the co-operation of man, and thus contributes largely to the forest fires which break out from time to

THE DISCOVERY OF FIRE

time. Turner was even informed by the natives of Nuku-fetau that according to their tradition they had discovered fire when smoke arose from two dry branches which had been rubbed together by the wind.

We need not, and should not, credit such legends as the last mentioned; but they have to be taken into account when it is a question of showing in what way and how frequently men have had an oppor-

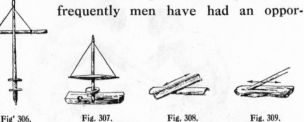

Fig' 306. Fig. 307. Fig. 308. Fig. 309.

306. Drill-borer, British New Guinea, here used as a shell borer, but in Micronesia for kindling fire. Melbourne Museum.
307. Fire-implement, West Malaysia. After Pleyte. Pump-borer.
308. Bamboo fire-implement, Malaysia. After Mason.
309. Implement for making fire by friction, Polynesia. The same form occurs on the Congo. This is the "stick and groove" process.

tunity of acquiring a knowledge of fire. Once man had learnt to employ fire, to make it useful and keep it alive, as we have just seen was the case amongst the New Guinea Papuans and the Central African Negritos, nothing more was needed than the actual discovery of a fire producer. But this, too, can be shown without any great difficulty.

The Wamolonge people, west of Lake Tanganyika, fasten the string to the bow by boring holes near its two ends, and this is done by bringing the bow to the ground and holding it firmly with the knees. Now they take a piece of hard wood which has been charred on the fire, and place it vertically on the spot where the hole is to

THE DISCOVERY OF FIRE

be made, and then between the palms of the hands twirl the piece of wood held vertically at one point hither and thither until the bow is bored through. When this is done, and it often takes several days, they rub oil vigorously into the spot. When my informant gave them an iron nail, and asked them to repeat the operation with this implement, they burst out laughing, shook their heads, and pointed out that the bow on being bent would split, even if it did not do so while the hole was being made.

In this same way nearly all Africans, Malagasy, and apparently all South Sea Islanders, too, bore fine holes. With the Wamolonge, for instance, the hole-twirling as such is an art which all do not understand. But among them it is done by the same persons who also kindle fire.

Fig. 310. Fire-maker in New South Wales; after Brough Smyth.

And thus we arrive at the great fact that fire is produced in precisely the same way.

The most widespread method of generating fire may be seen from the illustrations at figs. 299 to 304. In this process it is always a question of boring a soft with a harder piece of wood. For the most part, under the horizontal and softer piece, a little hollow is filled with any inflammable stuff, the tinder or touchwood, which is often inserted in the drill-hole itself. It appears that in exceptional cases even the borer may contain some tinder, that

THE DISCOVERY OF FIRE

is, may be a hollow stick or tube. The main point is to prevent the bored part from getting cold again, as always happens to the unexperienced. While they twirl with the palms and press downwards, the palms themselves also slip down with surprising rapidity and have to be brought quickly up again. But when once a little smoke begins to rise, the fire is soon obtained by blowing, introducing dry foliage and waving the glowing leaves to and fro.

Fig. 311. The fire-rubbing instrument of fig. 310, showing the direction of the movement.

The wild tribes have made the twirling process easier in many ways. For the hands a string was substituted. With a stick held obliquely, one man pressed the vertical twirler downwards while another coiled a string round it, working it backwards and forwards (fig. 305). After this step the pump-borer (figs. 306, 307) was not so far off.
It can be proved that all these fire implements are also simultaneously employed for drilling holes, but that the borers are always older than the fire instruments. In many places where the pump-borer is already in use for drilling holes, the natives still remain satisfied with the more primitive, less effective and simpler methods of producing fire.

If the development of the fire implement from quite a simple working tool can thus be indicated, the same is likewise possible with other methods. Such, for instance, is the simple bamboo fire-kindler of the East Indian Archipelago (fig. 308). The bamboo is divided lengthwise into two parts. The fine inside membrane, the "soul," that is, that tender film which is also found in our reeds, is rolled up into a little ball and shoved under the one half of the bamboo strip whose concave side lies on the ground. This strip is held firmly on the ground, while

THE DISCOVERY OF FIRE

with the other, that is to say, with its sharper edge, they keep "sawing" to and fro over the little filmy ball until the under strip is sawn through, in other words, until the heated bamboo-dust trickling through the slit falls down on the inflammable membranous mass.

The word "sawing," which has involuntarily escaped

Fig. 312. Fire by friction, New South Wales. After Brough Smyth.

from my pen, seems here also to give the key to the technical development of the fire implements. With the bamboo sawing the fire implement was "discovered." Many a South Sea process, the rubbing of a hard stick in a soft groove, as the Polynesians do (fig. 309), as well as the New South Wales methods (310-312), I trace back to the bamboo and similar sawing processes. These methods illustrate how the Australians of the seaboard facing the half-Melanesian Tasmania kept sawing with a hard stick on a groove filled with pith till the pith took fire, the groove itself being scooped out of a piece of wood or the stump of a tree.

In any case the remarks of Pleyte and of Rosenberg

THE DISCOVERY OF FIRE

that, in the bamboo process, instead of bamboo ordinary wood is sometimes used, justify us in believing that there is a connexion between the bamboo implement of the East India Archipelago and the stick and groove instrument of Polynesia.

But yet another form, that of New Guinea, I also bring into relation with the bamboo process. This is thus described by Finsch as practised in his time:

"Newära," as the chief instrument is called, is a short piece of a branch stripped of its bark, split lengthwise at

Fig. 313.   Fig. 314.

313. Fire implement, South-East New Guinea; Finsch Collection, Berlin Ethnological Museum. Above is the object as preserved in the Museum. Below its application, as conjectured by the Author.

314. Stone for striking fire. East Indian Archipelago.

one end and kept open by means of a stone inserted in the slit. The native takes a handful of dry grass, rubs it, rolls it up and puts it under the piece of wood on which he treads with his feet to keep it firm. With a long strip of split bamboo called "ana," which is passed through the gaping slit, he now begins to rub by drawing it backwards and forwards, whereby the grass is often set on fire in thirty seconds. All natives carry the ana with them, while wood is found everywhere, as any dry piece will do.

The specimen of the Newära brought back by Finsch, and now in the Berlin Ethnological Museum, I have above reproduced (fig. 313). But as Finsch writes to me that there is a mistake about this ana, which is not a bamboo but a strip of cane, I have endeavoured to show its application above in fig. 313.

THE DISCOVERY OF FIRE

Besides these, primitive peoples possess several other kinds of fire implements which, however, are all nearly related to the usual industrial technical appliances, and for the most part are directly derived from them. It will suffice to recall the method of striking fire. If we strike with a flint (fig. 314) against a bamboo or a potsherd, we may trace the process directly back to a practical experience. When the natives tried to fell a bamboo with their flint axes, the silicious bark of the bamboo spontaneously emitted sparks. In this way they came very near "discovering" a fire implement.

We need not worry ourselves any longer with the wearisome description of the implements. Let us rather conclude that the history of the discovery of these implements by no means implied the action of any great genius, that in fact nature herself first very impressively held the usefulness of fire before the eyes of mortals, that they then sought the means of acquiring it, that they learned to keep it alive, and that at last the simplest manual operations placed in their hands the simplest fire implements. That is all.

But in order to sum the matter up, if from the myths about the theft of fire we would really derive a lesson on the technical processes of fire-making and on its history, the lesson would be that in their myths the natives themselves never speak of such processes, never talk about fire implements being discovered, but rather always imply that these were brought to them by their god, that is, by a stranger.

Who was this stranger?

Can it possibly have been that people, that migrating race who spread the whole solar mythology over the northern hemisphere?

CHAPTER XXVIII
THE STONE AGE

HAVE you ever turned your thoughts to the Stone Age? Something almost fabulous lies in its very conception. This is doubtless mainly because we are from time to time reminded of those days, and yet know nothing about them. The peasant who when ploughing turns up a finely polished celt or an exquisitely fashioned spearhead; the Swiss farmer who on the lakeside or in the bed of a peat bog may bring to light the framework of a pile building, some old potsherds or remains of a net, may perhaps for a moment give a thought to the Stone Age, as I say, because we are so frequently reminded of a period which yet remains foreign to our thoughts.

In many parts of the world travellers have found people who had no knowledge of iron, and carved and flaked their weapons and implements with stones and bones. And they have told us what hard work it is to use such instruments, how the felling of a tree takes a full week, how after a few strokes the axe becomes blunt, and must again be ground, how nevertheless those men are eagerly engaged in producing the "beautiful," carvings pleasing to their eyes, all kinds of ornamental work and wonderful knick-knacks.

They have leisure!

They know nothing of the restless spirit of Europeans who pass from one object to another, hustling,

FIG. 315.   A PILE VILLAGE ON THE SOUTH COAST OF BRITISH NEW GUINEA.   From photographs

nervous, never quite satisfied. In this leisurely manipulation of the stone-axe there is a quiet enjoyment to which we have become strangers—for the toilers an enjoyment, for us, the observers, a magical charm.

Just think, for instance, of a pile village *rising out of the sea* (fig. 315). Here we have a great achievement —to recover from the sea the very ground on which to live, to create upon the flowing waters a stable dwelling-place. And even, apart from all minor questions, we must at least be astonished at the greatness of the works executed by the men of the Stone Age. I am not here thinking of the monumental monoliths, but refer rather to the Polynesian buildings, which from the constructive point of view are far more interesting, and one of which I am able to reproduce (fig. 317). What here rightly fills us with wonder is not so much the size and compass of the structure as the graceful and thoroughly thought-out plan of construction, displaying, as it does, the most refined use of the material, of the wood, the bamboo and the wickerwork. I will here also introduce a few other triumphs of native art. Let us take a South American bow, which sometimes may measure from six to nine feet. It is light, but very uniformly bent, tapering regularly towards the ends, and on the surface highly polished.

Now we should try to realize the amount of labour involved in the production of such a bow. In order to procure it, a whole tree, a giant of the forest, has to be felled, and then the wood is pared off down to the very heart. From this inner core a long staff has to be detached, and so far the stone axe has been available. But now small implements, such as the skull of a little rodent (fig. 317), or a sharp-edged shell, come into play. By

THE STONE AGE

their means the staff is smoothed, over the fire it acquires the desired bend, and at last is polished with a mixture of oil and pounded leaves. When it is finished the weapon betrays nothing of the incredible labour its preparation has required.

Fig. 316. Brazilian woman polishing a bow. From a Spanish woodcut.

And it is precisely in this that the greatness of the work consists.

Or let us picture to ourselves the spectacle of Tahiti's proud war-fleet (fig. 319), which has been preserved for us by the exceptionally trustworthy and singularly correct artist of Cook's expedition. I must confess that I have sat for hours before this picture; that often, when unable to comprehend the achievements of the "rude, wild tribes" of those times, I have pored wistfully over this engraving. And each time I have been again entranced by the grandeur of the spectacle; each time I have come to the conclusion that we have, after all, but

Fig. 317. A South American rubbing a bow smooth with the help of an animal's skull; after Crevaux.

little right to look *de haut en bas* on these "wild tribes."

There are three things that excite our admiration for the great works of the so-called Stone Age. The first is their massiveness. The huge structures of this period, such

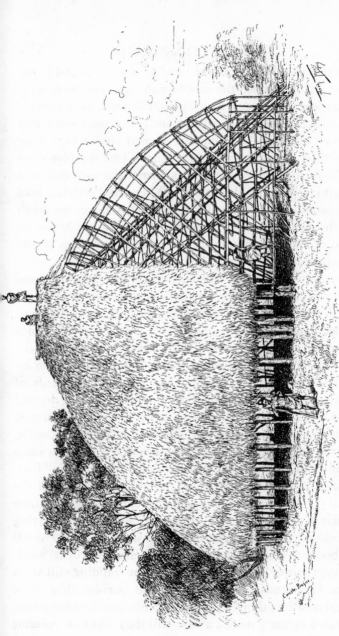

Fig. 318. House-building in Samoa. Drawn from a photograph.

as those of early Egypt, the temples of Mexico and Peru, have extorted from the observer the question how, with their incredibly poor technical appliances, those peoples could at all contrive to prepare such immense blocks, and convey them to the often very distant sites where they had then to be piled one on another? The question is not difficult to answer. There was formerly a very different organization of skilled labour. When the Peruvian Inca Yupanqui, who was called the Great, and was the tenth of the dynasty, began to build the fortress of Cuzco, he first of all summoned from the various provinces of the Empire 20,000 (twenty thousand!) workmen who, after three months' forced labour, were relieved by the same number, while during the service they were supplied with food by their own people. As many as 4,000 were employed at the stone quarries of Muyna, fifteen miles from Cuzco; 6,000 transported the enormous rough blocks hewn in those quarries to the site, mounting them on rollers and dragging them with stout cordage made of leather and agave fibre. The remaining 10,000 dressed the blocks on the spot and prepared the rocky ground on which they were piled up in layers to form the walls. These huge blocks, which had been conveyed over steep cliffs and across rivers, were called *Saykuska*, the "Fatiguing"; they might just as well have been called the "Slayers," for more than one of them cost the workmen their lives. One of the largest, so we are told, having broken from the ropes on a steep slope, slew 300 or 400 labourers in its downward rush. But however much "man-power" might be used up, the building still went on. Thousands of craftsmen might perish; they were replaced by others. Four Incas continued the operations. Half a century passed away; still they went on building

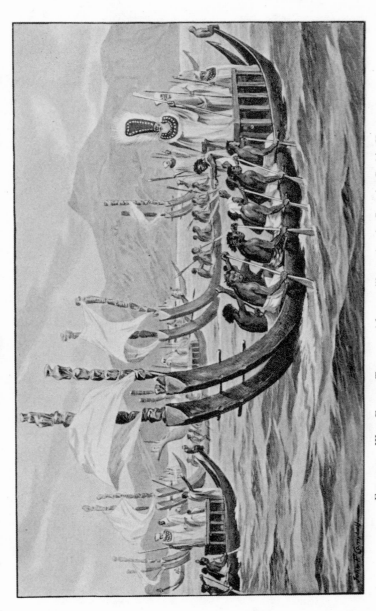

FIG. 347. WAR FLEET, TAHITI. After an illustration in Captain Cook's *Voyages*

went on building, till the great structure was completed.

Who would expect such a work from us nowadays? Therefore, I say, the achievements of the Stone Age were greater than our own!

The second point that must unreservedly impress us is the exquisite use of material. What we are able to execute by technical skill, or rather by technical means, they carried out by sheer industry. Of this I will give an instance. A small steamer of the Congo State, which was manned by a lieutenant and a few other Europeans, and supplied with axes and all kinds of other modern appliances, was commissioned to found a station, that is to build a house, at the mouth of the Luebo river. It must read very comically when I have now to say that these gentlemen failed to accomplish this, "because in erecting the walls the round logs always rolled asunder." Compare with this the intelligent performance, the technical ingenuity with which a house, such as that of fig. 318, was constructed.

After this, who will still laugh at the "rude" natives?

The third feature that strikes us in the works of the Stone Age is their extraordinary perfection of form. The natives *never* commit an error of style, either in technicality or in decoration. Every object that they have produced in the really uncivilized state, in the period before all contact with Europeans and their technical labour-saving appliances—I say every object, the most and the least important—they have fashioned, polished, decorated, with a devotion, a perfection of form which, as a rule, we to-day are most of us quite unable to appreciate. Yet these are the very qualities that ensure for such objects a permanent value, and in the history of civiliza-

THE STONE AGE

tion entitle them to the first "gold medal" for craftsmanship.

An example must also be given of the painstaking and
leisurely way in which the natives perform their work.
I refer to the method of preparing the shell bracelets that
are worn by the Papuans of New Guinea. These ornaments take a circular form, the inner diameter averaging
two inches, while the surface is polished smooth. In the
manufacture the inner circle is the main point, and for
this an implement is needed, whereas all the rest is executed with a free hand. The treatment of this inner circle,
the boring process, has been thoroughly studied and
described as under by the Hungarian explorer, Biro:

In its preparation there is needed quite a simple instrument, which is also applied in a very simple way. Thick,
solid and firm shells furnish the material, and the *eny*,
the boring-tool (fig. 321), consists of two chief pieces,
the upper borer and the lower block (fig. 326) which
serves to keep steady the piece of shell to be bored.

The borer itself consists of a bamboo, sometimes thicker,
sometimes thinner, to the upper half of which a longish
piece of stone is lashed with a thick strip of bast. Now
the operator grasps the two free ends of the stone and
turns the bamboo to and fro on the shell lying below,
whereby the lower end of the bamboo, the *Limbiye*,
begins to rub the shell in a regular, circular groove. The
friction on the piece to be bored is increased by the
downward pressure of both hands grasping the cross
piece of stone. Still the thick shell could not be pierced
through by the hollow bamboo of itself; hence sand from
the coconut-shell near at hand is strewn on it and kept in
place by the Limbiye as it penetrates into the shell. Moreover, water is sprinkled from time to time on the sand.

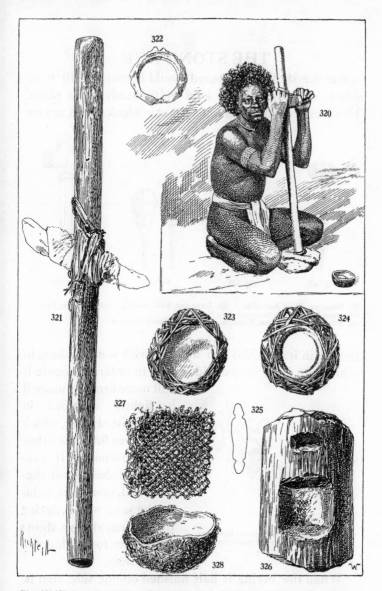

Figs. 320-328. A shell-ring maker and his implements, Berlinhafen in German New Guinea; after Biro-Jancko. Fig. 320. The Papuan boring; 321, the actual borer; 322, the ring after the boring is finished; 323, the ring packed in twisted osier before being bored; 324 shows the groove after the first boring; 325, section of the shell after slight boring on both sides; 326, the block with the rectangular incision; 327, shred of sacking; 328, the coconut-shell with sand.

THE STONE AGE

But the shell to be bored would certainly shift from side to side were it not kept quite steady in its place. This is effected by means of a wooden block with a square

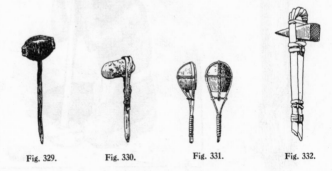

Fig. 329.   Fig. 330.   Fig. 331.   Fig. 332.

329. Stone axe, West Australia.   330. Stone axe, East Australia. South Oceanic type.
331. Stone hammer, Borneo; after Ling Roth.
332. Iron hammer, Katanga, Congo headwater. Tervoeren Museum.

hollow in it (fig. 326) and filled in with some sacking in which the shell is embedded. But in order to secure it

Fig. 333. Religious instrument, Bubi tribe, Fernando Po. Leipzig Ethnological Museum.

still more firmly, the shell is lightly wrapped in some twisted osier, which also serves for some other useful purposes. It prevents the shell from slipping, and, moreover, holds up the sand which, during the boring, always shows a tendency to trickle down at the sides.

When the boring is half finished on one side, that is, when the groove, as shown in fig. 325, is sunk deep enough, the shell is turned round and the boring begun on the other side. Naturally it depends on the borer's eyesight

THE STONE AGE

whether the two circular borings exactly coincide, that
is whether in the end the pierced shell comes out neatly

Fig. 334.   Fig. 335.   Fig. 336.

334. Stone axe, Entrecasteaux Islands.
335. Stone axe, Tahiti; Edinburgh Museum. North Oceanic type.
336. Stone axe blade, Polynesia; British Museum. North Oceanic type.

finished. When the osier twist is removed and the rim
ground smooth on a whetstone, the bracelet is finished.

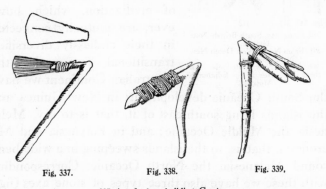

Fig. 337.   Fig. 338.   Fig. 339,

337. Axe for boat-building, Congo.
338. Stone axe, East German New Guinea, Middle Oceanic type,
339. Typical stone axe, East New Guinea. After O. Finsch.

It would betray a great lack of perspective, and very
little critical sense, were one unhistorically to regard all
peoples of the Stone Age as standing at one and the same

THE STONE AGE

level of civilization. We should rather say that the differences in the degrees of development within the limits of the Stone period are far greater than is supposed by those who separate the peoples of the Stone Age from those of the Iron Age.

In the next chapter I shall deal with the differences that exist between the peoples of the Stone and Iron Ages. Here I will only say that by means of the stone axe alone, which is the characteristic implement of the Stone Age, we are able to distinguish three stages of development. I will demonstrate this diversity at least in one region, that of the wide Oceanic domain. Oceania presents three different zones of civilization, which, however, are mutually connected in their endlessly diversified transitional forms. In the Australian Continent we have the South Oceanic development; in New Guinea and the islands lying south-east of it, that is to say, Melanesia, the Middle Oceanic; and in Polynesia and Micronesia, that is, in the islands sweeping in a wide bend round Melanesia, the North Oceanic. Corresponding with these we have also three types of stone axes (figs. 340, 341 and 342).

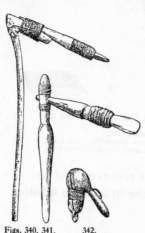

Figs. 340. 341.   342.
340. Stone axe, South British New Guinea.
341. From North West Dutch New Guinea.
342. From New Caledonia. All three stone axes in the Edinburgh Museum.

The South Oceanic Stone Axe (figs. 329, 330) is characterized by the *upright blade*, which is held fast by a piece of wood tied round it, or else is stuck into a mass of resin. This upright blade is never polished, but always only

THE STONE AGE

flaked off. We can show related forms as hammers from Indonesia also (fig. 331), and from Africa (fig. 332). Fig. 333 is a wooden religious instrument which in any case is related to these forms, since the blade does not lie flat. To the same group belong certain highly developed iron axes found amongst the Central African Warua and Wamarungu tribes.

The North Oceanic Stone Axe, which is shown complete in fig. 335, and the detached blade in fig. 336, so far shows a modification in that *the flaked and polished blade* is made fast *in a lying position* to a knee-shaped piece of wood poised at the back.

The Middle Oceanic Stone Axe has its blade, which is only polished, fixed in a casing, that is, enclosed between two pieces of wood. The casing which, taken alone with the stone celt attached, represents a chisel, is fastened to a knee-shaped piece of wood *bent forward*, or else, in the districts stretching towards South Oceania, is simply inserted in a hole in the handle of the axe in the South Oceanic manner (see fig. 341).

The last-mentioned form recurs also amongst the iron implements (see fig. 337).

But we reserve this transition to the Iron Age for a separate chapter.

CHAPTER XXIX
THE IRON AGE

STONE AGE and Iron Age—such are the old traditional eras. But strong objections have now been raised
against the expression Stone Age, and in place of it
attempts have been made to smuggle in a "Wood Age."
In a word, the credit of the "Stone Age" has sunk very
low in scientific circles.

But, viewed from a higher standpoint, neither the contrast drawn between Stone and Iron Age, nor the stress
laid on Wood or Stone or any other era, can be called particularly happy. For if I put these two questions: "Wherein
are these two periods actually distinguished one from the
other?" and, "What can we claim as really characteristic
of the Stone Age when contrasted with later developments?" nobody is able to offer a specially informing
answer of a positive nature. It would surely be an extremely superficial treatment of the history of human
culture to cut it up into chapters, to separate it into
periods, determined solely by the raw material preferred
at one time or another. It becomes rather ludicrous when
we take into consideration one very substantial fact.

When Europeans first became acquainted with them,
the Papuans of East New Guinea were still living in the
"unadulterated" Stone Age. On the other hand, the
natives of West New Guinea were already in close contact with iron-smelting peoples. From this one might

THE IRON AGE

suppose that the Papuans, possessing iron axes and iron knives, must be technically the more expert, and their

Fig. 343. Blast-Furnace, Moliro, South-East Congoland. From a photograph.

products the more artistic, the more polished and elegant. This, at least, would correspond with the current views regarding the progress indicated by the Iron Age.

Yet such views miss the mark!

THE IRON AGE

The case is just the reverse. This state of things may be observed not only in New Guinea, but also in Brazil and amongst the Eskimo. It is an established fact that, when primitive peoples who have hitherto worked with stone,

Fig. 344. Smithery, Katanga, South-East Congoland. From an original drawing of the Katanga expedition.

ivory, or shells, get possession of iron instruments, they may give up using the old ones, but the objects turned out with the new (the iron) instruments are infinitely inferior and more clumsy. The old elegance, the old perfection of form, the old fine finish is as good as lost.

A like experience is afforded by the peoples in the interior of Africa, who command a tolerably rich supply of iron implements. With their own soft tools they have carved most charming objects; but no sooner do they get

THE IRON AGE

hold of the strong European steel than all nicety and artistic finish entirely disappear.

This phenomenon, that peoples provided with superior implements do not immediately make any progress, pervades the whole history of civilization. Peoples have first gradually to adapt themselves to the higher stage of cul-

Fig. 345. Blacksmith's Workshop, Bassonge tribe. Model figures in the Tervoeren Museum. The dress is wrong; that of the crouching man belongs to the Northern Sankuru district, Congoland.

THE IRON AGE

ture presented to them. In their new clothing they behave at first as childishly and awkwardly as a youngster when first put into trousers; in his short "knickers" he gambolled gracefully and naturally, but in his new garb he struts about in a singularly ungainly and ludicrous way.

But let us for a moment compare the people who have obtained an iron instrument with the lad put into trousers. The trousers are merely an outward symbol of growing mental powers, the sign of a higher place in the school.

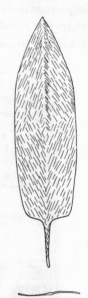

Fig. 346.

Fig. 347

Fig. 346. Double bellows, Lubenye district. From an original drawing. The lower picture, a cross section, shows the application. When two of the pistons are drawn down the other two are driven up. Every smithery always possesses two of such double bellows.

Fig. 347. Knife-blade as Money. Brandt Collection.

But the iron tool indicates absolutely no mental progress at all.

To this theoretical consideration the facts completely correspond. It has often been pointed out that the lands lying east of Asia, that is Oceania and America, had no iron before the advent of Europeans; that, on the other hand, the continents to the west of Asia—Europe and Africa—were in possession of iron implements. Attempts

THE IRON AGE

have been made to bring the whole history of culture into relation with these facts, and to show that it was just this possession of iron that secured the possession of the world to the Greeks, Romans, Spaniards and North Europeans. In connexion with this view it has been maintained that, had the Mexicans or Peruvians dis-

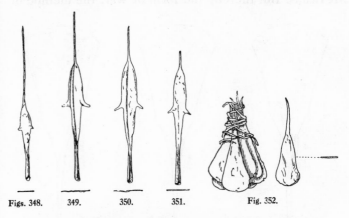

Figs. 348.   349.   350.   351.   Fig. 352.

Figs. 348 to 351. Unworked Arrowheads as Money, Lakembe in Ubanghi district. Brandt collection.
Fig. 352. Iron Money of the Banza people; is wrought into arrowheads. Brandt Collection.

covered iron before the Europeans, then *they* would have subdued the world, as we have to-day.

That is the fundamental teaching flowing from the classification of peoples as those of the Stone Age and those of the Iron Age. And this fundamental teaching is entirely wrong.

Let us only ask, for instance, what superiority the iron-using peoples of the Congo have to show over those of ancient Mexico?

It has been said that the superiority lay above all things in the improved agricultural appliances.

THE IRON AGE

Is it so? Is, then, the agricultural system of the Congo peoples higher than that of the ancient Mexicans?

Not in the least.

The weapons have been pointed to. Certainly these peoples have some additional iron weapons, and their iron weapons are more dangerous than those of the Mexicans. But thereby the form of war, the method of

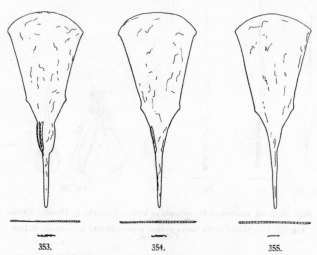

353.   354.   355.

Figs 353 to 355. Iron Money, tribes west of the Ubanghi-Congo Confluence. Is wrought into hoes. Brandt Collection.

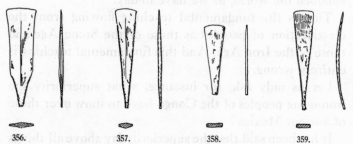

356.   357.   358.   359.

Figs. 356 to 359. Iron Money, Middle Ubanghi. Is wrought into axes. Brandt Collection.

444

THE IRON AGE

warfare, has alone been modified, *but mental culture not at all.*

Now when we further consider that the instruments of the Iron Age are much the same as those of the Stone Age, that all objects formerly made of stone are now

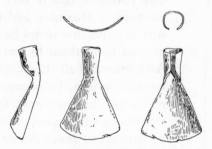

Fig. 360. Iron Money of a Mangbattu tribe. Brandt Collection.

merely made of iron (compare, for instance, the axes in the last chapter) we shall be fully convinced of the fact that the formula "Stone and Iron Ages" must be rele-

Fig. 361. Chiefs of the Lomami River, with "Money." From a photograph.

THE IRON AGE

gated to the lumber-room, like so many other old traditions of ethnology.

Africa is the classic land of the iron industry amongst primitive peoples. The reason of this is very simple. If the ancient Mexicans had no iron, it was because this metal had not been pressed upon them by nature. If the Africans are, of all rude peoples, the best workers in iron, it is because the broad plains of this continent are nothing less than a vast region of easily worked iron areas. Inner Africa is a great "laterite basin." Its very rivers are coloured brown and red by its brown ha-

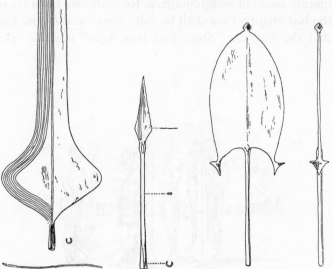

Fig. 362.   Fig. 363.   Fig. 364.

362. Iron Money, Lomami district, Brandt collection. Natural size about 5 ft 6 in. Is presumably used also as a rudder blade and as a show spear.
363. Iron Money, spearhead of the Mobali tribe. Brandt Collection.
364. Iron Money, Ughirri district. Brandt Collection.

matites and bog-iron ores. Thus it is not difficult to procure the ores. In a blast-furnace (fig. 343) with a tall clay chimney, which is provided with outlets at the base, layers of wood and bog-iron ores are piled up in successive strata. From below the whole mass is set on fire, and then it burns slowly out. Through the outlets at the base the molten metal escapes. Then comes the turn of the blacksmith (figs. 344 and 345). By means of a bellows, which usually takes the form shown at fig. 345, the iron is brought to a glow in the fire, and is then worked up with a simple iron wedge as hammer and a large stone for anvil. A length of rattan or cane simply bent round serves for the most part as tongs.

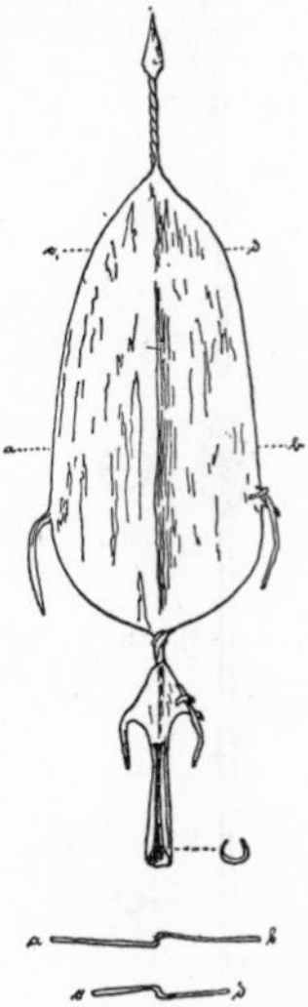

It is very important to notice that in Africa iron has exercised very great influence on trade. Of this the most practical proofs are afforded by Dr Brandt's splendid collection.

Fig. 365. Fig. 366.

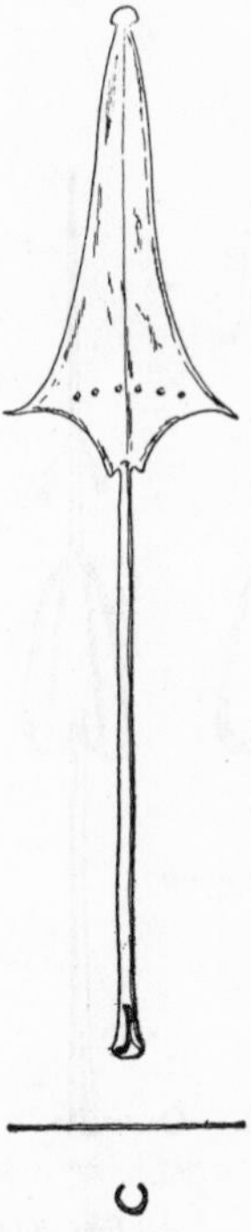

365 & 366. Iron Money of the Bolongole tribe; made for show. Brandt Collection.

Illustrations are given of a knife-blade in fig. 347; in figs. 348 to 351, of a series of arrow-heads; in fig. 352, a bundle of rough bars for making knives; in figs. 353

to 355, thin axe-blades from the South; in figs. 356 to 359, thick axe-blades from the North; at fig. 360, the blade of a Mangbattu hoe, showing how all these objects are traded as money. Such trading is quite intelligible.

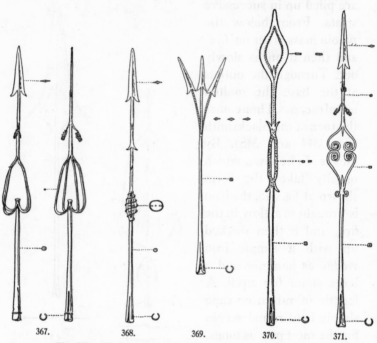

367. 368. 369. 370. 371.

Figs. 367 to 371. Show Money of the Bolongole tribe. Brandt Collection.

Some tribes live in rich iron districts, others in poor, and at fig. 53 (p. 60) I have an example of how such barter trade is arranged.

But I will here give prominence to another peculiar feature which characterizes this iron industry.

In the North-East Congo region, as well as in the Upper Sankuru district, the natives are no longer satis-

THE IRON AGE

fied with the simple serviceable iron money, which is without more ado wrought into implements and weapons. The love of show has brought about a wonderful transformation in this region. Here I introduce to the reader a group of well-to-do chiefs or village headmen from the Middle Lomami River (fig. 361). They are on a trading

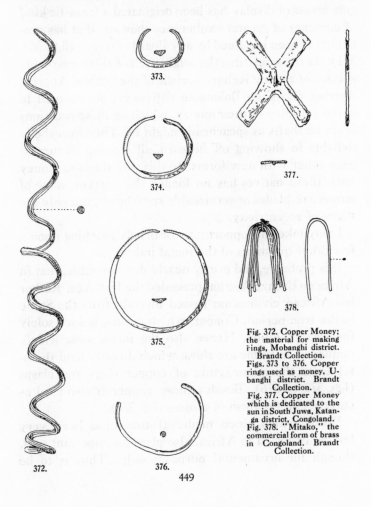

373.

374.

377.

375.

378.

372.   376.

Fig. 372. Copper Money; the material for making rings, Mobanghi district. Brandt Collection.
Figs. 373 to 376. Copper rings used as money, U-banghi district. Brandt Collection.
Fig. 377. Copper Money which is dedicated to the sun in South Juwa, Katanga district, Congoland.
Fig. 378. "Mitako," the commercial form of brass in Congoland. Brandt Collection.

449

THE IRON AGE

expedition, and make an ostentatious display of their wealth. So in truth it is. These thin spearheads, more than five feet long, are the money of these natives. A specimen of them from the Brandt collection is reproduced at fig.362.

Their artistic taste is no longer satisfied with the simple rough hoes and axe-blades. And thus amongst the Bolongole lovers of display has been originated a fantastic kind of currency of greater exuberance than any that has probably yet been imagined by any Board of Trade (figs. 365-371). At the same time the origin itself of this remarkable species of money is characteristic of the people. At great dancing feasts the Bolongole natives are accustomed to make a display of their money, which on those occasions is set on shafts as spearheads might be. Then everybody delights in showing off his own, all striving to surpass each other with new forms. In this way the iron money with these natives has no longer the current value of strong axe-blades or serviceable spearheads, but only the merit of eccentricity.

I may take this opportunity of briefly touching upon a few other questions of the metal industry.

It is probable, and pretty nearly demonstrable, that in Africa no Bronze Age has preceded the Iron Age. Rather has African civilization passed directly from the Stone to the Iron period. Copper, which occurs, is used solely for ornamentation. Hence also the forms most widely employed in traffic are those which directly lend themselves to the manufacture of copper rings and clasps (figs. 372 to 376). Besides these copper is also used as currency in the form of crosses (fig. 377).

Brass, which since medieval times has been very largely exported to Africa, also plays an important part, though for ornamental purposes only. Thus is to be

THE IRON AGE

explained the popular currency in Congoland, the so-called Mitako (fig. 378). That this bronze money very soon took the form of the copper coins may be taken for granted (figs. 379 and 380).

Probably in ancient Peru alone has bronze played an important part. Amongst all other peoples, in the East Indian Archipelago and in Africa, we see the direct transition from Stone to Iron. Coming now to the con-

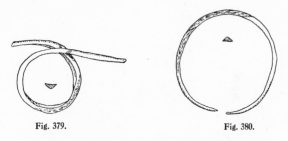

Fig. 379.   Fig. 380.

Figs. 379 and 380. Brass rings, a new money on the Ubanghi.

clusion of this exposition, I may say that iron has acquired no importance in the households of primitive peoples beyond a relatively insignificant increase of weapons and implements with a substantial improvement in their quality. Not even amongst the ancient Romans themselves do we find any extensive application of this material.

If we may speak of an Iron Age, if any form of civilization can be at all characterized by the use of a given material, then we may give the name of an Iron Age rather to our own epoch, an epoch of iron house-building, of iron rails intersecting the land in all directions, of iron ships ploughing the ocean. That, indeed, is an Iron Age.

THE IRON AGE

But all this was already preceded by the splendour of iron armour. If, however, primitive peoples have forged ever so beautiful arms (compare figs. 381 to 388), they still fall short of the highest excellence in this respect. For the finest examples of the armourer's work we must look to the sword and coat of mail of the medieval knight. So much we learn from the history of warfare.

CHAPTER XXX
EARLY HISTORY OF WAR

THERE was a time when men roamed the earth in pairs or in small bands. In those days the world was still but thinly peopled. Those were, no doubt, days of strife, of murder, but not yet of warfare.

Wars did not arise till the peoples had been constituted in stable societies, in tribes and states. In a word, wars first began when the world became more thickly peopled.

Thus the peoples who "lived before war" had as yet no warlike arms. They had no shields, not even any rules of warfare, no fixed abodes; therefore, when they came to fighting, they were marauders and murderers. But as murderers they were merely engaged in the hunt, only that the killing of game was for them an everyday and habitual occupation, and thus legitimate, whereas a comrade slain in a quarrel conjured up a blood-feud and the vendetta. But with the vendetta came war, and this settling of accounts by bloodshed has consequently persisted so long amongst mankind that they have learnt to regard an honourable war as a grave and justifiable legal proceeding and vindication of rights. When this theory was once established the vendetta disappeared, because in the great event of the victory or defeat of a whole tribe or State the wrongs suffered by a particular family were forgotten.

It is difficult to find instances from the early history of

warfare. A few, however, may perhaps still be noted amongst the most scattered of all hunting peoples known to us: the African Negritos and the natives of the Australian Continent. Here we still meet with quite plain and simple warlike relations, conditions which find their expression on the one hand in murder, on the other in the simplest of all forms of single combat.

There is no such thing as a South African Bushman "on the war-path." The Bushman goes out only as a marauder. Being absolutely indifferent to the rights of property, he can himself never be brought up as a stock-breeder. But being accustomed to lie in ambush for the game, in the same way he ensnares Hottentot and Kafir herdsmen; as he is wont to kill the game, he falls also on the ill-fated keepers of the cattle, and, finding them asleep, neither binds nor fetters them, but right away smashes their heads with a stone. Then, if he is pursued, he prefers to kill the oxen that he has lifted, or to hamstring them, rather than they should fall again into the hands of their owners. To the Bushman, man himself is nothing more than an animal. As he simply kills the animal, so he destroys a human life without giving it a second thought. The same relations prevail in Australia, where we have some interesting examples from the lives of the natives as described by Karl Lumholtz.

"One day," he writes, "when Yokkai (a Queensland native) and I were left alone in the camp, he suddenly broke out:

"'Poor fellow, white fellow!'

"Thinking that he referred to me, I, half angry, asked him what was the matter.

"He beat himself on the back of his head and said: 'Jimmy, white fellow in the water.'

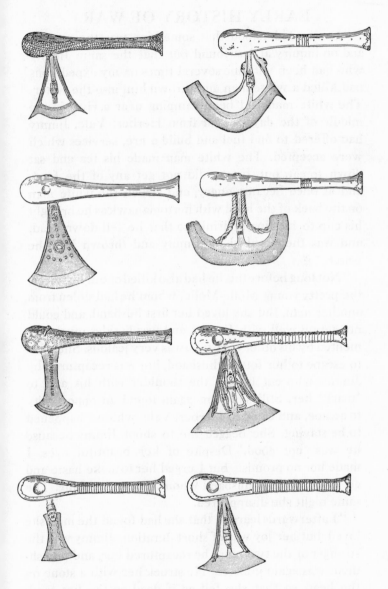

Figs. 381 to 388. Battle-axes of the Bassinge tribe, South Congoland. Brandt Collection.

EARLY HISTORY OF WAR

"I now understood that something was the matter, and on inquiry at last found out that the same Jimmy who had been with me several times on my expeditions had killed a white man and thrown him into the water. The white man had been camping near a river in the middle of the day, not far from Herbert Vale. Jimmy had offered to find fuel and build a fire, services which were accepted. The white man made his tea and sat down to eat, but Jimmy did not get any of the food, and at once became angry, and struck the white man on the back of the head with his tomahawk as he brought his cup to his lips to drink, so that he fell down dead, and was then robbed by Jimmy and thrown into the water.

"Not long before this he had also killed one of his wives, the pretty young Mólle-Mólle, whom he had stolen from another man. But she loved her first husband, and could not get on well with Jimmy, and was besides much tormented by his other wife, who was very jealous. She tried to escape to her former husband, but was recaptured by Jimmy who cut her on the shoulder with his axe to 'mark' her. Still she soon again found an opportunity to escape, and came to Herbert Vale, where I happened to be staying. She begged me to shoot Jimmy because he was 'not good.' Despite of her beautiful eyes, I made her no promise, but I urged her to make haste and go to her former husband whom she was seeking. The same night she disappeared.

"I afterwards learned that she had found the man she loved, but her joy was of short duration. Jimmy was the stronger of the two men; he recaptured her, and punishment was again inflicted. He struck her with a stone on the head, so that she fell as if dead on the hot sand.

EARLY HISTORY OF WAR

There he left her in the middle of the day, after covering her with stones, and she nearly died then. The next time I saw Mólle-Mólle she had grown very thin and pale, and had great scars on her head. She was on the point of going with Jimmy down the river to another 'land.' On this journey he killed her with his tomahawk and an old man buried her. This happened only three weeks after Jimmy had slain the white man."

Thus the same brutality with which game and cattle are killed prevailed in the times prior to regular warfare between man and man. The reason which is here given for the murder is doubtless also the same that occasioned the first beginnings of the first conflicts. The first cause of war is to be sought in the carrying off of women, in fights for women. For this also we have obtained a characteristic instance from Lumholtz.

Lumholtz had heard from some natives that a *borboby* was to be held three miles from Herbert Vale. Borbobys are gatherings at which these savages assemble from many districts to settle their disputes by single combat. "As I felt a desire to witness this assembly," writes Lumholtz, "I joined a company going there, and we all started in the afternoon. As we gradually approached the fighting-ground we met more and more small tribes who had been lying the whole day in the cool scrubs along the river to gather strength for the impending conflict. All of them, even the women and the children, joined us, except a small company of the former, who remained near the river.

"All were in their best toilet, for when the blacks are to go to dance or to borboby they decorate themselves as best they can. The preparations take several days, spent in seeking earth colours and wax, which are kept by the most prominent members of the tribe until the day of the contest. On the forenoon of the borboby day they remain in camp and do not go out hunting, for they are then occupied in decorating themselves. They rub themselves partially or wholly with the red or yellow earth paint; sometimes they besmear their whole body with a mixture of crushed charcoal and fat, as if they were not already black enough! Not only do the men, but the women also, though in a less degree, paint grotesque figures of red earth and charcoal across their faces. But one of the most important considerations on these solemn occasions is the dressing of the hair. It is filled with beeswax, so that it stands out in large tufts, or at times it has the appearance of a single large cake. This waxed headgear shines and glistens in the sun and gives them a sort of 'polished' exterior. All the natives were armed; they had quantities of spears, whole bundles of nolla-nollas (throwing-clubs) and boomerangs, besides their large wooden shields and wooden swords. The shield, which reaches to a man's hip, and is about half as wide as it is long, is made of a kind of light fig-tree wood. It is oval, massive and slightly convex. In the centre, on the front side, there is a sort of boss, the inner side being nearly flat. When the native holds this shield in his left hand before him, the greater part of his body is protected. The front is painted in a grotesque and effective manner, with red, white and yellow earth colours, and is divided into fields which, wonderfully enough, differ on each man's shield, and thus constitute his coat of arms.

"The wooden sword, the necessary companion of the shield, is about four inches wide up to the point, which is slightly rounded and usually reaches from a man's foot to his shoulder It is made of hard wood with a

EARLY HISTORY OF WAR

short handle for only one hand, and is so heavy that anyone not used to it can scarcely hold it perpendicularly
with half-extended arm, the position always adopted
before the battle begins.

"Near the edge of the wood our men and the savages
who had joined us on the road made a brief pause. One
of those who had last arrived began to run round in a
challenging manner, like a man in a rage. He was very
tall and his hair was closely matted together, standing
out in all directions. Shaking this heavy head of hair
like a madman, with head and shoulders thrown back,
he made long jumps and wild leaps, holding his large
wooden sword perpendicularly in front of him in his
right hand, and the shield in his left.

"When he had run long enough to cool his savage
warlike ardour he stopped near me. He was so hot that
perspiration streamed from him, and the red paint ran
in long streaks down his face. But he was again busy
taking great leaps and bounds; gradually the conversation became more lively, the warlike ardour increased,
and all held their weapons in readiness.

"Suddenly an old man uttered a terrible war-cry, and
swung his bundle of spears over his head. This acted, as
it were, like an electric shock on all of them; they at
once gathered together, shouted with all their might,
and raised their shields with their left hands, swinging
swords, spears, boomerangs and nolla-nollas in the air.
Then they all rushed with a savage war-cry through the
grove of gum-trees and marched by a zigzag route against
their enemies, who were standing far away on the other
side of the plain. At every new turn they stopped and
were silent for a moment, then, with a terrible howl,
started afresh, until at the third turn they stood in the

EARLY HISTORY OF WAR

middle of the plain directly opposite their opponents, where they remained. The women and children also hastened to the scene of the conflict.

"The strange tribes on the other side stood in groups in front of their huts, which were picturesquely situated near the edge of the forest, at the foot of the scrub-clad hill. As soon as our men had halted, three men from the hostile ranks came forward in a threatening manner, with shields in their left hands and swords held perpendicularly in their right. Their heads were covered with the elegant yellow and white topknots of the white cockatoo. Each man wore at least forty of these, which were fastened in his hair with beeswax, and gave his head the appearance of a large aster. The three men approached ours very rapidly, running forward with long elastic leaps. Now and then they jumped high in the air like cats, and fell down behind their shields, so well concealed that we saw but little of them above the high grass. This manoeuvre was repeated until they came within about twenty yards from our men; then they halted in an erect position, the large shields before them and the points of their swords resting on the ground, ready for the fight. The large crowd of strange tribes followed them slowly.

"Now the duels were to begin; three men came forward from our side and accepted the challenge, the rest remaining quiet for the present. The common position for challenging is as follows: The shield is held in the left hand and the sword perpendicularly in the right. But, owing to the weight of the sword, it must be used almost like a blacksmith's sledge-hammer in order to hit the shield of the opponent with full force. The combatant is therefore obliged to let the weapon rest in front on the

FIG. 389. BORBODY GATHERING IN QUEENSLAND. After Lumholtz

ground a few moments before the duel begins, when he swings it back and past his head against his opponent's head. When one of them has made his blow it is his opponent's turn, and thus they exchange blows until one of them gets tired and gives up, or his shield is cloven, in which case he is regarded as unfit for the fight.

"While the first three pairs were fighting, others began to exchange blows (fig. 389). There was no regularity in the fight. The duel usually began with spears, then they came nearer to each other and took to their swords. Sometimes the matter was decided at a distance, boomerangs, nolla-nollas and spears being thrown against the shields. The natives are exceedingly skilful in parrying, so that they are seldom wounded by the first two kinds of weapons. On the other hand, the spears easily penetrate the shields and sometimes injure the bearer, who is then regarded as disqualified and must declare himself beaten. There were always some combatants in the field, frequently seven or eight pairs at a time; but the duellists were continually changing.

"The women gather up the weapons, and when a warrior has to engage in several duels his wives continually supply him with weapons. The other women stand and look on, watching the conflict with the greatest attention, for they have much at stake. Many a one changes husbands on that night. As the natives frequently rob each other of their wives, the conflicts arising from this cause are settled by borboby, the victor in the duel retaining the woman.

"The old women also take part in the fray. They stand behind the combatants with the same kind of sticks as those used for digging up roots. They hold the stick with both hands, beat the ground hard with it, and jump up and down in a state of wild excitement. They cry to the men, egging and urging them on, four or five frequently surrounding one man and acting as if perfectly mad. The men become more and more excited, perspiration pours from them, and they exert themselves to the utmost.

"If one of the men is conquered, the old women gather around him and protect him with their sticks, parrying the sword blows of his opponent and constantly shouting: 'Do not kill him; do not kill him!'

"I went to the fighting-ground, and with the greatest attention I watched the interesting duels, which lasted only about three-quarters of an hour, but which entertained me more than any performance I ever witnessed. Boomerangs and nolla-nollas whizzed about our ears, without however hindering me from watching with interest the passion of these wild children of nature—the desperate exertions of the men, the zeal of the young women, and the foolish rage of the old women, whose discordant voices blended with the din of the weapons, with the dull blows of the swords, with the clang of the nolla-nollas and with the whirring flight of the boomerangs whizzing through the air.

"Here all disputes and legal conflicts were settled, not only between tribes but also between individuals. That the lowest races of men do not try to settle their disputes in a more parliamentary manner need not cause any surprise, but it may appear strange to us that aged women take so active a part in the issue of these conflicts. With the exception of the murder of a member of the same tribe, the aboriginal Australian knows only one crime, and that is theft, and the punishment for violating the right of possession is not inflicted by the community but by the individual wronged. The thief is challenged by his victim to a duel with wooden swords and shields; and the matter is settled sometimes privately, the relatives

Fig. 390. Barotse fighting with sticks. From a photograph.

of both parties serving as witnesses, sometimes publicly at the borboby, where 200 to 300 meet from various tribes to decide all their disputes. He who wins in the fight has right on his side.

"The stealing of women, who also among these savages are regarded as a man's most valuable property, is both

EARLY HISTORY OF WAR

the grossest and the most common theft; for it is the usual way of getting a wife. Hence, woman is the chief cause of disputes. The theft of weapons, implements and food is rarely the cause of a duel. I do not remember a single instance of weapons being stolen. If an inconsiderable amount of food or some other trifle has been stolen, it frequently happens that the victim, instead of challenging the thief, simply plays the part of an offended person, especially if he considers himself inferior in strength and in the use of weapons. In cases where the food has not been eaten but is returned, then the victim is satisfied with compensation in the form of tobacco or weapons, and thus friendship is at once re-established. Even when the thief regards himself as superior in strength he does not care to have a duel in prospect, for these savages shrink from every inconvenience. The idea of having to fight with his victim is a greater punishment for the thief than one would think, even though bloodshed is rare. In these duels the issue does not depend wholly on physical strength, as the relatives play a conspicuous part in the matter. The possession of many strong men on his side is a great moral support to the combatant. He knows that his opponent, through fear of his relatives, will not carry the conflict to the extreme. He is also certain that, if necessary, they will interfere and prevent his getting wounded. The relatives and friends are of great importance in the decision of conflicts among the natives, though physical strength, of course, is the first consideration.

"After such a conflict the reader possibly expects a description of fallen warriors swimming in blood; but relatives and friends take care that none of the combatants are injured. Mortal wounds are extremely rare. One only had received a slight wound from a boomerang in the arm above the elbow, and was therefore pitied by everybody. In the next borboby one person happened to be pierced by a spear, which, being barbed, could not be removed. His tribe carried him about with them for three days before he died.

"As soon as the sun had set the conflict ceased. The people separated, each tribe going to its own camp, all deeply interested in the events of the day. There was not much sleep that night, and conversation was lively round the small camp-fires. As a result of the borboby several family revolutions had already taken place, men had lost their wives and women had acquired new husbands. In the cool morning of the next day the duels were continued for an hour; then the crowds separated, each tribe returning to its own 'land.' While I remained at Herbert river four borbobies occurred with three to four weeks intervening between each, in the months of November, December, January and February—that is, in the hottest season of the year. During the winter no borboby is held."

To sum up: The notion of war does not yet exist for these peoples. On the one hand simple murder prevails, on the other a somewhat complicated kind of combat, which may perhaps not incorrectly be called "drubbing." These drubbings, or, if they are to be called by a more distinguished name, "duels," have still survived in more advanced conditions of civilization. I may recall the fighting scenes in the Malay Archipelago and in South Africa. Especially amongst the Zulus, the Barotse, the Basutos and a few tribes in the German colony of East Africa, the "knob-kerry fights" have retained the meaning and the character of a vindication of personal rights.

EARLY HISTORY OF WAR

On such occasions in South Africa each of the duellists wields two sticks, parrying with one, striking out with the other. Now he grasps with the left, now with the right hand. It is a game of pure skill for which one might perhaps have a certain measure of respect, if the brave combatants did not always select a particular object

Fig. 391. A Champion; Molucca Islands.

for the exercise of their skill. In fact they seldom aim at the head which is pretty well protected by their thick woolly pate, but rather at the shins where men are remarkably sensitive, much more so than is generally supposed (see fig. 390).

The weapons no less than the form of these fights have been preserved in certain kinds of single combat. This style of conflict originated in the period "before iron." Hence, they still lacked certain rudimentary kinds of

EARLY HISTORY OF WAR

weapons which were not invented till later times, and eventually exercised a most important influence on warfare. Especially did they lack knives, axes, one may also perhaps say the spear, and all warlike appliances such as slings, throwing-sticks, bows and darts. In other words, there were no missiles properly so called.

On the other hand, there were weapons which, strictly speaking, scarcely deserved the name. The bludgeon, or in its improved form the club, or else bearing for us the somewhat mystic name of boomerang, introduces such combats. These weapons unpleasantly remind us that European "street Arabs" also, when they know themselves at a safe distance, throw stones at people. The act is much the same. Hence, the weapon properly so called is found amongst the Australians. At least they have the wooden sword and the shield, the former of which has been transformed in the neighbouring East Indian Archipelago to the *kris*, that is an iron weapon which in the hands of protagonists plays a serious part, whereas the shield, certainly in its wooden form, has long held its ground with modifications. But this must be reserved for a separate chapter.

In conclusion I give fig. 391, which pictures a Malay champion with modified wooden shield and symbolic wooden staff, as representing a mimetic dance scene. Here again the pristine form of the duel or single combat receives full recognition.

CHAPTER XXXI
CANNIBALS

CANNIBALISM is commonly regarded as the most horrible and most repulsive of misdeeds, in fact the crime of crimes. It is even maintained that it is a sin against the laws of nature for one species to feed on creatures of the same species, hence, for man to devour his fellow man. But cannibalism can no longer have anything incredible or horrifying for us who have been studying the history of human warfare and the warlike implements that man has devised against man, for us, I say, who have just been investigating the original causes of murder. But with cannibalism another question still presents itself. It is the most contested question in ethnology.

"To what is cannibalism to be traced?"

The most diverse causes have been advanced as the real origin of the practice; it has been based by some on religious motives, having arisen simultaneouly with human sacrifices; others find its motive in gluttony, the most refined of all dainty food being human titbits. Or recourse is had to hatred, to famine and so on.

I hold the question in most cases not to be so very difficult, especially when we bear in mind that timid, spiritless, indolent, "really tame" peoples are not cannibals as a rule. On the other hand, energetic races, men who have become great in the very struggle for existence,

CANNIBALS

peoples distinguished by their achievements, are, in the wild state, for the most part man-eaters. I shall give an instance from the natives of the Australian Continent. In the South are met kindly, weak and feeble groups, quite exceptionally indolent, but well-disposed. None of these were cannibals, and they stood in the most violent contrast to the Queenslanders, about whom Lumholtz reports roughly as follows:

"In the Herbert river district it even happens that expeditions are organized for the express purpose of procuring human flesh. With this object in view there assembles a small band of the most daring men, who enjoy a great reputation for courage. There are not many, as these raids are usually directed against small families of from four to six individuals. The journey is very slow, and supplies have to be obtained on the march. When they have found a likely family they go

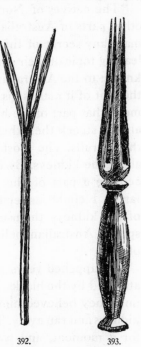

392.   393.

Fig. 392. Fork for human flesh; Fiji. In the possession of Reuleaux.

Fig. 393. Fork for human flesh; Mobati tribe. Brandt Collection.

very cautiously to work, encamp secretly in the evening at some distance and begin the attack before sunrise, when the family wakes up in a fright. Each one tries to save his life as best he can; resistance being out of the question, there is no gallant defence of women and children. Each one has to look after himself; and it is generally

CANNIBALS

worst for the old people, who are killed and eaten. A woman is, as a rule, splendid booty; if she be young her life is generally spared, but if she be old she is killed and eaten like the rest.

"The natives of Northern Queensland and of many other parts of Australia are cannibals. My people never made any secret of this, and in the evenings it was the leading topic of their conversation. The greatest delicacy known to the Australian native is human flesh. The very thought of it makes his eye sparkle. When I asked my men what part of the human body they liked best, they always struck their thighs. They never eat the head or the entrails. The most delicate morsel of all is the fat about the kidneys. By eating this they believe that they acquire a part of the slain person's strength, and so far as I could understand this was even more true of the kidneys themselves. For according to a widespread Australian belief, the kidneys are the centre of life.

"It happened years ago that a white policeman was attacked by the blacks. They struck him with their clubs until they believed him dead, and then they took out his kidneys and ran away. The man recovered consciousness for a moment, and was able to relate what had happened, before he died.

"The natives on Herbert river are particularly fond of the fat of a dead foe, which is not only eaten as a nourishing delicacy, but is also carried as an amulet. A small piece is done up in grass and kept in a basket and worn round the neck, and the effect of this is, in their opinion, success in the chase, so that they can easily approach the game. A man told me that immediately after beginning to wear a small piece of human fat, he

CANNIBALS

waded across the river and came at once to a tree where he found a large edible snake.

"As a rule, the Australian natives do not eat persons belonging to their own tribe. Still I know instances to the contrary, and I have even heard of examples of mothers eating their own children. Mr White has informed me that the natives living south of the Gulf of Carpentaria are also cannibals to some extent. But they kill nobody to eat him, although the women eat those who die a natural death, and at Morton Bay the dead are consumed by their own relatives.

"The blacks do not like to eat white people. When Jimmy had killed the white man near my headquarters, my question as to whether the dead man had been eaten caused great surprise.

"The answer was: 'No, indeed! horribly nasty!' At the same time the person pointed, with a grimace, at his throat, to indi-

Fig. 394. Chain of human teeth with fork for human flesh, Mongola River. Brandt Collection. Each tooth is supposed to represent the remains of a cannibal repast.

CANNIBALS

cate his disgust for the flesh of a white man. The other persons agreed with him. I have often since heard them say that the white man's flesh is not good. This may be owing to his constant diet of salt beef, tea and bread, which possibly gives his flesh a different taste from that of the blacks.

The black man lives on vegetables nearly all his life. I have heard it stated by 'civilized' blacks that the white man's flesh has a salt taste, which the natives do not like.

"This also seems to harmonize with their fondness for the flesh of the Chinese, whose food consists largely of rice and other vegetables. Farther north, in Queensland, it twice happened during my sojourn in Australia that the blacks killed the Chinese in great numbers. It was said that ten Chinamen were eaten at one dinner. All strangers who travel through the land of a tribe are of course their enemies. This is true both of the white man and the Chinese,

Fig. 395. A Congo man-eater.
After a drawing by
Ward.

both of which races are looked upon as another kind of black who come from distant lands, and are killed when the opportunity presents itself. Human flesh, however, is not the daily food of the Australian. On the contrary, he seldom gets a mouthful of this delicacy. During all the time I spent on Herbert river, only two blacks were killed and eaten. One of them was a young man who had ventured to go into the territory of a strange tribe, where he was surprised and killed. The other was an older man

474

who was not able to run fast enough when his tribe was attacked, and he was stoned to death. His flesh was brought in baskets to Herbert Vale."

Here we have the lowest aspect of cannibalism. Just as the Australian negro eats with relish his herbivorous

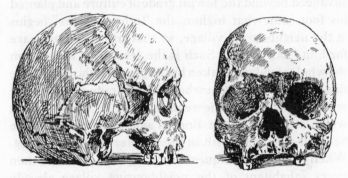

Fig. 396. Skull of the devoured man-eater Si Gallak.

Fig. 397. Si Gallak's hand.

kangaroo and his herbivorous neighbour, in the same way he dislikes the salted body of the European. In this, apparently, mere outward attitude and preference of the native gourmet is already embodied the inner fact established by force of habit.

It has been said that it was immoral and sinful, in the sense of being "unnatural," for one creature to eat

CANNIBALS

another of its own species. If we think only of nature that may be so. But if we think of men, that cannot be said, since man has once for all entered with all his vital energy into the struggle with nature, just in so far as he is susceptible of civilization. For the man who has advanced beyond the lowest grade of culture and planted his foot somewhat higher, the "other species" begins at the neighbouring village, so that his neighbours are for him "fair game." Such is the lesson we learn from the whole standpoint taken by the peoples who have made this advance to a somewhat higher grade of culture. I will merely remind the reader of the social conditions which are prevalent in Borneo and Sumatra, and have been already dealt with in the chapter on head-hunting. When it comes to a question of capturing a head, then every inhabitant of the neighbouring village already belongs to "another species," and that is true not only in the matter of head-hunting, but also as regards cannibalism.

I shall now give an example to show how cannibalism looks in this second period of culture. I take it from an entry in Von Brenner's diary.

According to all appearances Si Gallak is a wealthy chief. His teeth are gilded, and in a bamboo box covered with writing there was a gold ornament, a necklace of strikingly beautiful and tasteful workmanship, which he gladly showed us, but would not trust me with to take a sketch of it. In the lid of this box was set a tooth which, as he said, came from an enemy whom he had killed and eaten. This man he hated beyond measure, and even after his death pursued with his vengeance, for whenever he shut the lid of the box, which he always carried with him, he banged the tooth, declaring that

CANNIBALS

each time he had the pleasant feeling of giving his enemy a real blow.

Yet withal, he gave us the impression of being a genial sort of man-eater, for he willingly let the Toba people chaff him, or laugh at his broad and drawling speech, not seldom joining in the laugh himself.

When we asked him, in case we should visit him in his home, whether we too might not perhaps get eaten and our skulls hung up as proud mementos, he replied that we might rest assured, as not a hair of our head would be hurt.

A few years later Meissner met a Batta who was just setting out to bring him a human skull and a smoked hand. When purchasing these remains Meissner inquired particularly as to their origin, and one of his companions there and then took down verbatim what passed at the interview. We are thus enabled to communicate the further history of the chief Si Gallak, who took such pleasure in striking the tooth on the lid of his box, with the feeling that he was hitting his enemy straight in the mouth.

Meissner asked:

"Whence come the head and the dried hand that you have there?"

"These are from an enemy who fell into our hands three years ago," replied the Batta.

"And whom no doubt you have eaten?"

"Of course; why not?"

"Who then has eaten him?"

"My brother-in-law and his people."

"Tell me, how so, why? His name?"

"His name was Si Kemat Si Gallak. He had fled with his brother, his wife and his mother from the fore- land where he had been raja; then he wanted to seize

CANNIBALS

the rule in Pantjo, my brother-in-law's village, and called himself a magician. Then my brother-in-law declared war against him, and he was conquered."

"Did it then come to a fight?"

"Fight? No! We captured him. We lurked for a few days close by the road, hidden in the rice fields until we could catch him alone. Then we seized and bound him, and brought him to our chief, who had him locked up."

"And his brother?"

"His brother fell in the war."

"How in the war, since he was alone?"

"Well, yes; we shot him at night when he was asleep. The bullet hit him in the right arm, and he defended himself holding a knife in his left hand; but we remained conquerors. We cut him down and sent his head to the chief. Do you call that no war?"

"And what became of his body?"

"Well, that we ate."

"And then what became of his head?"

"That our chief put on the ground under the nose of Si Kemat Si Gallak, that he might know what awaited him."

"Could he not buy himself off?"

"Buy himself off? No question of that; he had to die."

"But did he not cry out?"

"O yes; but that did not help him at all; he was bound."

"And then?"

"Of course we ate him."

"How was that done?"

"Next day, when the sun was no longer rising, and was not yet setting, we brought Kemat out of the prison, pressed him down on the ground face uppermost, and my brother-in-law struck off his head—no, he only cut

478

Fig. 398. Mona Kakesa's Ancestor, equipped with his own teeth which were broken from his head after the body had been devoured by his own tribal associates. In the Author's possession.

through what remained. He got the heart and as much flesh as he wanted; whoever else cared for it, held a slice over the fire and ate it. The rest we cooked with pepper and salt, and ate it at home (?). The larger bones were tied up together and hung up with the others in the *bale*. Next day we drove off his *begu* by shooting, and buried his head on the way to the *bale*, so that his friends might tread on it and thereby make an enemy of him."

"What became of his wife?"

"Her I sold for my brother-in-law in the market for the price of 120 dollars."

"So he completely covered the cost of his war?"

"Certainly, and something to boot."

"What became of his mother?"

"His mother! Bah! The *guru* said she was as bad as her sons, so we cut her throat a month afterwards."

"And ate her?"

"Of course. Why not?"

"Why are there so few teeth in the skull?"

"The rest were knocked out by the people to set them on the lids of their sirih-lime boxes."

"Why so?"

"Well, when they shut the lid they have the same feeling as if they were hitting Si Kemat himself in the mouth."

Probably there is scarcely a more characteristic account of the cannibalism of the Battas than the foregoing. For what is here specially noteworthy is the introduction of the reference to war.

As war is here described—in one word, *murder*—this removal of any troublesome person as a matter of course is typical for this period in the history of warfare, when the "other species" always begins in the neighbouring

CANNIBALS

village. And to this view of society cannibalism inherently belongs. Hence, there is no need of our casting about for more remote motives for the practice. Here the whole connexion, the whole warlike attitude of social life, plainly shows that we have here to do with a simple feature of brutality and bloodthirstiness. At the same time it need not be denied that religious motives may also be adduced for the practice of anthropophagy, and for this the following proofs may be advanced.

As in the skull-cult we have to notice both a warlike and a religious motive, and to recognize that on the one hand the skull is a memorial of war, a trophy, and on the other that the head is hunted in order to procure a soul as a slave for the next world; so also in cannibalism, warlike and religious ideas are often intermingled with other groups of customs hard to disentangle.

There is certainly no doubt that amongst the lower peoples, the so-called wild tribes, the religious and everyday life cannot be separated, because the lack of the consciousness of a real purpose, the intense predominance of a symbolic way of viewing things, exercises a thoroughly confusing influence on the whole sphere of thought. We have seen how the history of the discovery of fire has become interwoven with the solar mythologies, how the trade of the blacksmith has become a sacred avocation, how in fact the world is no longer estimated from the natural and actual standpoints of practical life, but in accordance with spiritual notions, with the laws determining the relative position of animals and the belief in spirits.

Hence, we need no longer be surprised that cannibalism also plays a part not only in the sphere of practical war-

CANNIBALS

fare but also in the religious life of primitive peoples. Now, if we connect with skull-cult a group of moral acts which in their underlying motive are closely akin to cannibalism, we are at once struck with a case in point mentioned in the chapter dealing with skull-cult. I refer to the fact that in South Guinea the people devour by preference the brain of some highly honoured member of the tribe, in order in this way to acquire the spirit and the strength of the deceased. Here we have already the beginning of a certain kind of cannibalism. The custom assumes even a more repulsive form when the survivors, that is the deceased's own relatives, consume the maggots developed in his decaying body. To them these maggots appear as the "life" thus undergoing metamorphosis. Nor is the notion so very extravagant. With it is closely associated the horrible custom of pressing out and swallowing the moisture of the mouldering corpse. The practice is not at all rare amongst the natives of the East Indian Archipelago, of West Africa and North-East Brazil.

Let us recall the practices connected with the embodiment of spirits which are mentioned in the chapter on secret societies, that is to say, how the members of the societies endeavour to gain possession of another's soul, and how this is effected by swallowing a part of another man's body. When we think of all these things, we shall no longer feel so puzzled at the next step, that is, at the natives eating the bodies of their own tribespeople.

On the basis of these manistic views there has arisen a group of cannibal practices which may be best studied amongst the North-West Americans. With them is frequently met a class of priests or shamans who are called *hametses*, a word which is divided from *ham*, meaning to eat. Thus they are already called eaters, that is, according

CANNIBALS

to the sense, man-eaters. Of them Jacobsen writes as follows:

"Cannibalism appears to have been practised till recent times by the Indian tribes living south of the Kolushes and Tlinkits on the coasts and islands of British Columbia. So lately as the year 1860 it happened in Vancouver Island itself, although held by the English, that at a feast a prisoner of war, who was tied to a stake, was disembowelled in presence of a European, whereupon the Indians took up the flowing blood in their hands and drank it; probably the whole body was afterwards consumed. In this instance the British authorities took such drastic punitive measures that such a scene does not appear to have been witnessed again, at least within the range of their gunboats." Yet, in 1882, Adrian Jacobsen was present at a pantomime which exhibited the same incident on the West Coast of Vancouver.

"On the other hand, another remarkable reminiscence of anthropophagy has survived till the present day. Amongst those Indians the highest social rank is taken by a class of holy persons who are known by different names in every tribe, and among the Quakiutls in Vancouver are the hametses just mentioned. Admission to the society may be claimed by any youngster of a distinguished and well-to-do family, that is, of one possessing a great many blankets. If found acceptable on the ground of his family connexions, the candidate enters on a four years' period of probation full of severe trials and painful castigations. But during the last four weeks of this novitiate he remains alone in the forest, in order by bodily privations to prepare himself for the ceremony of reception. In the eyes of the other natives of the place he is then already a more exalted person, possessed and guided by the god Pae-Pae-Kvala-misiva, whose proper abode is the air; and with a certain feeling of awe every one moves away on hearing the notes of his flute and pipe in the bush.

"The act of reception into the society consists in the hamets suddenly rushing from the wood into the village, and then, in a festive gathering prepared by the other hametses, with his teeth tearing a piece of flesh from the arm of one or more of his tribal associates, and swallowing it; or else biting pieces out of dogs' throats. The men who may get injured by the hamets thus falling upon them in blind fury no doubt let him have his way, either because they are unwilling to contend with the god working with him, or because they are indemnified with a number of blankets, often as many as forty.

"Although the presence of hametses at festal gatherings is much desired, they have to be four times formally invited by four chiefs before they condescend to give a promise. Then the hamets thus invited prepares himself for the feast by fasting and seclusion in the darkest corner of his house, for custom requires that such a saintly person should look pale and haggard. Then when he has to repair to the banqueting place, decked in all his finery and preceded by the four chiefs, he moves at a snail's pace, very slowly putting one foot before the other, and taking hours to cover a distance of perhaps not more than 100 paces; and all along the tedious route he is gazed upon by his fellow villagers with profound silence and veneration. Even at the feast itself he is the object of universal attention and esteem, and accepts all these marks of homage with self-satisfied complacency.

"The hamets's greatest privilege, however, consists in his right to share in feeding on the corpses of his dead associates, since his mere partaking of these meals raises him, in the opinion of his fellow tribesmen, to the highest

CANNIBALS

pinnacle of worth and holiness. In the deep recesses of
the woods the hametses gather together for their cannibal
banquet, which no outsider dare approach, and at which
they produce a body either from the wooden boxes suspended on the trees, or else from the raised wooden platform where it has been dried by the action of the wind.
Then they soften this mummified corpse in water, after
which they bite off and swallow large pieces of the loath-
some 'fare.' When the bodies are old enough, that is,
belong to persons who have been dead at least one or two
years, such food appears to be not unwholesome. On the
other hand, it has repeatedly happened that hametses
have died of blood-poisoning from consuming still comparatively fresh corpses. For each participation in such
horrible repasts the hamets receives in confirmation and
indication of the fact, a death's head artistically carved
from wood, and this he wears as an ornament on a large
necklace made of cedar-bast. A genuine representative
of this amazing custom, who was 'exhibited' some years
ago in various German towns, could boast of no less than
eight of such 'medals.'

"I may now state that I was twice present as an onlooker
at hamets feasts. On the first occasion pieces of flesh were
torn from the arms of five men; on the second a hamets
bit out pieces from the throats of sixteen dogs. At the
former feast the hamets began by singing and dancing
the first four dances usual on such occasions. But towards
the end of the fourth he was like a madman, howling like
an enraged bear. Then he tore off all the blankets from
his body and rushed on an Indian standing in the vicinity.
He defended himself with all his strength, and at first
even successfully. But the hamets, to whom his frenzy
seemed to lend supernatural power, soon flung his oppo-

CANNIBALS

nent on the ground, bit a large piece of flesh from his arm and swallowed it.

"In the same way he behaved towards his other tribesmen, until he had bitten five of them, when the rest 'seemed to have had enough of the gruesome game,' as a number of other hametses tried to bind him. But he sprang over the heads of those who wanted to hold him, and was not to be restrained. Then they went off to fetch the shaman or medicine-man, who for fifteen minutes practised all kinds of hocus-pocus on the madman, and at last brought him round. I can assure you that the whole proceeding presented the most disgusting spectacle that it is possible for a man to behold, one I shall never forget to the end of my days. Quite fiendish was his glance when, in his frightful excitement, he sought out a fresh victim. He came at me, too, and acted as if he wanted to rush on me; but I held myself ready to deal him a knock-down blow, and it is quite possible that he guessed my intention, for he passed on and selected another victim. Many of the natives fled through fear.

"After the feast the injured parties were, according to custom, compensated with blankets for the resulting fever and the worry they were put to. The horrible spectacle, however, gave me the opportunity of making an interesting discovery. I found that the hametses do not always use their teeth alone, as we had heard and believed, but now and then slice the flesh from the arm with the help of a knife. This may very well escape the notice of the crowd of spectators standing a little distance off, since the victim lying on the ground and his assailant are usually closely surrounded by several other hametses.

"At the second feast sixteen dogs were bitten by a hamets, who tore out a piece from the throat of each.

CANNIBALS

While hunting them down he wore a large mask representing a wolf's head, the eyes and lower jaw of which were movable. When there were no more uninjured dogs at hand, he pretended to be sick, and apparently vomited through the wolf's jaws large pieces of flesh which he had kept concealed under the blanket. At the same time a second hamets seized with his teeth and pulled out by main force the pieces which were too large to pass easily through the narrow jaws of the mask. At the end a number of Indians joined in a dance which represented how the wolf, who grew longer and longer by several of the men creeping under the blankets, tried to escape, while the crowd sought to lay hold of him. It all made a tremendous uproar."

In the scenes just described religious cannibalism finds direct and unmistakable expression. Hence we can with comparative ease separate this series from the sphere of warlike customs, and contrast them with the history of Si Galak, which on its part affords the best illustration of warlike cannibalism.

This warlike cannibalism still calls for a remark. It is certainly strange that those very peoples who have shown the most remarkable developments in other directions should be the worst and most pronounced cannibals. Here I may take instances from Africa, and refer to the A-zandehs (Niam-Niams), the Mangbattus, the Bassonge, the Bakuba, who are all peoples that have developed an astonishingly wide range of the industrial arts. The velvet fabrics, the wood carvings, the iron hardware, the basket-work which these peoples turn out represent all that is most perfect in these departments that has ever been produced by the so-called wild tribes.

CANNIBALS

They are objects whose artistic value in some respects even surpasses that of the high-priced wares that go to adorn our boudoirs. This I assert with full deliberation.

Yet they are all cannibals!

How is the riddle to be solved?

On this point I have but one thing to say. I can only compare it with the moral conditions of the Renaissance period. The Renaissance was a time when the ethical energy manifested itself in the overthrow of all moral laws. It is certain that these peoples, with their great and free sense of art, peoples who had broken loose from the fetters of rigid convention in the artistic domain, had also shaken off all the fetters of morality, and committed the wildest excesses that have ever been perpetrated in the way of murder, treachery, fraud and robbery, and this always whenever they had some object or other in view. Thus, the Renaissance movement was an instance of the ethical force of a process directed towards emancipation from ethical shackles.

I have the impression that something similar is the case with the African wild tribes just mentioned, with those great craftsmen of the Dark Continent; they, too, supply an illustration of ethical energy. There is something appalling, and, despite the horror of it, something imposing in the daily returning cannibal meals of a King Munsa, or a King Gapech.

It even seems to me as if in this cannibalism there lay a real historical document. If it be true that, as I have just stated, cannibalism occurs not only as the crime of dull-witted peoples, such as the Australians, but that in it we must also recognize an indication of ethical energy, of a great and untrammelled warlike spirit, then it would almost seem as if cannibalism should be brought into

488

CANNIBALS

association with the sanguinary human sacrifices which were practised during the first period of the solar view of the world. And then we should like, once for all, to cast a rapid glance over the earth, and ask ourselves how all these things are related to each other. To the question put in this way we get quite a surprising answer:

Over the earth there has prevailed a vast period of time, the time during which were born the colossal solar ideas, the time of the highest mythological efflorescence. It was the same time when in the ruddy glow of the setting sun was offered up the blood of human victims; the time when the first stone effigy was erected, when the first product of the loom enveloped the human body; the time of the first delight in dainty craftsmanship. It was the time when mighty rulers held sway over strong nations, when peoples harried each other to death, and when the wild lust of power could be sated only with the cannibal feast. It was the time of a King Munsa, or a King Gapech.

Such is the first Renaissance era of mankind, the first period when the ethical sensibility was stronger than the force of the commonplace. And an illustration of this period may also be afforded by the cannibal repasts of a King Munsa, or a King Gapech.

CHAPTER XXXII
WARLIKE PEOPLES

NOBODY will doubt that a difference, wide as the poles, exists between the predatory raid of a band of Australian cannibals and the attacks of Masai or a Zulu horde. When we unfold before our eyes all the varied scenes from the warlike life of primitive peoples, we get such a diversified picture of the historic development of warfare itself as could scarcely be presented by the history even of civilized nations.

To reduce all these forms of war to a single system would scarcely be at all possible. Hence, in this department also we can but again consider the several incidents from definite points of view.

Here we have the South African Zulu people who one day suddenly abandon their kraal, and with wives and children start with bag and baggage to found new homes in some more favourable part of the world. That means breaking through the defensive works of other tribes, for they have to support themselves on the march and to feed their numerous followers. In a wild assault the horde breaks over the land like a swarm of locusts. Where were before seen thriving crops and well-filled granaries, now there is nothing but the smoke of glowing embers. Where before women frolicked merrily over their work and children gambolled playfully about, there now prevails the dreary silence of solitude and desolation. But

FIG. 398. AN ONSLAUGHT OF MASAI WARRIORS

the migrating people have passed on, perhaps the weaker
by a few killed in the fray, but all the richer in women
and slaves, and so the flowing avalanche rolls along, with
fresh hopes ever before it, and behind it smoke and ruin.

Or take another picture.

Closely penned together in their fenced village are the
natives, none of whom venture to cross the nearest en-

Fig. 400. War-dance of the Wute people. After Morgen.

closure, because there is a standing feud with the neighbouring village. If it becomes necessary to migrate, the
convoy starts under strong escort. But what avails the
escort! An arrow whizzes almost noiselessly through the
air, and one of them falls to the ground. Thenceforth the
friends of the slain lie in wait for their neighbours with
redoubled cunning. And even if it be only a woman
whom they surprise while drawing water, they are jubi-
lant at being able to score a murder, or, as they would
call it, a deed of war on their side.

Or again!

493

WARLIKE PEOPLES

A frontier dispute has arisen; two tribes can no longer
settle matters peacefully, so they send each other the
signal for war. Now all preparations are made. The cattle
are driven in from the fields, a palisade is run up round the
hamlet, arrowheads are forged, stones collected for the
slings, and information eagerly sought as to the direction
from which the foe may advance. Now they approach,

Fig. 401. Declaration of manhood, coming of age, of the Yaunde people ; after Morgen.

and there are mighty surprises by the assailants and sorties
by the besieged. At last a single combat, or a new commercial agreement, may again make peace possible.

Thus property and organized society must be indicated
as the factors that control and determine the conditions
of regular warfare. Raiding and plundering of opulent
neighbours on the one hand, and on the other the defence
of one's own property, determine as a rule the form of
warfare amongst the settled and organized rude peoples.
But how the wars may be carried on depends on the most
varied elements, such as the training of the people, their

warlike spirit, their weapons, and last, not least, the geographical features of the seat of war.

Everywhere the less civilized societies effect by the organization of masses of men what is achieved with the help of more developed military resources by the tribal groups which are more advanced, or, if you like to call them so, in a rudimentary sense, more civilized. I need but mention the Zulus and the Masai in Africa. What is lacking in military aptitude is dexterously made up for by an outward "get up" as truculent as possible, an intense excitement strung to the highest possible pitch. The warriors, in fact, dance themselves into the frenzy of the battle-field (fig. 400).

Amongst rude peoples the military training pretty well represents the whole education of the "rising generation." I may remind the reader how those who are admitted into the secret societies also for the most part pass through the "military academies." It is precisely the fighting element in him that amongst the ruder peoples raises man so "sky-high" above woman, a fact which indeed often assumes a ludicrous aspect. When, for instance, the Younde youths attain their majority the event is celebrated by a general feast, in which the standing joke consists of their being attacked and spoiled of the female garments that they had hitherto worn (fig. 401).

A fresh illustration of the saying that "from the maiden state the youth tears himself proudly away."

I cannot undertake to treat of the weapons of primitive peoples. Their historic development would lead us too far into the early history of war, and real warfare does not belong to the Childhood of Man.

THE END

INDEX

INDEX

INDEX

INDEX

INDEX

INDEX

New Pomerania, The dewarra of, 57, 59; the *Kinakinau*, 61; the drum-language, 86; relic worship in, 170; skull-masks in, 219

New Zealand, Tattooing in, 34; the god Maui, 273; creation myths of, 382

Nganga, "Knowing Ones," members of a Secret Society on the Lower Congo, 202

Ngombe village, A solar ceremony in a, 337

Niam-Niams, Tattooing among the, 36

Nigerland, Spider stories of, 365-370

Night, *Quat*, The creator of, 297

North American myths: the raven and the whale, 277; the mink and the whale, 278; Kanigyilak and the monster Tsekis, 279; the grampus and the fishermen, 281; the raven and the fisherman, 283

Northern Philippines, Signal-drums in the, 90

Nose, Piercing the, among the Australians, 41, 54; among the Aztecs, 53; among the Motu of New Guinea, 54; on Florida Island, 54

Nyankupong, the embodiment of the sky of the Yorubas, 380

Obatala, the chief god of the Yorubas, 374

Oceania, Secret Societies of, 217; creation myths of, 381

Odudua, the chief goddess of the Yorubas, 374

Okomfus, Priests of the, 336

Old Calabar, a funeral ceremony in, 162

Olokun, the sea god of Yorubaland, 294

Olorun, the sky god of the Yorubas, 374

Olosa, a sea goddess of Yorubaland, 294

Oobé, a mythical people of the Bushmen, 122

Ordeal, The, on the Lower Congo, 190, 193

Ornaments for personal adornment, 26; animals' teeth, 27

Orungan, a god of the Yorubas, 376

Otter, The, a sacred animal of the North American Indians, 228

Oya, wife of Shango, the sun god, 294

Ova-Herero, Creation myth of the, 380

Pahu or war-bell of the Maoris, 93

Peruvians, The building achievements of the, 428

Peruvians, Ancient, flattening of the head by, 39

Phaeton, The myth of, 327

Pictorial Script of the Uncpapa Dakotas, 103

Picture-writing and decoration among the Dakotas, 103

Poison cup at funeral ceremonies, The, 157

Polynesia, Tattooing in, 36

Polynesian buildings, The construction of, 425

Puka-Puka, Solar myths in, 330

Purrah Secret Society, Sierra Leone, 205

Pygmies of Africa and their smouldering trees, 414

Pygmy races, 130

Quanciquchaa, a mythical hero of the Bushmen, 118

Quasavara and Quat, The myth of, 300, 326

Quat, a Banks Island god, the creator of Night, 297; his encounters with Quasavara, 300; his heavenly wife, 305; his canoe, 307, 325

Queensland, Cannibalism in, 471, 474

Rarotonga, Creation myths of, 382

Raven and the Fisherman, the, a North American myth, 283

Raven and the Whale, a North American myth, 277

Raven Rattles of North-West America, 256

INDEX

INDEX